IDLE WOMEN

IDLE WOMEN

by

Susan Woolfitt

B

M & M BALDWIN
LONDON
1986

This book was first published by Ernest Benn Ltd in 1947. The text of this new edition has been reprinted from the original text without alteration. The original edition had but a single photograph, which has been omitted from this edition; instead, a carefully selected group of photographs, some previously unpublished, has been added, along with a new Introduction.

The originals of photographs 2 and 18 were provided by Harriet Graham, and those of photographs 6 and 7 by Ruth Clements. Photographs 9, 12 and 13 were taken by A. Pritchard. Other photographs are reproduced by courtesy of the BBC Hulton Picture Library, Kit Gayford, K.L. Henderson-Begg, Times Newspapers Ltd, and The Waterways Museum. Prints of photographs 1, 6, 7, 9, and 12 – 15 were made by Richard C. Packer, and that of photograph 8 by Hugh McKnight Photography.

ISBN 0 947712 03 8

Published by M & M Baldwin, 98 Kenyon Street, London SW6 6LB

Printed by Redwood Burn Ltd, Yeoman Way, Trowbridge, Wilts BA14 0QL

CONTENTS

ILLUSTRATIONS

(between pages 96 and 97)

INTRODUCTION

It is now more than forty years since the end of the Second World War, and in the time which has elapsed since the first publication of *Idle Women* in 1947, much has changed on the inland waterways of this country. The transport of cargo by narrow boat has virtually ceased, and where hundreds of boats were once employed the picture is now one of a few isolated boats doing an occasional run. Few, if any, of the craft on which the author worked are still in existence, and few boaters are still able to make a living on our canals. But along with the death of freight traffic a new interest has been gradually awakening in our waterways. Just when it seemed as though weeds and silt might choke for ever many of the canals which were cut by our eighteenth- and nineteenth-century forefathers in pursuit of trade, a whole new generation of enthusiasts has discovered that, in the immortal words of the Water Rat in *The Wind in the Willows* ... "There is *nothing* – absolutely nothing – half so much worth doing as simply messing about in boats." It is thanks to these enthusiasts that narrow boats still ply up and down the inland waterways of Britain.

This book is the story of one woman's contribution to that gigantic national effort which the people of this country were called upon to make during the Second World War. To most people it was simply known as 'war work', and in the author's case it was undertaken at a time of great personal as well as national crisis.

As a young woman Susan Woolfitt had joined the Old Vic Theatre School, and it was during her time there that she met and fell in love with the actor, Donald Wolfit.* They were married in 1934, but by 1944 their marriage was in severe difficulties. With the war then in its fifth year, and my brother and myself both evacuated to a boarding school in north Devon, she very much needed a fresh perspective and some absorbing interest into which she could pour her considerable energies and talents. The advertisement which she saw in the evening paper in September 1944 must indeed have seemed like an answer to prayer. The Ministry of War Transport were doing a recruiting drive for women to work on the canals and, as she describes at the beginning of the book, it was the photograph which caught her eye: a picture of a girl standing on a boat with a boat hook in her hands. Up until that time Susan Woolfitt's experience of boats had been confined to holidays spent on the Norfolk Broads with friends during the nineteen-twenties and early thirties, but the recollection of those idyllic times and the knowledge which she had gained were enough to persuade her that she had discovered an area where she, too, could contribute to the general war effort.

---

* This difference in the spelling of the name is not an error. The original spelling of the name is Woolfitt. The alternative, shorter, form was adopted by my father early on in his career and retained by him. On publication of *Idle Women*, my mother reverted to the original spelling.

The year which followed, and which is described in this book, was to prove truly liberating as well as being totally absorbing and personally satisfying. Her enthusiasm spills over on to every page, just as it did when, as children at boarding school, we received her letters, written after a long and arduous day's work on the boats. Those letters were always full of detail about the boats and the boaters, and often illustrated as well. We looked forward to them avidly and begged to be taken to see the boats. But it wasn't until after the war, during an unforgettable canal holiday in 1948, that we witnessed at first hand her competence and physical dexterity at the tiller, and began to learn for ourselves the mysteries of the locks. That holiday also introduced us to a different countryside, seen not in set-piece fashion from approved viewpoints, but constantly changing and unfolding as the canal wound on, following the contours which the land had dictated, equally at home with the heronry and the back of the the gas works. We learnt to appreciate the unique back-door vistas which the canals present to those who travel them, and we discovered how homely and beautiful were the fixtures and fittings that surround those who made their homes on narrow boats: the shining brass and black lead of the range, the water can and dipper traditionally painted with fairy-tale castles and vast, pink cabbage roses, the flowing brickwork that ornamented so many of the smaller bridges, and the charm of the lock-keepers' cottages.

But by then the war had ended. Women were no longer needed to work on the canals, and Susan Woolfitt was never to return except as a holidaymaker. Her interest and enthusiasm, however, did not fade away. She was an early member of the Inland Waterways Association, which had been founded in 1946 and, following the publication of *Idle Women* in 1947 and a children's book *Escape to Adventure* in 1948, she lectured extensively about her experiences on the boats. By then she had become actively involved with the Women's Institute movement, and this gave her the opportunity to return to drama. She directed and performed in many productions at her local WI in Surrey, and did a great deal to establish the good reputation which the County came to have in amateur dramatic circles. This led her eventually into adjudicating, and for a while she was an adjudicator for the British Drama League, as well as being on the board of directors of her local repertory theatre. Towards the end of her life her grandchildren, her garden, and her many hobbies absorbed most of her attention until she was overtaken by her last illness and died at the end of August in 1978.

Long before the days of Women's Lib, Susan Woolfitt and the other 'idle women' who worked on the cut proved that they could take on the arduous job of keeping the cargoes moving and see them safely delivered to their destination. We are delighted that *Idle Women* is being re-published, and that a whole new generation of boaters will have the opportunity of reading it and learning, perhaps, from its practicalities as well as discovering something more of the cut as it was, and of those who worked on it during the Second World War.

Harriet Graham
Putney, December 1985

Chapter i—HOW IT ALL STARTED

It's funny how the most momentous things that happen in life seldom have momentous beginnings. Nothing could have been more unexciting than the way I walked right into the picture in the evening paper that set me off on my year as a canal boatwoman.

It was the end of the day; all the innumerable evacuees and visitors had gone to bed and I was sleepily tidying up downstairs before going up myself. Someone had left a paper on the table in the hall; it was folded back at a picture showing a girl, standing on top of a barge with a boat-hook in her hand, in a kind of "Come to the Broads" attitude. I love boats, so it caught my eye. That was all. . . .

The photograph was published at the instigation of the Ministry of War Transport, who were doing one of their periodic recruiting campaigns for the Women's Training Scheme. Women were being trained to work as canal boatwomen (or "bargees" as most people mistakenly call them) in order to release men for the Armed Forces. This much I learned from the paper and instantly started to wonder if it was work that I could do?

Both the children would be going off to boarding school in a week or so's time and I should then be free to do some real war work, which had not been possible so long as my small son was still at home. I knew a bit about boats, having had many holidays on the Broads before I was married, and this seemed a heaven-sent opportunity to have a lot more to do with them and yet be doing war work at the same time. I did not know a thing about canals, where they ran or hardly what they were; I could only guess at the kind of work it would be. With a good deal of doubt but with a burning desire to know more, I sat down and wrote to the Ministry then and there before I went up to bed.

To give any very clear impression of the way in which events tumbled over one another, once I had started the ball rolling, I ought to write the rest of this chapter like a telegram, but as it would be very tiresome to read that way I will make it as brief as I can, to show how I rushed headlong into the next year's experiences.

A*

The doubts I had were on account of my age (I was thirty-seven, which seemed rather old to begin this sort of thing) and because I felt very uncertain if they would take me as a part-timer; I *had* to be free in the school holidays for the children.

Anyway . . . my letter was answered by return.

22nd September, 1944.   M.O.W.T.,
                                                           Stratton Street,
                                                           Mayfair, W.1.

Dear Madam,

I enclose an application form and an explanatory letter about the Women's Training Scheme for work on canal boats.

Before taking up your application it will be necessary for you to consult your local Labour Exchange . . . etc, etc.

If you can do this in time and can arrange to come here for an interview next Wednesday, kindly phone me at this number on the Tuesday, and I will give you all instructions. The medical examination would be the same day to save you two journeys. You would not be free to leave London until about 5 p.m.

Hoping to hear from you one way or the other,

                                                  Yours faithfully, etc.

Things seemed to be on the move . . . with one hand I got the children off to school, with the other I waved good-bye to my visitors. I dealt with the Labour Exchange and duly rang the Ministry on "the Tuesday."

I was fully prepared to have an awful time getting through to the right person, in what I visualised as a vast building teeming with earnest myrmidons all on war effort bent. It was something of a surprise, therefore, when the extension number produced instantly: "Oh, yes, Mrs. Woolfitt. . . . can you come?"

Well, the answer to that was: Would they take me when they heard my terms? So I broached the question of "term time only" without delay.

There was a very nasty pause and then the telephone said, in quite a different voice: "Oh, no . . . that would be quite impossible, you see." I didn't see and I said so, forcibly, and with a good deal of why and wherefore. Warming to my subject I pointed out that there must be many women placed as I was who could give nine months' work a year . . . was that to be turned down out of hand? I talked wildly about a volunteer reserve such as the Forces had, and said how valuable we should be as spare-wheelers in case of sickness. In effect, the burden of my song was: See, hear and argue with me in the flesh, and then leave the rest to me. It was very impressive, I thought.

The voice seemed to think so too, though possibly not in the same way as I did; she said she was still afraid it would be quite hopeless but would I hold on for a moment? Guessing, correctly as it turned out, that she had gone for reinforcements to deal with the lunatic on the line, I held on and thought up some more excellent reasons why the war couldn't possibly proceed without me as a canal boatwoman. When someone tells me that something is "impossible" for me, I immediately want to do it more than anything on earth. This utterly mulish trait in my make-up has got me into trouble before now; this time it did me a good turn.

The Reinforcements Voice turned out to be of the opposite sex; with joy I plunged into the fray, getting more determined every minute to have a crack at the job. We argued for some time until, finally, the penny dropped and he asked me if I would be in town again soon and could I go and see him?

This was much the most satisfactory thing to do from every point of view. I can argue much better face to face with someone and he, rather naturally, wanted to have a look at me and see if I was the right type. So off to town I went the next day and saw both him and the owner of the Front Line Voice. They gave me a cigarette and we all proceeded to hurl questions at one another.

I discovered, first, that the things I was hoping to learn to manage were not barges but BOATS; that these long-boats, monkey-boats or narrow-boats (whichever you like so long as you don't call them "barges") are seventy feet long and seven feet wide; that they work in pairs, one with a heavy-oil engine towing the other which is called the "butty-boat"; that three women made up a crew, working the boats entirely from the moment when they set off down to Limehouse to load with cargo, to the time when, having emptied in Birmingham and picked up a second cargo of coal in Coventry, they empty again somewhere in the London area and come back to the depot for fresh orders. I was told that this whole round trip took something like a fortnight, that the crews lived entirely on the boats and were responsible for their own feeding arrangements, and that I should be entitled to a short leave after every two trips.

Further, the boats were capable of a speed of about 5 m.p.h.

empty but only 3–3½ m.p.h. loaded; that there are 152 locks between London and Birmingham, all of which we worked our-selves. (I received this piece of news quite calmly, without the faintest idea of its magnitude.) The training trips were two in number, worked under a woman trainer with two other recruits like myself, after which we should be drafted off elsewhere to make up fresh crews of our own. And so on and so forth. This certainly seemed as if it was going to be vastly interesting. My excitement grew.

They evidently thought I might be worth a trial because they arranged for me to go down to Southall that afternoon, to the offices of the Grand Union Canal Carrying Company, who were co-operating with the Ministry in the Women's Scheme. I should find the Front Line Voice down there, and I could look over some boats and see if I still liked the idea. I thought it sounded heavenly. I had missed the medical for that week, but there would be another that I could attend later.

From the centre of London there are several ways of getting to Southall, all equally deadly and all involving at least three different modes of locomotion terminating in a half-mile walk. Even on that first day, borne up by the excitement of the chase, I took a very poor view of this Approach to Adventure . . . later on, when I had done it a score of times, and nearly always draped in heavy kit-bags and even my complete bedding roll, it had developed into a phobia. My friends, kindly asking: "How do you get to Southall?" would wish they hadn't. . . .

My impressions of that first trip are very confused; overlaid as they are by what I now know to be there, it is hard to pick out anything clearly and say for certain: "I remember *that*. . . ." But I can distinguish a few:

The line of corrugated iron sheds, the open fields and allot-ments the other side of the road . . . where, oh, where! was the canal? . . . getting myself lost in the yard and caught up in the stream of blue boiler-suited workmen hurrying here, there and everywhere, suddenly spotting the ENQUIRIES sign I had been looking for, over the office door, the extreme hardness and narrow-ness of the seat inside (which Time, the Great Upholsterer, did much to improve); the shrewd bright eyes of the young man inside a sort of barricade, who took my name and said the F.L.V. would be along soon; and the two women . . . yes, the two girls in the office.

One was very dark and sunburnt, the other was very fair and equally brown. A very technical conversation was in progress about an injury to the fair one's knee and the word "butty" was mentioned frequently. I did at least know what that meant and to my disgust found myself glowing with pleasure. Obviously these two were part of the W.T.S. . . . my future colleagues, so to speak. I studied them, I hope unobtrusively, with the deepest interest but I could not make out how she had got hurt.

Then the F.L.V. suddenly walked in and even more suddenly I found myself being introduced to the other two who turned into Daphne (dark) and Margaret (fair) and "Could I be shown over Daphne's boats ? . . . yes, of course . . . you've got all the particulars you need to make the claim, haven't you, Mr. Kempton ? . . . right. Come along." And we all went out of the office and through the yard till we came to the water's edge.

There it was . . . the Grand Union Canal; just for that one brief moment of introduction it bore its full title. Because for ever after it was simply "the cut." All the time I worked on it I never heard anyone say anything else; nor did I ever hear the word "bargee." I cannot make out where this word has come from because nobody on the cut uses it. The men and women who live and work on the boats are called "boaters," or "boatmen," without fail; the workers on a barge are called "lightermen."

I don't really know if I had had any preconceived ideas about the boats; if I had, I was almost certainly disappointed. The pair we were visiting were tied up abreast, and parallel to the tow-path on which we were standing, so that it was impossible for my layman's eyes to tell where one stopped and the other began. I only remember that they looked huge and vast, high out of the water and like nothing I had ever seen before.

Daphne, it turned out, was one of the trainers and into her cabin we now went, down two steps into the smallest living space . . . "in the world," I was going to say, and I am not at all sure that it's an exaggeration. An enthusiastic conversation had started on the question of baths and biscuits, so I had time to look around.

I was sitting on a wooden seat to the right of the doorway*; it extended to the far end of the cabin and was built-in underneath to form lockers. Opposite me was a miniature range, from the

* See plan on page 220.

top of which a flue-pipe ran up and out through the roof; the wall behind was painted bright blue and the space between range and door was occupied by shelves, bearing the paraphernalia of washing-up. To the right of the range was an open cupboard, its three shelves packed tightly with groceries and china, its door hinged at the bottom and now flapped down so as to form a table round which the other three were seated. Beyond the cupboard lockers and drawers from roof to floor reached to the far end of the cabin. ("Far end" is quite the most unsuitable expression in the world to describe the doll's house atmosphere of the cabin. I could almost reach the "far end" from where I sat!) The fourth wall contained another doorway whose purpose I couldn't even guess at, and to the right of this again was a built-in bookshelf over the end of the "side-bed" on which I sat. Behind my head was a porthole, for light only, and a similar one was placed in the centre of the ceiling. The distance from my knees to the stove was perhaps eighteen inches.

I took all this in so much more quickly than it is possible to describe it but a careful description is necessary if the reader is to get a clear picture of how we lived. The furnishings and colour schemes varied from one cabin to another but basically the design was exactly the same. I am filled with admiration for the amount the designers packed into them; there was really very little that could be improved on.

The other three were sitting on my right, Margaret on the bed beside me and the other two on the cross seat. This is really only a plank of wood which fits into grooves on either side of the cabin but it never ceased to please me by its extreme simplicity and usefulness. It could be whizzed right up to the table, as it was now, or shoved back out of the way or lifted out altogether.

Biscuits had now been produced out of the bursting cupboard, and Daphne began to tell me about the work in the gloomiest possible terms. This technique was always adopted by the trainers when an aspirant fell to them for interview, in an endeavour to sort out the sheep from the goats as early as possible. So many applicants came with the idea that the life was one long glide through sunny meadows, an arm thrown lazily over the tiller and a good spice of romance to brighten things up. It was very desirable that any girls who thought that way should be got rid of before they started and before they had a chance of changing their minds in the middle of a trip.

I am quite sure that I never thought it would be like that . . . that sort of picture doesn't appeal to me anyway . . . and every word Daphne said made me more and more keen to try it. Actually it turned out far more colourful and interesting than I had imagined and for that I may well have Daphne's gloomy little talk to thank. She told me of the dirt, the difficulty of learning to manage the boats, the wet and icy hands of winter-time boating and the primitiveness of it all. She said nothing about plumbing, any sign of which was conspicuous by its absence. I didn't like to ask.

One of the trainees materialised at this moment and I was hauled off to have a look at the engine-room. I think the others wanted to have a chance to give me a good pick over; it was very hard to tell at first sight if you had a dud or a winner, and if they made a mistake it was sure to result in a loss of time and money and labour. The engine-room left me quite cold, but I plied my guide with questions and learned that it was an excellent life with no fixed hours and your evenings to yourself. That sounded all right . . . I liked the whole idea more and more.

When I got back they had decided to give me a trial; the F.L.V. said she would go into the question of letting me off for the holidays and when she had talked it over with the G.U. she would let me know.

Nothing more happened for some time and it began to look as if the ball had rolled so far and then changed its mind. I waited, and thought about it a great deal and wondered if I was mad to attempt it, but whichever conclusion was reached I was always quite certain that I wanted to try it, provided I could get through the medical. . . .

This was worrying me more than a little. I had been over-hauled recently by my own doctor and knew that I was perfectly fit but for a semi-detached kidney. This produced no symptoms, adverse or otherwise, and if he had not told me I should not have known anything about it; so perhaps I might get away with it at the forthcoming medical. It all depended on how thorough it was . . . but I felt pretty sure that if it was spotted I should be turned down.

About ten days later I got sick of waiting and phoned the Ministry for news. The upshot of this was that I went to London again the next day . . . for the medical. I called at the Ministry for instructions, armed with a long list of questions, which I have

just found amongst the clutter. It reads: "Civvies ? Fare home ?
How long will first trip take ? Leisure at night ? Leave kit
during leaves ? Address for letters ? Saucepans ? Cash if no
letters ? When do we get paid ? Pyjamas ? Fuel for Primus ?"
All these questions have a tick against them, so I must have done
a good deal of talking. Apparently the G.U. were prepared to
take a sporting chance on me as a spare-wheeler; with this
heartening piece of news I set off to the dreaded medical.

For the rest of that day things happened like a news reel put
through the projector at top speed. Out of the train, wait for
the doctor, unpleasant sinking feeling, enter doctor bustling,
into surgery, rip open top buttons, "say ninety-nine," "have you
had any serious illness ? . . . when did you have your appendix
out?" . . . "when I was seven!" . . . here it comes, a violent kidney
punch . . . "did that hurt ?" . . . "not more than I should expect,
doctor ! . . . Ha ! Ha ! Ha !" . . . (that's perfectly truthful but
will he fall for it ? . . . breathe again . . . he has !) " Have I passed?"
. . . "I am not permitted to divulge the result of the examination"
. . . "WHAT ??" . . . "You will be notified by the Ministry . . .
(don't be daft . . . is it my body or the Ministry's we're talking
about . . . better put that more gracefully) . . . "Well, doctor, I
quite see your point . . . the only thing is that I shall certainly not
bother to return to the Ministry and waste their time and my own,
if I've failed . . . yes, regulations I know . . . certainly I'll take a
note to them . . . do I have to travel all the way to Mayfair without know . . . Oh ! I *have* passed ? . . . thank you, thank you *so*
much . . . not at all, good-bye, GOOD-BYE." Back to London
with the road clear before me . . . into the office waving the doctor's
note . . . I'm through, I've passed, I'm in . . . "How soon can I
start ?"

"Can you be ready by Tuesday ?" said the F.L.V. (No, not
possibly but I shall.) "Your trainer will be Miss Gayford" . . .
(what about Daphne ?) . . . "your boats the *Battersea* and the
Uttoxeter" . . . (so much for romance !) . . . "you will take
the 2.7 train from Paddington to Hayes where Miss Gayford will
meet you with your luggage . . . have you got a mattress ? You'll
have to get one somehow. The other trainee will be another
term-time mother like yourself . . ." (so my idea *had* worked?) . . .
"don't forget the strong belt . . . it's very important . . . good-bye
and good luck !"

A frenzied week-end getting rid of the livestock, notifying the school authorities how they could get hold of me . . . (within an hour if Mr. Kempton at Bull's Bridge was on the job. Many of us had reason to be grateful to him for the marvels of ingenuity he performed on the end of the phone in this respect) . . . dashing once again to London to buy a mattress, digging out my husband's discarded flannel trousers and as many pairs of socks as I could find, washing, ironing, darning, calming down friends and relations who were now quite certain I had gone off my head, cancelling the tradesmen, packing, shutting up the house, writing to the children, ordering the taxi, piling my kit into it . . . I was off !

Whatever happened I was for it now; I had got to go through with it however awful it turned out to be, and quite suddenly I was certain it *would* be awful and I would have given anything to be able to rush back into the house . . . well, at all events it would be something new to occupy my mind and all the wits I had, and I wanted nothing so much as that.

And so it started; all from a picture in the paper. The most interesting, original and enviable year I ever spent in my life; a year that I never could have spent if it hadn't been for the war; a year that I wouldn't have missed for anything in the world; a picture of a life that I had no knowledge of, of companionship and gruelling hard work, of learning how the other half live and love and make friends . . . a picture from the paper.

PASSENGERS for Southall and Hayes have to take off from the extreme back of the station. I didn't, and my arrival at the front entrance and subsequent pilgrimage through the sprawling terminus was something of an ordeal, nobly shared by the fatherly porter on whom I hastily shed my unspeakable luggage.

After what seemed like several days we landed up at the suburban line and here a surprise awaited me. While I was busy getting my stuff into the van, a woman of about my own age came up and asked with enthusiasm, "Are you the new trainee?" I had not expected this and with a sinking heart confessed that I was and was thereupon led into the carriage where she was already established. She said her name was Vera and she had been told to look out for me, adding: "You can always tell new trainees by their bedding, so as soon as I saw your luggage I knew it must be you !" (I was becoming increasingly doubtful if it *was* me, setting off on this wild idea, but I felt her point with all the concentrated venom already engendered by my detestable bedding roll.)

We settled down in opposite corners of the carriage, I to ask a spate of questions and poor Vera to answer them as best she could. She had done one trip and had loved it and would now be the semi-trained third on Miss Gayford's boats, the other mother and myself completing the crew. She had not seen the other trainee and I had not seen "Miss Gayford"; from both our points of view present fears were less than horrible imaginings and we forthwith decided to share a cabin; on the motor boat, Vera explained, because "Kit" always lived on the butty. I asked who Kit was, stupidly, I suppose, and learned that Miss Gayford answered to that name. It all sounded very matey and slightly hearty, and I wondered if I should ever arrive at such terms of easy familiarity. I need not have worried. . . .

I went on and on at Vera, finding out from her at first hand all the things the F.L.V. hadn't been able to tell me, I elicited all there was to know on the subject of sanitation (despite the horrified looks of the other occupant of our carriage) which can be briefly summed up, once and for all, by the word Bucket. I have a joyous recollection of Vera's face as she earnestly assured me: " . . . really, ours is *awfully* comfortable." This superb line upset me completely and at the same time dispelled my last doubts in a wild fit of giggles which, once over, left me restored and confident again.

By the time we reached Hayes I felt I had learned a good deal and got out of the train ready for anything. Vera immediately began to fuss like an old hen, in an endeavour to locate the other mother and bring her safely into the fold. Between us we got my quantities of luggage to the far side of the station and there we found "Mother McCrea," similarly laden and waiting for us. Owing to some domestic upheaval, the details of which I forget, she wasn't going to join us for a couple of days but had arrived, wisely I thought, to make sure that her equally repellant luggage was stowed on the boats with mine. Vera went off to find "Kit" and arrived back to say that she was waiting, so we all loaded up and set off.

Much sooner than I had expected, in a few yards in fact, we came to the steep bank that leads from the station level to the water side. At the top of the bank stood "Kit" and I nearly laughed out loud . . . she was so very different from what I had expected her to be. Very small and slim, dressed in sailor's trousers and a faded brown sail-cloth fisherman's blouse, with very dark short hair and gold rings in her ears, she radiated a sense of unbounded vitality, the whole effect making me seem like a well-intentioned but extra clumsy elephant. This feeling has never worn off and even to this day I feel much too large when I meet Kit. I was more than relieved to see that she didn't look at all "hearty". . . .

"Have you got much more?" asked Kit. "Right . . . I'll whistle up and help you. Vera, put your stuff on the motor and come back and give us a hand, will you?"

Saying which she "whistled" . . . and when Kit does that most people of ordinary proportions have to run to keep up with her. I ran. Backwards and forwards we went till all our stuff was stowed away on the motor lying tied beside the towpath, and Mother McCrea had arranged where and how to meet us in two days' time.

Kit had already "winded" the boats, so, with Vera steering, she let go at once and we started for the "lay-by," the stretch of cut at Bull's Bridge where the boats lie up to wait for fresh orders. To "wind" a boat means to turn it; owing to the narrow-

ness of the cut and the length of the boats this can only be done
in specially prepared places. At this particular spot you have to
take the boat on about half a mile beyond the "arrival" bridge
and wind it down a short little arm of water which just there
gives the width required for the operation. (It is not pronounced
navy fashion but like the wind that blows.)

As soon as we started Kit showed me where to stand to get
out of Vera's way, so that I should not be swept off if the tiller
came across suddenly. This was lesson number one and a very
important one, too. The tiller handle is breast high and long
enough to reach right across the little piece of deck space called
the counter, at the stern end of the boat; when you are steering
and want to move the tiller from one side right across to the
other, going round corners for instance, you must get your body
out of the way first.

This is achieved by stepping as far forward as you can (till you
are nearly falling down the cabin steps) and letting the tiller
pass behind you from one hand to the other; or else you can
duck underneath it, which isn't elegant but is a good deal
quicker. You obviously cannot do either of these things with
two other people on the counter beside you, so that anybody, other
than the actual steerer, has to stand forward on the gunwale.
This runs from the counter to the far end of the engine-room
down either side of the cabin and is about four inches wide; it
struck me as being a very precarious perch but I very soon got
quite used to it and found it a good deal safer than it looks. The
cabin sides slope inwards so that you can lean against them, and
well away from the water which looms a few inches below the
foot you are balancing on; the cabin top has a kind little ledge
running round it which offers a finger-hold. It was while I was
engaged in balancing and gripping like mad that Kit suddenly
said:

"What's your name?" I told her it was Woolfitt.

"Yes," said Kit kindly, "but I meant your other name. We
only use Christian names on the cut."

I must have looked a little blank because she added:

"You always call me Kit, of course."

Now, I have an intense dislike of using people's Christian
names unless and until I know them really well, and it fills me
with embarrassment and cold panic to be asked to address someone like that straight off. When Kit said that about Christian

names I knew I would be lost if I paused for a second to think about it, so I plunged into the "Kit" and "Vera" business without delay and hoped I sounded more natural than I felt. Lesson number two.

We had been travelling quite fast all this time; the butty had been left behind in the lay-by, so naturally the motor could get along faster without her. The cut bends and winds a bit round here but there was no other traffic and I do remember thinking how brilliant Vera was to be able to steer so well. She was not, of course, being at that moment anything of the kind and I am sure she won't mind me saying so; it was only due to my total ignorance that it looked so expert. If anybody had told me then that I should learn to steer the motor and simultaneously prime and light a Primus, boil a kettle and make a pot of tea, at the same time dodging bridge-holes and avoiding other boats and think nothing of it at all, I should have thought them raving mad. Yet I did. We all did.

The cut isn't very attractive between Hayes and the depot. On the one hand there are fields and hedges running down to the towpath but the other side has a series of wharves and ware-houses letting out every variety of smoke, smell and noise, mostly unpleasant; the grand exception being the perfectly entrancing smell which emanates day and night from the Nestlé's cocoa factory. Hot chocolate blended with the scent of roasting coffee is wafted on the air till the longing for the abolition of the sweet ration becomes nearly unbearable.

This smell and the sight of the huge grey buildings are a signal that one has nearly arrived at the lay-by, and very soon Vera was told to slow down while passing the boats tied up there. If you go past at full speed the wash is apt to suck the stationary boats away from the kerb and snap their tying-up straps; a mad-dening thing to have done to you, especially if you are out at the time.

I am afraid there will have to be an interlude here to allow me to explain a little about the cut language and the jargon of the boats. I had hoped to be able to do it bit by bit as I went along but I can see that it is going to be very irritating for the reader if I don't break the ground first.

To start with, then; there are practically no nautical terms in use on the cut; there is no port or starboard, you "tie-up" and "let go," your ropes are called "straps" and "lines," the bows of

the boat become the "fore-end!" the boat-hook is the "shaft,"
and the operation in which it is used, of which *very* much more
later, is called "shafting." Every single part of a narrow boat
has its own special name which in nearly every case is quite
different from that used on sea-going or river craft. The boaters
for the most part refer to the cabins as their "houses"; the towpath side of the cut is called the "inside" and the other bank the
"outside"; if you want to tell the steerer to get in closer to the
towpath you say; "Hold in," or for the reverse: "Hold out."

I have been told, though I have never actually heard it, that if
you wish to be particularly rude to another pair of boats, usually
with reference to their untidy appearance, you greet them as you
go past with: "How d'you do, *sailor!* " . . . from which it will be
seen that anyone coming to the cut as I did with a smattering of
nautical language and a deep reverence for the Senior Service
will have a rude shock in store. The first thing I had to do was to
un-learn everything I knew or had picked up about ordinary
boats and begin again at the beginning of this bewildering new
vocabulary. I shall come to more of that later.

We moved very slowly past the dry-dock, the slipway
and the oil store and then came upon the line of tied-up
boats I had seen on my first visit. The next thing, of course, was
to find our butty. I expect Kit knew exactly where it was but it
took several trips before I could go unerringly to the right spot;
it is not as easy as it sounds when you are approaching from the
water.

As many as twenty pairs of boats all tied up in a long line, with
their stern ends to the kerb and their identical fore-ends face you
in the water; all looking as like as peas, the only distinguishing
marks being newer paintwork or some individual decorations
here and there. To make it harder still they are named and
numbered on the sterns only, far out of sight; since you went
away the "hole" made by taking your boat out has neatly closed
up again, the fore-ends swinging and swaying together cheek
by jowl as other boats have passed by. There are not many landmarks on the bank to help either, but of course none of these
things worried me that day. Kit was in charge and l watched with
fascinated admiration while she and Vera backed the motor into
its proper hole, shafting the other boats out of the way to do so.

Even here the cut is not wide enough to allow much manœuvring of a seventy-foot boat (four feet longer than a cricket pitch),

but the method used to get in is extremely simple when it comes off . . . and very much the reverse when it doesn't.

One person stays at the tiller; putting the engine "astern" she steers for the hole with as much acceleration as she can muster, but this alone is not enough. A second person goes down to the fore-end with the "long shaft," which is twenty feet long and weighs about a ton. Braced on the tiny bit of deck space with her back to the steerer but keeping one eye trained on her (a complicated position, this), the unhappy girl plunges the shaft into the water, to the bottom, and with all her weight and strength pushes on it till the nose of the boat has moved round a little; she then pulls the shaft out, hand over hand, and begins again. This goes on until the boat is at right angles to the kerb, when it should be an easy matter to back her gently into her place.

The finer shades of this particular performance were wasted on me, but with Kit in charge of it I have no doubt whatever that it was done superlatively well . . . I wondered if I should *ever* learn to do anything so gymnastic.

When Vera had tied the boat up Kit told me I could go below and unpack. This I was delighted to do because I had been burning to see what I was already thinking of as "my cabin."

The cabin of the motor is slightly smaller than that of the butty for three reasons. First, it is not so wide owing to some of the total width of the boat being taken up by the gunwale outside. (There is no gunwale on the butty.) Secondly, it has no door at the far end, which is an iron bulkhead separating the cabin from the engine-room. Lastly, it has to be shorter so that the inclusion of the engine-room doesn't detract too much from the hold space. Later on I measured the *Battersea* cabin and found it was eight feet long by five feet wide.

Into this snug little apartment I started to fit my belongings. Each girl had one drawer and one locker for her clothes but we used to use the side-bed, which was made with removable top boards, for boots, frying-pans, oilskins, saucepans and other impedimenta. If you didn't do this, all these things had to hang up in the cabin, which besides being very unsightly got horribly in the way. In addition to this space, there was also the little locker under the table-cum-cupboard and a second one to the right of the door which was generally used by us for our washing things.

By moving out the cross-seat, a big flap door let down from

under the lockers and fitting into a groove in the side-bed opposite formed the second bed, at right angles to the other in an L-shape. During the day all our bedding, blankets, pillows and mattresses had to be packed away in this cupboard and woe betide anyone who turned up with an enormous quantity of stuff. She was hideously unpopular, because it meant a fearful fight every morning to get the cupboard to shut. Vera's mattress was huge and, as well as the daily struggle to put it away, about a foot of it used to lie on my feet every night.

She chose to sleep across the cabin with her feet in the cup-board. I slept with my head facing the stove and my feet in Vera's face, an arrangement which she didn't seem to mind; and so long as it was her face that was walked on and not mine I wasn't complaining. By virtue of her seniority she had first pick and could have had my place if she had wanted it.

I'm glad she didn't because, in my opinion, my position was far and away the best and whenever I had any choice in the matter I always chose it. In the summer you could have the sliding hatch open over your head so that you got the maximum of fresh air, and in the winter you had the remains of the fire about eighteen inches from your bed, which was extremely comforting. And all the year round the grate was my ash-tray and the coalbox lid my bedside table ! The only snag was if it started to rain in the middle of the night, when you woke, rather belatedly, to find your pillow and shoulders soaked and knew there was nothing for it but to get out into the puddle on the floor and pull the hatch over. But this didn't happen often and I never got so wet that I bothered to change my pyjamas.

Across the bulkhead at the end of all motor cabins ran a shelf. Ours was decorated by a bottle of ink (Vera), some books (me), a small mirror and the kind of metal tea-pot that becomes so hot when full that you can't possibly pick it up. Both these last possessions were Kit's and only lent to the trainees on the motor.

We also sported an alarm clock, which went off like the Last Trump every morning, and a very efficient Primus. And that was all that was visible to the eye. Later Vera proudly displayed a couple of saucepans, a frying-pan, a bottle of disinfectant (very necessary), a quantity of bars of washing soap, some potatoes and a few sticks of firewood. Oh, and the milk; evaporated and tinned and supplied to the boat people and to us "off points," it was our pride and joy, representing the only official recognition of our peculiar mode of life where even the ration was unobtainable. It lived in the side-bed in both boats, though in the butty it had to share pride of place with a colossally heavy wet battery which supplied the electric light and which constantly had to be heaved back and forth into the engine-room for recharging.

We had lunch in the works canteen that day; at the same time I dropped talking about "lunch" and referred ever afterwards to "dinner." I think in all branches of heavy work it is "dinner" that takes the limelight; people simply don't know what you are talking about if you call it lunch, or else they think you mean the hasty snack which you grab between ten and eleven o'clock in the morning.

I cannot remember what we had to eat but I am sure it was good, filling and very cheap. It was all those things every other time I took advantage of it; very thankful we used to be for the canteen facilities when we got in exhausted at the end of a trip with an empty larder. The women who ran it were all destined to become great friends (they always took an intense interest in my children for some reason) and would give us a rousing welcome when we arrived for our first shore meal for a week or so.

There was a long table right down the middle of the room, at which were seated all the mechanics, carpenters, painters, glaziers and office staff of the depot, all with large steaming plates in front of them. Some were more advanced with the meal than others, causing the air to be thick with cigarette smoke, and as you came in at the door you walked straight into the middle of a game of darts which always seemed to be going on. There were small tables down the sides of the room and the far end was all serving counter. The manager used to have one of the small tables and, if he was lucky, a cloth, but everyone else gravitated to the counter, leaned on it, passed the time of day, ordered, waited, was served, and, after collecting suitable implements out of a box, moved off to any space that was free.

I had changed by this time into a very old pair of trousers and a shirt, and 1 felt more in the picture as I took my place with the others against the counter. I remember that the wireless was on at full blast and that the after-dinner cups of tea, saucerless, were of a very high standard of excellence and comfort.

When Kit thought we had sat long enough Vera was sent off to Southall to do the necessary shopping for the motor menage; bread, fresh milk while we could get it, and rations. I was led

back to the boats for a personally conducted tour of them, but
on the way Kit took me into every single workshop in the place,
introducing me to the foremen and telling me where everything
was stored and where to go for this, that and the other.

The tour started at the stern of the motor where the first
thing you come to are layers of fat fenders, sticking out beyond
the counter by a yard to protect the propeller blades in the water
below from getting knocked. The first fender is like a very
thick footstool and is hung on to the counter with strong chains;
inside it are two more, fat in the middle and tapering to points
at both ends, which rejoice in the delightful name of "tipcats."
The whole thing is rammed together quite tight so that instead of
hanging down it sticks out rigidly, just where it is most needed.
It also weighs an incredible amount if it wants altering at any
time, but Kit didn't mention this. . . .

The tiller is called the "ram's head" and is curved like a swan's
neck towards the steerer. It is metal, on the motor, and is painted
in sections with the G.U. colours of red, white and blue; at the
top it straightens out and an extension fits on with a loose pin so
that it can be removed in a lock. If it didn't do this it would swing
across and jamb against the walls. I found afterwards that the
tillers on both the boats are taken out every night when you tie-
up; it is a sort of signal that work is over. On the butty the tiller
is alternatively reversed in its socket so that it points heaven-
wards but it is quite a different shape. I shall come to that later . . .
we are still on the motor now. . . .

We walked round the gunwale till we had passed the engine-
room, Kit telling me the name of everything as we went. Beyond
the engine-room comes the hold, the largest proportion of boat
space. About a yard is cut off this next to the engine-room by
loose planks which fit across the boat and form what is known as
the "back-end." Words fail me with which to describe the inestim-
able value of this little bit of space snatched from the cargo;
into it goes the coal to be used in the cabins, the brooms
for sweeping out the boats after unloading, the odd bit of rope
waiting to be spliced, the coal shovel and any other unwanted
bit of tack that cannot be kept tidily anywhere else. The butty
achieves an even better back-end but I will come to that later, too.

(This is all horribly technical and I strongly advise anybody
who is already yawning to skip it. It will be possible to get on
without it, but it is all so very much part of our lives that I

feel I must include it for those who are interested in the running of the boats.)

When the gunwale came to an abrupt stop we climbed on to the cabin top, which made me feel very guilty as if I were walking on the dining-room table. But far worse was to come. From the roof of the cabin, planks lead the whole way down to the fore-end of the boat and there is no other way of getting there. There is nothing to hold on to and only the width of the plank to walk on, while underneath the empty hold yawns to receive the stumbler. The hold is divided into three by cross planks, called beams, on which the top-planks are supported. Each beam has a slot in the centre through which passes a flat upright, so that if you can make the intervening gap you can clutch the "stand" as you go by.

The real fun begins when the boat is prepared for loading; then all the top-planks are elevated away on the top of the stands, where they form an uninterrupted path from cabin-top to fore-end with a sheer drop into the hold on either side. In addition the planks bounce in a lively fashion as you walk, and if you ever achieve running, the levitation is quite remarkable !

The last upright is a solid square affair and is called the "mast" . . . one of the few nautical terms, but quite unlike an ordinary mast. It telescopes into itself so that it can be pulled up to take the last of the top-planks in their highest position, and is topped off with a natty little contrivance to which is fastened the pulley-block when the overhead towing-rope is in use. I *never* discovered a satisfactory method of fixing this pulley and the operation was destined to become one of my Waterloos.

The top-planks end about six feet short of the extreme fore-end, and before you is a tent-shaped affair with semi-solid sides and a flat and solid top. This is the cratch and you get to know it very well, as it has to be climbed over on every journey to the fore-end of either boat . . . a journey that is made with great frequency. The cratch has a shelf inside it where Kit used to keep the tarred sheets which cover the cargo, and round the edge is a very narrow gunwale round which I now crept, holding tightly to the "top-strings" (which are lashed over the cratch to keep its tarpaulin flat).

If and when you have succeeded in getting round the cratch, you are at last on the fore-end of the boat; a nice flat comfortable surface marred only by the raised iron hatch cover and the thought

of your return journey . . . This space is called the "deck" and
the hatch, also called the deck, lifts up to reveal a dark hole of
Calcutta in which are coiled all the straps and towing-ropes not
used when the boats are empty. The deck also carries the headlight on an iron stand and, on the extreme front, a T-shaped stud
for towing.   Hanging down from the actual prow is another
fender, but this is quite a ladylike affair and in locks is easily
heaved on board.

All the time we had been making this perilous journey Kit
had kept up an unceasing fire of information and, I now realise,
had been watching me like a lynx to see how I got on with the
gymnastics. It was the first time I had been from one end of a
boat to the other, and you could tell a lot how people would
shape from the way they "walked the plank" at the first go.
Luckily heights don't worry me, but any poor soul with a bad
head for them might just as well have packed up and gone home
at once.

(Well, that's the end of the technical part . . . for a bit, anyway.)

When we had regained the cabin, Kit sent me off to the Labour
Exchange to complete the formalities there. I was badly in need
of a change of environment to clear my head a bit; if this has been
muddling to read about, it was fifty times worse to look at and
try to take in intelligently. There seemed to be so much of it at
the same time, and the life going on all round in the other boats
was highly distracting. I was dying to stop and watch them but
I knew I should have to keep my wits about me if I was to take
in all that Kit was saying. I went off to Southall on the bus feeling
as though I had just been let out of school.

On returning from the Labour Exchange I found Kit had
produced tea in her cabin; I was seeing it for the first time. It
was the nicest cabin I ever saw. The woodwork was very dark
and gave the impression of an old inn bar parlour. Some of it
was picked out with a green line and the port-hole had a miniature
red cotton curtain over it. The cross-seat was red, too, with a
picture of the traditional castle in the middle, and at the end of
the side-bed stood a large box with more castles on the top and
its sides covered with roses. Every available piece of flat wall-
space was hung with brass, shining in the dark little cabin with the
glow from the fire. Horse-brasses of all shapes and sizes, a brass
rod over the range, three handsome brass knobs in a proud line

inside the door lintel, all throwing out little moving gleams of orange-coloured light. The range was polished like black satin; even the enamel kettle on the top shone with the rest.

Above the side-bed Kit used to hang a row of beer mugs, pale blue and grey and pink, and her "party" cups, mottled green with flowers on the handle. At the head of her side-bed she had had a shelf fixed, so that it would just clear the pillow at night, and on it was a candle in a small green candlestick, her cigarette box painted with roses and a copper mug filled with those bright-coloured tapers.

It was with real pleasure that I saw this cabin for the first time and realised that one could have comfortable, and even beautiful, surroundings on the boats. I hate the word "snug" but I must admit that I cannot think of a better one to describe what these cabins could be. On a cold and wet winter night with the doors fastened and the slide pulled over, the fire roasting hot, a good supper and comfortable slippers on one's weary feet, with a sense of the job done for the day, life could be very pleasant indeed. On one trip we had the luxury of a wireless and could lie back at the end of the day and listen to the Proms, or whatever else fancy dictated, in far greater comfort than at home where it is not usual to go to bed in the drawing-room !

I am sure the party cups were not got down for me that day; they were only used for visitors and very special occasions and I wasn't either . . . that was a really stirring thought. I belonged to these boats now; it was going to be part of my work to look after them, to keep them clean and running properly so that they could do their job. Suddenly I felt a warm rush of affection for them.

My diary says: "Bed by 9 with head in complete whirl." It is not to be wondered at. This was a New Life with a vengeance; I was dead tired mentally when at last I got into my badly made, brick-hard, strange new bed, so tired that I couldn't sleep at all because my brain would *not* stop working.

Some late home-comers made a fearful row around midnight, passing within a yard of my head; I thought how truly extraordinary it was that I should be lying there, practically in their path, with nothing but two half-open doors between me and complete publicity . . . if I had known a little more I should have said "with nothing but the boat people's great natural courtesy between me and complete publicity. . . ." Vera and I were as

private that night as if we were the only occupants of a house at
the end of a long drive.

And it was only I who had the peculiarity not to be able to
sleep . . . the new trainee. They were not being inconsiderate
when they came home singing; they simply didn't know I existed.
Why should they ?

CHAPTER III—FIRST DAY

IT was with great relief that I heard the alarm go off, and Vera's smothered grunt as she reached out to stop it. I looked at my watch ... 6.30 ... what an hour ! but thank heaven the night was over.

We clambered out, and dressed sitting on the edge of our beds. We had to: there wasn't room to do anything else. While we did this Vera had got the Primus going for the coffee and, as soon as we could, we got rid of our beds by simply rolling them up and thrusting them into the cupboard. The exponents of turning the mattress every day would have had a stroke but there was neither time nor room for stripping one's bed and the best you could hope for was to hang everything out in the sun while waiting to load.

I don't remember my ablutions playing any very important part that morning but I daresay there were more of them than at any later date till I had my first leave. All water had to be carried in big red eight-gallon cans which were kept on the cabin top; this was all we had for all purposes till we came to the next fresh water tap. For obvious reasons we never used cut water for anything except, possibly, to remove the top layer of grease and dirt from hands and legs before coming into the cabin. Tied up in the lay-by we could use as much as we liked to carry from the near-by taps, but even then we thought twice before lugging eight-gallon cans about too often.

Breakfast on the boats was always the nicest meal of the day. There was a little more time for it than for the other meals and we got up earlier than we need have done for the exquisite pleasure of dawdling over a cigarette afterwards. It was a very simple meal; invariably coffee and toast and marmalade, and it took place at the unbelievable hour of 5.45. . . . We kept our porridge for 9 o'clock, by which time we would have been working for a couple of hours and would be very, very glad of it. Eaten out of the saucepan with tinned milk and treacle, as you steered, it was very good.

So, although I did not know it, I was being broken in most gently that morning, waking up a whole hour later than usual.

Everything felt queer, rather like a fairy-story or living in a

doll's house. I sat on the edge of my bed and laid the fire and
then, without shifting my position, I could turn and take my
breakfast mug off its hook above my head; I let down the table
and laid that by moving the things from the cupboard six inches
forward: the cutlery was kept in a drawer beneath. Still without
getting up, I reached the biscuit tin that was our bread bin, the
jug for the coffee and the top of the stove where the kettle was
by now boiling, all without moving a step. It was almost too
easy, I thought, standing up to stretch . . . and caught my head a
hearty crack on the ceiling. "Too easy" was the word; now I
had found the snag. For a whole year I had to brush my hair
sitting down, which I never got used to, and there was only one
butty in which I could stand completely upright. At other times
I walked about with a permanent crick in the neck.

Vera spent breakfast telling me how Kit expected her trainees
to keep the motor cabin: no dirty washing-up left about, range
polished and hob emeried and if possible she liked us to have
something ready to heat up for dinner; there would probably not
be time to cook anything later and she well knew the value of a
hot meal when we were tired.

I learned, too, how the shopping was worked. We both put a
fixed sum, usually ten shillings, in the "kitty"; whoever went
shopping took the "kitty" with them until it was all spent, when
we each put in an equal sum again. It sounds very simple but in
practice we always seemed to be in a state of owing money to,
or being owed money by, the "kitty," but there didn't seem to be
a better way to work it and I think everyone used the same system.
The shop people up and down the cut got accustomed to the
sight of us paying for our purchases out of a treacle tin.

We had washed up and cleared everything away when Kit's
voice suddenly called out:

"Can I come in ?"

This was my first introduction to cut manners and I remember
thinking it funny that she should bother to ask. After all, she
was the boss.

You never, under any circumstances whatsoever, went into
someone else's cabin without an invitation and if you could not
wait for one then you asked before going in or knocked loudly
on the cabin side and stood looking into the middle distance
until you were invited in. If, in the course of the day's work,
you had to walk past or over another pair of boats (as very often

happened) you asked first for permission to cross and if possible did so beyond the cabin, or failing that you crossed or went by as quickly as you could, with your head turned the other way so that you should not see inside.

Kit was always fearfully particular about this until she had got us properly trained to it; there is nothing the boaters object to more than prying into their homes. The fact that you live within a foot or two of the public pathway makes you very vulnerable but it is surprising how few people seem to realise what a breach of manners they are committing when they do their utmost to stare in. I have actually had people on the top step, craning their necks into the cabin to get a better view, people who certainly wouldn't dream of pressing their noses to the front window of a house . . . but what is the difference ?

It is a thoughtless piece of rudeness arising, I daresay, from the intense interest felt about those whose homes are on the water. Don't we all like to look over the living quarters of a ship ?

I must admit that the boaters' cabins are *very* well worth looking into, with the profusion of brass, the pierced and painted plates, the lace curtains and every flat surface covered in "boat painting." Kit was well aware of this and she explained to me once and for all, as she did to all new trainees, that to give way to the temptation was simply not done. She *always* asked before she came in to us and so I quickly learned to do the same.

"How did you sleep ?" she asked, seating herself on the bottom step, which was also the lid of the coal-box. . . .

"Rottenly, thank you," I answered, "in fact I didn't. My brain was going round and round all night."

"I know," said Kit, "you don't know if you're coming or going to start with, do you ? Well, now . . . I think this morning we will go and have a little instruction in the engine-room, only a very little because you're going to have a proper talk from Mr. Curtis this afternoon—you've never had one, have you Vera ?—and then we will go up and have a look at Cowley."

I asked, what was Cowley and what was there to look at there ?

"There is a lock at Cowley," said Kit and I am surprised that there was not an off-stage clap of thunder or some other awful phenomenon to accompany her words, so momentous an utterance was it.

"Do you know how a lock works ?" she went on.

B

"Only vaguely," I answered. "I've only been in a lock on the Thames and you sit and wait till there are enough boats in and then a man comes and does things."

"Yes . . . er, yes . . . " said Kit. "Well, on the cut you don't wait because there is only room for one pair of boats at a time and there is no man to 'do things.' We do that ourselves. We will go up and look at it and then I'll explain to you how it works. Are you all cleared up ? Good . . . then come on" . . . and out she went with us at her heels. (I have never seen Kit move slowly and if I did I should be quite sure she was ill.)

The engine-room is very small and there is barely space for three people to see properly. I was shown how to turn the engine over, with someone to help me; how to push down the compression lever at the right moment, when the others were starting her; how to stop her, and the names and functions of various bits and pieces. I hope I looked intelligent: I did not feel it. Kit always kept her windlasses in a methodical pile on the oil tank in one corner; under one door was an iron ladder and under the other was the tool-box; on the wall hung a huge ship's lantern for use if the electric light failed before a tunnel. We never carried a riding light as other boats are forced to do.

The talk did not take long and then Kit told us to get coats before starting for Cowley.

We took both boats this time so that I could be taught to steer the butty. They were unloaded, of course, and the fore-end of the butty was tied up close to the stern of the motor, in which position the butty doesn't really have to be steered at all, except to keep her away from the kerb in a bridge-hole. Happily I didn't know that my efforts were entirely superfluous and madly strove to do as I was told.

The big, curved, wooden tiller seemed unwieldy to a degree and it felt very odd to be steering with my hands behind me. Our little motor cruiser on the Broads had had a wheel like a car and was similarly steered. Now, it was all behind or beside me and the handle was capable of going right over the water until I felt I *must* go with it, only my feet staying in the well of the butty hatches. And the direction was all back to front: if I wanted to go to the left the tiller had to go to the right . . . it took me literally weeks before I could steer instinctively without having to work it all out first. Kit said some people are born steerers and then, I suppose, it is quite natural for these happy few to do the opposite to what appears necessary; I was very dull about it, though it was not for lack of interest: it fascinated me beyond measure to see the great boat obeying my hand.

There are no bad corners or other excitements on the way to Cowley; beyond Hayes and the "arrival" bridge the cut becomes very countrified and by the time we had arrived at Cowley it was beautiful, with the massive beeches below the lock reflecting all their October splendour of colour in the water below. The cut is very wide here and we tied the boats up just short of the lock and walked up the towpath for my initiation.

From the direction of the lay-by Cowley is an up-hill lock and for some reason that I never fathomed, is always left ready for up-hill traffic, so it was empty when I first saw it. The big bottom gates were open, and inside the lock the water was black and still from the reflection of the high walls, slimy with weed and wet in the sunshine. We walked to the edge of the lock and I looked down: it seemed a long drop to the water.

At the far end were the top gates, massive wooden affairs, built so that they met in an apex pushing out into the enormous weight of water above the lock. The bottom gates are similarly built to point inwards: it would be impossible for them to bear the weight of the water if they were straight. Out across the towpath on either side reached the balance beams of the gates, white painted tree trunks, usually of elm or oak, sometimes planed to a roughly rectangular shape, sometimes left their natural roundness.

Across the top of the gates runs a narrow wooden platform with a metal hand-rail: this is the only way across the lock and is always used when working through in the boats. Close to the hinges of the gates are the all-important paddles, by means of which the lock is emptied or filled: actually, the work of winding up and down is done by ratchets, but we got so used to referring to the visible ratchet sticking up in the air as "the paddle" that I was forgetting. The paddles themselves are shutters in the bottom of the gates and are always below the water out of sight. They are attached to the gate by long iron bars terminating in the ratchet that you can see and are wound up and down with an L-shaped metal handle, the omnipresent windlass.

While Kit was explaining this to me and I was trying to take it in, a distant pop-popping was heard, a sound that I already recognised, and a pair of boats came in sight round the corner, from the same direction as ourselves.

"Good !" said Kit with relish, "here are boats. Now you will be able to see them working through the lock. Watch and see how quick they are and try to understand what they are doing and for goodness' sake don't get in the way . . . they are always in a hurry and you will be very unpopular if you hold them up."

As the boats drew nearer the pop-pop of the engine grew softer and slower as the motor slackened speed to enter the lock. Slowly and almost silently she nosed in against the wall, the steerer with his eye fixed on the dwindling distance to the top gates. Then he stooped and, lifting the towing-rope off the hook at his feet, deftly threw the coil on to the fore-end of the butty as it glided in beside him. A moment later the motor came to rest against the top gates and almost in the same second of time the man turned and shinned up the wall beside him like a cat, moving down quickly, to shut the gate on his side.

On the opposite side of the lock a girl was already up and tying a thick strap round a squat wooden stump on the lock side: then she, too, went down and shut her gate. The man by now was at the top gate: flicking his windlass out from under his coat collar he started to wind the paddle up. It took him under ten seconds and then he was across the gates and winding up the other one while his "missus" dropped back on to the butty cabin top, to prepare the dinner no doubt.

The door of the office behind us opened and out came "Syd" with his gauging stick in his hand. The most extraordinary shuffling of the boats then ensued which I couldn't follow at all but it ended up with Syd and the boater retiring into the office, an exchange of papers and cheery greetings and I saw suddenly that the two boats had changed places, the butty now being on our side of the lock. The steerer was back on the motor again, the engine pop-pop-popping at top speed, and the gates opening as the nose of the motor pushed them out of the way; as he came abreast of the butty fore-end he stooped again and picked up his tow rope, fastened it to the hook once more and they were off—one lock nearer to Birmingham and the next cargo.

Before the butty left the lock the woman had reappeared, put back her tiller handle and called to me as she passed:

"Like your jersey, mate. . . . Where did you get it ? . . . Wish I'd got one like that !"

I just had time to yell back:

"Afraid it came from Norway . . . if I ever go there I'll bring you one" . . . which produced a broad grin and a parting wave.

"All right, missus !" called Kit suddenly, "we'll see to it for you."

I did not know what on earth she meant but the woman obviously understood for she waved again in acknowledgment and signed to her husband on the motor. Both boats moved quickly away into the shadow of the bridge ahead and then were gone altogether.

"Well, now . . . " said Kit, "do you feel you know anything more about it ?"

I couldn't pretend that I did, the whole performance having taken at the outside four minutes and having left me breathless with the blur of impressions I had received—but simply delighted that a boater had called me "mate" on my very first day. I wondered if Kit or Vera had noticed ? I thought I probably should be able to sort myself out a bit when Kit was explaining the drill to me later: having watched it was bound to be a help.

"Now," said Kit, "go and shut the gate on the other side."

I started off obediently as I had seen the boater do . . . and realised, too late to stop feeling a fool, that the top gates were now wide open and uncrossable. I quickly ran to the bottom gates, crossed them somewhat gingerly, and ran up the lock side to the top ones.

"Get your back against it as soon as you can," called Kit. "It can be very dangerous if you don't."

I stooped and pulled at the balance beam, lying above the edge of the wall; it was very heavy and I had to jerk and heave at it till I got it going, then I nipped round and leaned against it, walking backwards to push it shut. This was much easier, I found, than dragging it and I was soon rewarded by a bang as it met its fellow.

Kit called me over to her side again and showed me how to drop the paddles . . . windlass *just* caught on the end of the spindle, a half-turn back, release the safety-catch, off with the windlass quickly and with an ear-splitting rattle the ratchet dropped down. Vera had already dropped the opposite one so Kit took me to

the bottom gate, fitted her windlass on the spindle and bade me
wind.

I could hardly move the thing and really thought I must be
doing something wrong: I am fairly strong in the arm and I
recollected how easily Vera had got hers up. With infinite grunt-
ing and puffing, and very slowly, I got it to the top. It seemed
ages before it got there, and it was an awful strain on the muscles
of my middle. . . .

"Come and look," said Kit.

Outside the gates the water was eddying and boiling as the
water from inside the lock rushed out to mingle with it below the
surface. The whirlpool grew, boiled and churned for a moment,
then slowly died down to a ripple, then to nothing. In the lock
behind me the water had sunk to its lowest level and we could
open the bottom gates leaving the lock ready for up-hill traffic
again.

"You always have to leave Cowley ready for up-hill boats,"
said Kit. "If we hadn't done it for them they would have had to
stop in the bridge-hole, come back and shut the gates and wind
one paddle up . . . one's enough when there isn't another pair
behind you: by the time other boats get here the lock will be
empty and Syd or the lock-keeper usually see that the gates are
open. We did it all properly, because it was such a good chance
for you to try it yourself. It was a great piece of luck those boats
coming through, because of course we couldn't waste a whole
lockful of water just to demonstrate how it works. Now, come
on . . . we'll get home and you can come on the motor with me
and try to steer her."

Back on the boats I watched, and tried not to get in the way,
while Kit and Vera winded them: then, with much inward trepi-
dation, I took the tiller from Kit who, mercifully, remained on
the gunwale beside me, with one of her hands on the tiller too:
a wise precaution!

It felt completely different from the butty; for one thing the
tiller, as I've already said, is made of iron and is set quite horizontal, it is much thinner to grasp and vibrates slightly all the time.
It answers more easily with the power of the engine behind it,
and the nose of the boat responds accordingly and more
quickly.

There is also a good deal more responsibility, for where the
motor leads there must the butty follow, with no chance of

initiative when she is tied up so tight behind. I nearly died with terror when boats came towards us, and tried to hand the tiller to Kit who declined it and merely told me to steer as close to the other boats as I could—but she left her hand where it was. This nearly resulted in a free fight, my one idea being to keep as far from the oncoming pair as I possibly could and Kit, determined that I should learn properly, pulling me over and over till I was sure a head-on collision was coming. Naturally it didn't, but we passed so close to the other motor that I don't think there was room for a piece of three-ply to be slipped between us.

The man at the tiller of his motor jerked his head in the conventional form of greeting as we passed and said: "How d'you do?" Kit answering with the same expression: presently I discovered that it was always "how d'you do" from one boat to another unless they were particular friends, in which case you wasted no precious seconds in a greeting, but as soon as they were within earshot embarked without delay on everything you had saved up to tell one another since the last few-seconds meeting perhaps a month ago—both talking at once and generally hearing nothing ! They were unbearably tantalising, these mid-stream meetings, with only a second or two when the boats were abreast and after that the distance getting wider and wider till there was no hope of being heard although you were still plainly visible to one another. The butty people came off best, without the noise of the engine to drown their voices.

The boaters have a dialect all their own that is very hard to understand at first, being compounded of North Country, or what sounds like it, Birmingham, and bad enunciation, liberally interspersed with the traditional "bargee" language. This combination, shouted rapidly and at full pitch of their lungs, with the wind blowing the opposite way and the gap widening all the time, doesn't make for better understanding, one of the other. I used to smile encouragingly and hope to heaven that what I *had not* heard was not important, which it very often was, relating to how many locks we could count on being ready "just round the corner" and who would be coming down the cut that we might like to look out for.

My diary says that coming back from Cowley I learned "to breast-up." That I most certainly did not though I may have believed I had . . . after one lesson. I always found it difficult and can't believe that I was at all clever at it the first time. It turned out to be the reddest of red rags between Kit and me. It was her job to see that I learned to do it and do it properly, and the more she tried to teach me the stupider and more idiotic did I become till, by the end of my second trip with her, it had almost taken on the nature of a personal insult when she gave me the order. I blamed the boats, the butty steerer, the way the cut was designed, anything but my own stupidity, and invariably lost my temper completely. Kit was at all times a model of patience and fairness . . . which only made it fifty times more mortifying . . . the pangs of bitterest shame were mine as well as the burning knowledge of my incompetence. Therefore, I am doubtful if "learned to breast up" is, in any meaning of the word, true. . . .

To "breast-up" is to slow down the motor till the butty has caught up and then, by skilful judgment, to tie the two boats together, fore-ends and sterns, without ever actually stopping the forward movement of both boats. Like practically everything else on the cut it is purely a matter of judgment and co-ordination of hand and eye, together with a knowledge of what your engine can develop and an ability to do at least five things at once. A second person is running about like a stag doing the actual tying but the success of the operation depends entirely on the steerer of the motor: the procedure is gone through, with very few exceptions, every single time you tie-up, so it may be seen that I had plenty of practice.

When we got back to the lay-by it had started to rain but we had our dinner in the canteen before we changed. Dry once more, Vera and I had a lesson in knots and splicing, learning to make the knot which is used for everything on the boats and which all the women used to call a "boater" . . . what the boaters called it I don't know ! It is very simple and is not really a knot at all. I was fascinated with splicing and always found it fairly easy: I used to enjoy doing it and never minded a strap breaking so long as I had a bit of leisure time to splice it together again. We were expected to make good any breakages of this kind; only in extreme cases would it be possible to get a new strap out of the store-keeper and before he parted with it he'd look up and see how long it was since you had the last new one. What was not such fun was breaking a strap in a lock and having to repair it before the next lock, which in all probability was very near; wet and cold frayed rope is not the easiest medium when one's hands are wet and cold too, and I have a strange preference for being able to use both my hands for splicing which is not practicable when the boats require steering as well, but somehow it used to get done and I don't remember any of my splicing ever giving way on us.

That first lesson in Kit's cabin was great fun; I'm knot-minded, I think, and love doing things with pieces of string; it was something of a blow to have to go and have the engine-room talk with Mr. Curtis, especially as I didn't understand a word of it. I tried again to start the engine and did manage it with someone to help me, but try as I could I could not do it on my own and was green with envy of Kit who did it quite effortlessly. I did not realise that it would be some weeks before my muscles had hardened up enough for such an unaccustomed strain to come easily. Kit had been on the cut training people for three years and her arms and legs were like steel although she is only about half my size.

When Mr. Curtis had done his stuff Vera and I retired to the motor cabin and made ourselves tea while Kit went home for the night. We still had no loading orders so there was nothing to do for the moment: I was thankful for a rest and a chance to think over all I had done that day; writing home, I tried to compress into a letter the confusing blur of the new things that I had seen and done. Sitting in the cabin with the doors wide open and the evening sun streaming in, a mug of tea at my elbow and a large slice of bread and jam to hand, while down the lay-by went an endless stream of children, boaters, mechanics, women with bursting shopping baskets, the loud insistent life of the boats sounding all round, was a very pleasant end to the day. I was filthy dirty, but what of it? The moment I touched any outside portion of the boat I should be dirty again so why bother to clean up before bed-time?

Vera and I walked down to the pub at the bus stop after supper and there I met the first of the other women that I had so far seen, not counting Daphne and Margaret. She was just as untidy as we were, I was glad to note, and yet the man behind the bar did not seem to think there was anything odd about any of us.

Kay was in the throes of moving into new boats; when we had finished our beer we all walked back to the lay-by where her boats were tied up in the dry-dock. She and two others had made up a crew and were collecting their bits and pieces before

B*

starting on their first trip together. I was fearfully envious of Kay's cabin: brand new, cream paintwork, new saucepans and jugs and china, new lino on the floor and new curtains at the porthole. Each steerer was given a cash grant to fit out her boats before she took them over, though it usually didn't cover all the things one was dying to do to the cabins, and a great deal of stuff had to be bought to make them even reasonably comfortable.

We gratefully took three superfluous mutton-chops off Kay and returned home, thinking deeply of the day when we should each have our own boats.

My bed was a great deal more acceptable that night and I slept like the proverbial log after a last cigarette, smoked in the dark by the light of the dying fire.

Chapter IV—LIMEHOUSE

THE water frontage at Bull's Bridge must be over a quarter of a mile long, so a microphone is installed in the office with loudspeakers at strategic points to get hold of people quickly. Sometimes it is calling for the head mechanic, sometimes for the manager to come to the telephone, sometimes for the carpenter, but generally it is: "Calling Tom Smith . . . calling Tom Smith . . . will you report at the office for orders, please" . . . or whichever steerer is wanted.

It was half-past four next day before we heard what we'd been waiting for.

"Calling Miss Gayford . . . calling Miss Gayford . . . will you come to the office, please, for orders. . . ." Kit went flying off on her bicycle and Vera said: "We had better get everything cleared away in the cabin . . . we shan't have time to breathe from now on."

We had only just got done before Kit was back, the bike was flung into the empty hold and we were letting go.

We turned left as if we were off to Cowley again but just opposite the dry-dock there is a bridge . . . Bull's Bridge . . . and the cut goes off at right angles. It takes a bit of getting round this angle and there was much blowing of an instrument rather like a hunting horn, before Kit was reassured that there was no other pair on the far side of the bridge-hole. The boats are fitted with electric horns but they all carry the hand ones as well. Kit used ours mainly to call to us from the butty and it was known to all her trainees as "the sackbut."

I was, needless to say, not allowed to steer till we'd got safely round the corner; after that I had a good bit of practice and began to get the feel of it. The cut goes through Greenford and Perrivale up to Alperton, which we made by six-thirty. It is a grand tie-up, close to the Underground station so that one can buzz up to town on the Piccadilly line and be in the centre of London in half an hour. This is exactly what I did that evening, after some supper and a good wash-up: I went to see some friends and came back all the better for the break into civilisation again. I also collected a quart of milk I remember, so Vera was very fond of me that night. It was pouring with rain when I got back but I had a mac and sou'wester so it didn't matter and I was in bed, dry and warm, in a very short time. This was accelerated by Vera's goodnight blessing which took the form of announcing that she had set the alarm for five-thirty . . . which made me turn out the light very quickly indeed.

The next day was the first morning that I had had the "breakfast at 5.45" time-table tried out on me and I don't remember taking at all to the idea: nevertheless, one of the clearest impressions I have of those early days is of the exhilarating feeling on waking up each morning, *longing* for what the day would bring forth. For five years life had been a matter of just getting through the day as best one could; rations, mending, fuel restrictions, queues . . . all the innumerable irritations that made up the daily round. Now that was all a thing of the past; there was very little waiting about and so far no signs of rules and regulations . . . instead there was a permanent rush, activity, a job to be done under my nose, here in the boats; a question of ropes, tillers, judgment of eye and hand, movement, novelty and excitement.

For it *was* exciting—it was thrilling and I was enjoying every second of it, even though I was being clumsy and ignorant and inefficient. It was all new: sights, sounds, people, drill, clothes, food . . . the whole pattern had changed and I felt as though an enormous double window had been flung open, allowing me to breathe in great gulps of fresh air, while away in the distance a huge and unknown country lay at my feet.

Another thing, which other housewives will perhaps understand, was the perfectly blissful sensation of being bossed about by someone else, for a change! Thinking for the family all day and every day in war-time left you more exhausted than you knew, till you got away from it. It was really heavenly to be given orders and not be expected—in those early days—to think for myself or make decisions for other people.

The journey from Alperton to the Regent Canal Dock in Limehouse might have been designed especially for the new trainees to give them some idea of the whole round trip: it has everything that they will meet later on, locks, tunnels, bridges, a bit of mud, a lot of traffic, S-bends, but all in a nice, gentle, initiating way. For instance, the eleven locks, that are all fairly close together, gave me a very good idea of how locks worked by the time I was through them, but in every case the lock-keeper dealt with the paddles. They are double locks down here; that is to say, there are two locks side by side, the water emptying from one to the other as one pair of boats come up and another down, thereby saving a great deal of water. Traffic is very heavy with many boats and barges of every description and the lock-keeper's presence is very necessary to control the filling and emptying.

Kit had been training for three years by the time I got there and she was a familiar figure to the lock-keepers. Some of them were anxious to help and showed me the meaning of the curious iron machine in between the two locks . . . we used to call it the "sewing machine," which is not a bad description. By winding the handle of this a paddle is raised between the locks, so that the empty one is filled from the full one. When the same level is reached in both locks the paddle is dropped, and only then is water taken from the "pound" above to fill one right up.

There is a perpetual bustle about the canal down here: barges with their super-intelligent horses and lounging lightermen, other Grand Union boats, easily recognisable in their red, white and blue; green and orange "josser" boats; more horses; barges shining with black coal; on the towpath men and bicycles and children; in the streets women with shopping bags, small children shoving smaller ones in front of them in rickety prams or swinging in public playgrounds; the clang and rattle of trams, the thundering roar of a train as we pass under a railway bridge, the pop-pop-pop of our own engine . . . on the other side tall houses and strings of washing, blocks of flats, factories, wharves, timber-yards, rubbish dumps, a hospital, a school; more horses and barges, goods yards, marshalling yards; a sudden jet of boiling water from a factory steaming and spurting into the dirty cut water, a cemetery, a Lock hospital, a barge loaded with timber, a piercing whistle from yet another train, more barges, more horses, more boats . . . and in the midst of it all our own particular pair of boats, our home at night, our work by day, threading in and out of the noise, dirt and smell with a definite job to do, on National Service and playing its own tiny part in the upheaval of the world's titanic strain and stress.

I never got used to the incredible idea that I really belonged to all this: it was a perpetual marvel to me that I should be *allowed* here, part of it all and accepted by the men of the cut, boaters and lock-keepers and toll-office clerks. Gold braid and red tabs could not have made me prouder than I was, in my nondescript

sweater and trousers, dirty, untidy, muscles aching and fingernails torn and split, dead tired and often ravenously hungry.

Gold braid was not ever part of the boater's lot but later I was
presented with that which made me prouder, if possible, than I
was before . . . the little blue plastic, rather inconspicuous
National Service badge of the cut workers. No one ever knew
what it was—it was only seen on the cut—and if we wore it on
leave we always had to explain that "I.W." stood for Inland
Waterways . . . until someone hit on the bright idea of suggesting
that it really meant "Idle Women, because we do no work." We
all got one at a test that took place after we'd finished training and
there was no special distinction about it unless you were as
sentimental as I am!

We got to our destination at two-fifteen after a very genteel
trip down, compared with what it was on later occasions. I tried
a little bit of everything: first, steering the motor into a lock, Kit's
hand beside mine on the tiller and my other hand moistly gripping
the accelerator; then, a turn on the butty, all quite different
again and back to the beginning; then down into the cabin
to make cocoa, to make tea, to hot up baked beans for dinner,
up to steer again, down to wash up, up to splice a snapped
rope . . . the pattern began to take shape.

Surprisingly, they started to load us at once, with aluminium
bars which look so like chocolate bars wrapped in silver paper,
with neat little nicks in them to make them easier to break!

Before the men could start we had to get the boats ready; that
means that all the stands and top-planks come out and any stray
brooms and shovels are hastily put elsewhere. The beams are
knocked out, the rigging chains are unscrewed and the hold is
left completely empty ready for the cargo.

I was fascinated by the electric cranes, by the precision and
control exercised by the man far above our heads in his little
box, looking ridiculously small beside the infinite length of steel
and chain that is the crane. When people ask: "Did you have to
load the boats yourselves?" (which they often do) I always want
to laugh. . . .

One man in a little box on wheels, two men on the quayside
to slip the slings under the piles of metal, a shout and up goes
the great arm, pauses in the air and hovers a moment, then slowly
pivots, flattens itself and drops to the waiting men in the hold of
the boat, swinging gently over the exact spot that is waiting to

receive it; they steady it and hold it firmly while the steel arm bends yet a little more and there is the aluminium resting on the bottom of the hold without a bump. Of course, the balance of the boat has been altered considerably . . . woe betide the foolish virgin who has anything cooking on the Primus; the saucepan will at once capsize and generously spread its contents over the floor and surrounding furnishings of the "home beautiful," with all the attendant agony of trying to clear up with a limited cold water supply.

When the first boat was finished the men started on the second and we retired for a cup of tea.

"We will have tea first," said Kit, "and then sheet up. We shall feel stronger afterwards and I expect the men will like some." Saying which she disappeared into the butty and Vera and I began our own preparations in the motor.

"What exactly *is* sheeting-up ?" I inquired in my innocence.

Vera produced a mirthless laugh and said that I should "soon know." We ate our tea thoughtfully.

It is not really bad when you get used to it but, at the start, sheeting-up comes very hard on the hands and knees; it also requires a good deal more brute force than I could muster that day, honest brawn and muscle that were not yet mine to command.

First, the beams are replaced across the boat and the rigging chains screwed as tight as they will go to pull the sides of the boat together. The stands are next dropped into position and wedged; then the top-planks go back, promoted to the top of the stands, instead of halfway up at gunwale level: it looks rather as though the boat were covered in scaffolding. The gunwale itself has now dropped down to water level so that the hold and its cargo are well below. When the top-planks have been firmly secured with screws and ropes and are safe to walk on (for they are to act for many days as the only pathway for the crew on its way to the fore-end) then the sheeting-up proper begins.

Down into the congested hold go Vera and I; we take a side each and work steadily up the length of the boat, clambering over the aluminium as we go, untying the knee-strings that are holding the side-sheets in a tight roll along the gunwale. As we finish Vera calls out to me to work back again, unrolling as I go. When I have done this I see that the side-sheets are really one length of tarred canvas, nailed to the inner edge of the gunwale and now sagging into the hold. At intervals this edge has long, tarry strings threaded through eyelet holes and when I have freed them all I am told to chuck them over the top-planks above my head. Then Vera goes to the other side of the boat and threads each one through a corresponding eyelet in the opposite cloth. And then Kit takes charge.

We mount the top-planks—I attempt to look nonchalant but do not risk a glance into the distant hold beneath me. On hands and knees we crawl slowly down the planks, Kit showing me how to pull the side-strings tight (so tight that I'm no good at it), take a turn round the plank on which we kneel and finish it off firmly. When we reach the end I can see the side-cloths as tight and hard as boards, and a pleasing vista of sloping strings and hanging knots that reminds me of the Kentish hop-fields.

We then heave the top-sheets up aloft; they are also black and tarry and are boldly stencilled with the Company's initials— G.U.C.C.C.—and the number of the boat : they weigh a ton and it isn't easy to hoist them above your head but, nevertheless, you do, three of them which are to cover the hold from cratch to cabin. Vera hands up more strings and I become paralysed as I see her proceed on to the gunwale, which is certainly not more than three inches wide here and practically in the water. She takes each string in turn and laces it through a metal ring in the gunwale and passes it back to Kit. I am transfixed with horror and wait breathlessly for Vera to disappear with a splash . . . instead, I am told to go and help: Kit speaks in a voice which does not suggest that there is any choice open to me. I go.

When all the top-strings are tightened and tied off, the boat is finished. She is now completely covered in from fore-end to cabin and has a lovely, long, lean line that I like very much. If we crash a bridge-hole or a bank now, we shan't be able to ship water; we are safe too from a deluge of rain which would soak the hold if it were uncovered. I think we look lovely, and then remember that there is still another boat to be done and my hands are already raw from the strings and I shall undoubtedly have housemaid's knee tomorrow.

It was a pleasant change, when we had done, to wash ourselves free of the strange liquid which had squeezed out of the sheets and strings (known affectionately and resignedly as "gravy") and go off shopping down Salmon's Lane. This was the first time I had ever been in Limehouse and I looked about eagerly for the traditional slit-eyed Chinese. I did not see one; instead, I found an excellent and cheap shopping centre with a great variety of shops and choice of food. The shop-people were Cockneys and Jewesses . . . but they were a great deal more anxious to be helpful and obliging than many I had met in my home market town or in the smart West-end stores. We were universally addressed as "mate" or "duck" and came groaning back to the boats under the load of our goods.

Coming back to the Dock was always rather an event. Down a narrow lane off the Commercial Road and through a small gate set in the big ones, we were pounced on at once by our "own" policeman. I say our "own" because, although looking exactly like the ordinary brand of copper, they have a discreet little "G.U.C.C." on their shoulders instead of the usual "M.P." It is their job to see that no one without authorisation gets past the gates and it is just bad luck if you try to smuggle in a perfectly innocent visitor without written permission from the harbourmaster, as I found out later.

Kit took me with her to the local after supper to show me the sights and because she hoped she'd meet a man who was mending her wireless for her. In this she did not succeed but we spent a very amusing evening, listening to a highly detailed and intimate description of how our drinking companion came by his tattooing, and just how painful it had been. He certainly had a magnificent display of pierced hearts and anchors, roses and snakes and, as a *piéce de résistance*, a complete dancing lady, dressed only in garlands of very unlikely-looking flowers. She extended nearly to his shoulder and he practically undressed so that we should not miss the treat!

I reflected that I was certainly seeing a side of life that was new to me and could not imagine any other circumstances that would give me quite the same view of Limehouse or, may I add, of the dancing lady.

After a pint and a half consumed in an atmosphere that appeared to be solid, I was distinctly drowsy and with gratitude stumbled home through the cold night air. The sirens kept up their usual racket but I was far too tired to take any notice of them.

Suddenly it dawned on me that I was not just "tired" . . . I was *dog-tired*, mentally, physically and muscularly, in a way that I hadn't felt tired for years . . . a way that can be absolutely satisfying. I pulled off my clothes and tumbled into bed without

noticing its hardness and lay still and relaxed, revelling in my
bodily exhaustion.

Later, I used to do a good deal of reading in bed, but I don't
remember opening a book on that first trip, partly because the
light was in the wrong place and I did not get it reorganised at
the start, but mainly because I was always too perfectly "out"
to be able to concentrate. To begin with, the pattern of the day
was: work, learn, eat, work, learn, eat, sleep, repeated over and
over again like the play of the street lights on the nursery ceiling
when one was small and tucked up in bed. It had the same
hypnotic quality and charm and I did not want anything else
that would break into the pattern.

I was very often in trouble from Kit, who thought I might
have done something better than I had . . . (and how right she
was!). I had nasty moments when I *knew* I had messed things
badly, when I waited to be cursed and knew I had deserved it
heartily, moments of sheer delight in an unexpected picture, as
the boat rounded a bend; other moments of almost animal
satisfaction when hunger, thirst or tiredness were appeased; silent
moments when I went up on to the step to have a look at the
stars before getting into bed, but never sad or unhappy or doubtful
moments. It was with a shock that I realised what a time it was
since I had thought a thing about my own personal worries.
This existence was more completely satisfying than anything I
had known for years—in fact since the hours following the births
of my two children, six and nine years before, and for the same
reason; it was bodily work accomplished naturally, with no more
emotional complications to mess it up than are felt by the animals.

There is a vast deal of difference between steering loaded and
unloaded boats and the next day provided a series of shocks for
me. I thought I was beginning to know something about steering
and here were the beastly boats feeling quite different and refusing
to behave as I had learned to expect.

The butty was now a long way behind the motor, separated
from her by seventy feet of coconut fibre rope, as thick as my
arm, and well named the "snubber." Snubbed just about described my feelings as I strained at the tiller, realising that with
all this new weight I had left it too late to turn as I wanted to.
Kit was with me all that first day, changing from one boat to the
other with me when we came to the locks. She always had a
marvellous way of knowing, far better than we did ourselves,

when we had had enough; it came as a surprise to hear her say: "All right . . . I'll take her for a bit now, if you'll go down and put the kettle on and get a bit of a rest."

I used to protest that I had only just begun and felt as fresh as a daisy, and I would go below to do as I was told feeling slightly injured . . . until I realised that Kit was right . . . I *was* tired, tea sounded heavenly and I would put my feet up on the side-bed and go straight off to sleep while I waited for the kettle to boil. After a bit I didn't argue but was thankful for the chance of a break.

We got back to the lay-by that evening before it was dark and tied up there for the night. Mother McCrea was supposed to be joining us next day so it would not be an early start; we should have to wait for her. It must have irked Kit terribly to be tied-up unnecessarily when we might have been "whistling": I never knew her stop willingly for anything and to hang about waiting for people to turn up was her idea of purgatory. Still, it meant an early night for us and a lie-in in the morning. We rushed to the office for our letters and had a "lazy" evening, writing home, darning, and washing our clothes while the water supply was nice and close.

Next morning, while waiting for the new arrival, we cleaned out the cabin thoroughly, black-leaded the stove till it shone, cleaned all the brasswork, chopped the fire-wood, cooked enough food to last us two days, exchanged gossip with the neighbouring boat families, learned a few more knots from Kit, did our "homework," which consisted in making out a route-book of our own copied from a model supplied by Kit, and several other odd jobs, in all what Kit called in disgust "a morning off" . . . !

CHAPTER V—UP THE CUT

It was the last "morning off" for a week so I hope we made
the most of it. Mother McCrea turned up at dinner-time and
we let go at two o'clock. I was feeling very superior, five whole
days older than the new trainee. I was probably showing it;
at any rate, it was not very long before Kit threw me and the
bicycle off at a bridge-hole, and told me to go and see if the next
lock was ready, and if not, to get it ready. That was a nasty
moment; it was also the first time I had ridden Kit's bicycle, which
was nastier.

It really does deserve a paragraph to itself, that bike. Kit said
it was thirty years old and I never found any grounds for dis-
believing her. It had no mudguards, no brakes, practically no
paint, and would have been more comfortable with no seat.

Learning to ride this machine was really an entirely separate
piece of training. The seat, like my kidney, was semi-detached;
that is to say, it was attached at the apex of the triangle in front,
while the base floated free and wide, which was not apparent at
a casual glance. Unsuspecting, the novice mounted and sat
down—at once to rise rapidly with a sharp scream of agony,
which quickly turned to hysteria as the brakes refused to work.
One then fell off in the manner best suited to one's own fat
distribution, and examined the seat with interest, not to say
resentment. It became clear that one had not sat upon the seat
at all but upon the iron upright of the cycle frame, the seat having
swung away from under one at the critical moment. You gave
a quick look round to see how many people were watching,
laughed heartily and tried again, with the cut ready to receive
you on one side and the hedge on the other: there was really
no choice and the brambles were particularly luxuriant that year.

This went on until one had mastered the hedge, the cut, no
brakes, and being thrown violently over the handle-bars now
and then, owing to the windlass, worn tucked into the belt in
front, getting caught up in the middle of the upward lift so
essential to mastering the errant seat and the immobile iron spike.

"Bloody but unbowed," the first phase would be overcome
and zigzagging furiously and dangerously down the narrow path,
you steered with one hand and with the other arranged the seat

52

beneath you, in mid-transit as it were. With what a sigh of pleasure you relaxed cautiously on to the firmly held saddle— with what a merry laugh did you discover that the little pet had yet another trick in store.

As there was nothing whatever to hold the back of the saddle up, it very naturally hung abruptly downwards and backwards, the front part pointing straight into the sky. Apart from feeling unpleasantly like a piece of cheese as the grocer's wire goes through it, one's balance became very odd indeed, if one had succeeded in retaining it at all. Knees up to the chin, backside on a level with the heels, hands, seemingly, some miles away and, of course, the towpath is no dirt track. In most places it is filled with miniature bomb craters, in others the water had encroached to the very hedge, so that sudden canyons yawn for the delirious acrobat. And at all times one is riding through a dense and tangled succession of thorn bushes, brambles and briars, dodging as one swerves and sways, between water and quick-set hedge . . . . ("What did you do in the Second Great War, Mummy?" . . . "Rode Kit's bicycle from London to Birmingham, darling!")

But the very oddest thing of all was that nobody else seemed to mind that bike! Kit herself rode it like a trick cyclist, albeit she did *look* very peculiar and could be instantly identified in a busy High Street, full of bicycles, by the unique stance she, and everyone else, was forced to adopt. I did, in time, get better at it, but at an early date organised a newer saddle on to Waltzing Matilda, which gave rise to no great excitement to anyone but me.

Being faced with a lock, by yourself for the first time, has awed stronger women than me. I arrived panting, flung myself off the bike and gazed at the silent water with eyes that saw, but a brain that refused to co-ordinate anything I had been taught with the scene now before me. Was it ready or wasn't it? After all those London locks I ought to be able to tell at a glance. I couldn't . . . my brain still would not do its stuff and I was further fussed by the terror that the lock-keeper would appear from his cottage and see me standing there, gawping like an idiot, and know me for the greenhorn that I was; even more terrified that a large, black rough boater would come round the corner and start doing things to the lock so that my boats would have to wait . . . just a minute, though . . . I was supposed to go and warn them if a wait was necessary, so that Kit could choose a suitable place to hang about in, where our boats wouldn't be in the way. Complete silence. No lock-keeper . . . no boater . . . no nothing . . . not even a brain: just the lock and the still watching water . . . and me.

Realising that all instruction I had received was firmly embedded in my subconscious, and unlikely to emerge until I had no immediate use for it, I decided, belatedly, to apply common-sense to the question.

Was the water inside the lock on the same level as the water outside, on which my boats were at this moment floating nearer and nearer ? that was the question. The answer was clearly: NO. Then the lock was *not* ready and I must rapidly do something about it. Inside, the water was right up to the top of the lock; my boats would arrive below . . . very well, the water had got to be let out. I tore to the bottom gates to wind the paddles up and remembered, just in time.

The top gates were wide open and the paddles up; reversing quickly I tore back to the top, shut one gate, dropped the paddle with a rattle that froze my still uncertain blood, rushed to the other end, over the gates, up the other side, shut the second top gate, dropped the paddle, back to the bottom gates, on with the windlass and up . . . up . . . Lord, it was stiff . . . up . . . the first paddle was dealt with: over the gates again and up more slowly still with the second paddle, there . . . at last I could pause; there was nothing else to do for a moment . . . (except be consumed with gnawing doubt). From below the bottom gates there was a rushing sound: inside, the water was sinking rapidly and soon the whirlpool died to a gentle eddy, to a ripple, to nothing . . . I could swing open one bottom gate. After I had opened the other I heard the boats coming; in a moment they rounded the bend, but it was all right . . . the lock was ready.

Kit came in first on the motor, Vera behind on the butty with the new trainee trying not to get in the way. Kit swarmed up the wall and came over to me.

"Was it ready ?" she asked. I shook my head and opened my mouth to speak. . . .

"Well done," said Kit, "shut your gate," and ran up to the top paddles.

Now, in case I am thought to be exaggerating my stupidity, I can only say that I really am not. People who know all about locks from watching them worked will no doubt put me down

at once as a mental defective (which is possible) but I have heard
lots of other people say that they became mentally paralysed
when they met their first lock.

Although I had been, at that time, five days on the cut, I had
not carried out a single operation without supervision; added to
this, I was definitely not lock-minded before I came on the cut
and finally, I was haunted by the fear that I should do one or
both of the Unforgivable Sins . . . keep the boats waiting or,
far worse, leave a paddle up at both ends at once. The iniquity
of this latter cannot be over-emphasised. A lock, like these of
which I am speaking, holds 56,000 gallons of water and will
probably be emptied and filled between fifty and a hundred times
a day. All the water passing through the locks has to be pumped
back again, at night, to the summit level; so, it will perhaps be
realised just what is involved by leaving a paddle up at *both* ends
of the lock at once, thereby allowing the water to run straight
through and, unless it is discovered in time, ultimately draining
the upper level quite dry, and, in any case, lowering the water to
such an extent that progress will be considerably slowed down
even if the boats don't actually get stuck on the mud, which is
common during a drought. The fear of being guilty of this dis-
graceful crime was an ever-present shadow to us and fearful
consternation would be caused by the news: "HAVE you heard
that So-and-So has left a paddle up ? ? ! !"

Even though I was lucky enough to get on all right at my
baptism of fire, it was ages before I could take in at a glance all
that a lock had to tell me and learn to read the signs as a detective
reads footprints.

After this the rest of the day was uneventful; we only did one
or two more locks and then tied-up in a lovely wooded spot
above Black Jack, the fifth lock from Bull's Bridge. Mother
McCrea was bewildered and silent and did not seem to be enjoying
herself very much. She had her unpacking to do in the butty and
it was nearly dark at five when we got to Black Jack, so Kit
called it a day and we knocked off.

Next day, poor Mother McCrea's first proper one, we did
twenty-three locks. Vera was on her second trip and knew what
she was about, I was, at least, willing to do as much as I possibly
could, and, of course, Kit was everywhere at once—teaching,
encouraging, ticking-off, chatting with lock-keepers, swearing at
some inefficiency of ours, darting to a pub by the cut side to buy

a cabbage, opening gates, shutting gates, winding paddles incredibly quickly, shooting down into her cabin to find some toy she had promised to a boater's baby "two or three trips back," popping up again and calling instructions to me as she ran past: the effect was to make me feel completely breathless but I must admit it was infectious, and from then on I could never go slowly through a lock without feeling guilty.

This stretch of cut was very lovely in the October sunshine. It winds from Denham through Rickmansworth to Croxley Green, and meanders pleasantly through Cassiobury Park where the beeches made a picture, in spite of the rain which elected to fall thereabouts.

Rain is about the worst thing that can happen to you on the boats. If it is a really heavy downpour you have to shut the sliding hatch-cover to keep the cabin dry, and steering becomes very difficult: rather than bother, one usually tries a compromise and the cabin floor becomes a shambles. We had to keep running in and out in our wet things, too, and every single bit of us was wet at the end of a few minutes. Hands wet from the paddles and climbing up lock sides, mackintoshes wet from the same cause, boots (if you were lucky enough to have them) soaking from the puddles, sou'wester dripping down the back of your neck, bottoms of your trousers clinging damply round your ankles ... altogether horribly uncomfortable and only one small range and the line above it to dry two people's wet clothes on. They never did get really dry till the weather changed, and each morning presented the problem: Which are my least wet things?

In spite of all this and a phenomenally cold winter that followed the autumn, I did not get a cold of any kind the whole time I was in the job. A doctor friend and I were discussing this the other day and I said I was sure it was due to the constant fresh air; he said unsympathetically, that it was more likely to be because I was "*disgustingly* well." Perhaps he is right; I certainly felt as fit as a fiddle all the time, and had an appetite like a horse.

Shopping on the boats was a fine art. Practically all of it was done from shops close to the locks as we went through. The lock-wheeler was responsible for getting it done in any spare seconds she could wring from preparing the lock for the oncoming boats. She would shut the gates and get the paddles up, and then tear into the general store with string bag and ration books, giving the order as she ran. Then, out again to make sure that no one else had appeared to pinch the lock from her and back into the store to collect the stuff. It probably was not ready, so she would entreat the shop-keeper to HURRY, and dash back again to open the gates for the boats, and then back into the shop, and so on till the stuff was collected and paid for and the boats were leaving the lock.

If she was late she would have to cart her purchases on to the next lock with her on the handle-bars of the bike; she would have to hurry up, too, because it would have to be prepared and the boats were ahead already. Her cabin mate, in the meantime, in addition to working through the lock (which is a more complicated business than I have so far explained) would probably be mixing mugs of cocoa ready for the kettle and spreading thick hunks of bread for "elevenses." The jaded lock-wheeler, seeing the boats disappear, would hang her bags of groceries on the bike and ride furiously off down the tow-path to the next lock. With any luck she hadn't gone far when another pair of boats would appear coming towards her and she would be able to relax, knowing that the next lock was ready.

Sometimes we had to stop of course; for instance when we needed new Emergency Cards and had to go to the Food Office for them; but Kit was a genius at organising in advance and if it *had* to be a stop then at least six other crises would be dealt with at the same time.

Fenny Stratford was a favourite all-round halting place. The Food Office was not far off, the shops were good and the pub at the lock-side was a depot for our tinned milk, besides being a positive home from home as regards gossip and good cheer from the innkeeper and his wife. There was also a water-tap close by, and a butcher who sold fresh milk as well as excellent meat.

There *was* an extra allowance of, I think, one pound of tea and one or two pounds of sugar per pair of boats per two trips, but this worked out at such a minute quantity per head that it was hardly worth bothering about; apart from tinned milk off points and doorstoppers known as "boaters' pies," which we could occasionally buy, we had no extra rations of any kind. It was fearfully hard to make the food go round and I, personally, was frequently very hungry.

I cannot imagine how the boatmen managed: three lamb cutlets a week is *not* a sufficient ration for a grown man doing over a hundred hours very hard work a week. They did not even get the agricultural cheese ration which would have helped a bit. The answer was bread, bread and again bread . . . but after the first week of the month it was bread with not much on it: one pound of preserves for boat-people as for everyone else. Many of the boaters have large and young families and I can only suppose that the "missus" would see to it that "Dad" got the lion's share at every meal. But that is hardly what the Ministry of Food intended for the children.

I am very hot on this point because I always felt it was a gross injustice. There were both men and women in all the Forces with sedentary occupations who were infinitely better fed than these cut people who, although in a job which the Government had "reserved" because of its importance, were without uniform or coupon allowances other than the "industrial ten," and were palpably underfed. The boaters' wives perform miracles of cooking ingenuity, making-do, and mending, which would compare favourably with the efforts of the proudest British housewife; and all this, remember, in a cabin measuring nine feet by six feet and in addition to rearing a family of four or five young children and acting as their husband's first mate, which office entails as much hard work as his.

Is it surprising that some of the women, without the strength of mind to compete with these devastating conditions, give up the unequal fight and degenerate into the dirty and ill-kempt boat-loads familiar to the towpath loafer ? To those who have looked with a sneer at these boats I would say: Go and ask if you may see inside a clean boater's cabin. You will have to ask very humbly and even then you will probably be met with refusal but if you should be fortunate enough to be asked in, then look well and ask yourself how they do it. If you can come out and honestly say, that under the same conditions, you could do one hundredth part so well I shall be surprised. I know I could not, and what's more I did not, even with no one but myself to see to.

The problem of boat conditions always causes me to side-track. On my first trip I had no idea of all this, though the domestic side of it loomed large in Kit's training methods. Not only did she try to teach us management of the actual boats but tried to plan and think ahead for us, until we were able to do it for ourselves. Housekeeping on dry land is far easier than the same job mixed up with the work of the boats, and any amount of home experience that we may have brought with us was of very little use in these changed conditions: though it was very useful to be able to cook, I must admit, and I did not go hungry through inability in that direction.

I had the most awful mackintosh on my first trip. It was too big and too loose and it wasn't really waterproof. It kept catching in the windlass and the balance beams of the gates, flapping and getting generally in the way; but it was a poem compared with that sported by the unhappy Mother McCrea, who appeared later in the day draped in her husband's Home Guard rubber cape, which was never intended for the job, and was tastefully embellished with camouflaging. I can well remember the poor thing getting caught up at every turn, and getting thoroughly wet into the bargain because her "cape" fitted nowhere. At intervals she would become inflated like a child's balloon as the wind got under her floating draperies and blew her up. It was a fascinating sight.

There are two locks in Cassiobury Park which are called, simply, "Albert's Two" after the lock-keeper who, as may be imagined, is something of a character. The locks themselves are only a hundred yards apart and are nice, gentle little affairs, but beyond them lies a Z-bend which is a teaser. I was steering a lot by now but I had not met anything like this before. I think Vera must have been by herself on the motor; it would be the third time she had done the bends and Kit would have helped her on the previous occasions. At any rate, I was on the butty and dis-covered what misery a sharp corner with a loaded butty can be if you judge a single thing wrongly.

I shuffled all round the first angle with the nose of the butty bumping along and scraping the concrete edge, having taken the turn much too closely. Once on the kerb it is practically impossible to get off again. If you do try to steer the fore-end away from the edge it only has the effect of putting the stern on, which produces shuddering bumps and welts close to where you are standing, so you quickly shuffle the nose back again to where it was before.

Even if this does not happen, and the boat is fairly well-placed in the middle of the water, you have still got to "row" her round the bend. This is done with the huge wooden rudder (the boaters call it the "elum," a corruption of "helm"). The elum goes deep into the water and the tiller handle is in the top. Facing the

tiller, and holding with both hands, you push it right out over
the cut and then draw it quickly back again towards you, then
out, then back, and so on. If the boat were on the stocks this
would be child's play but it is not. It's in the water and the pushing
and drawing is all done against the pressure of water over the
whole area of the elum's surface. In effect, what you are doing
is imitating the flick of a fish's tail as he turns a corner; and oh,
do you envy the fish the ease with which he does it! It's very,
very hard work; as I strained and strained and cursed my weak
arms, I could hear Kit shrieking, like the Red Queen: "Faster . . .
Faster!", but it was no good. There was a bump and I was in
the bank again.

When the butty decides to take a walk in a field the person
on the motor should be watching carefully and at once reduce
speed, if necessary going into reverse. If she doesn't, one of two
things will happen. Either the towing rope will snap under the
strain, or the butty will be pulled over sideways till the screams
of the butty steerer bring the motor person to earth and a realisa-
tion of what is happening. Truly, never a dull moment. . . .

I waited for retribution.

"Well now . . . I'm very glad that's happened," said Kit with
zest, "it will show you how *not* to do it next time and you can
learn what to do if this happens when you are on your own
boats." She was climbing on to the cabin top as she spoke and
pulling the long shaft out from under the top-cloths. Carrying
it in both hands she ran along the sheeted top-planks and jumped
down on to the fore-end. I followed cautiously but was promptly
ordered back again, to my great relief. I hadn't yet learned to
run like a chamois down those planks, with the sheets sloping to
the water on either side and not a thing to hold on to. (But I did
in time: indeed, three trips with Kit nearly made me a professional
acrobat, and at my age, too.)

Kit shoved the shaft into the bank and pushed with all her
weight and strength; several times she did this and then stood
up and called orders to Vera marooned in the middle of the cut
on the motor. Cautiously Vera put the engine into gear and with
her tiller hard over and away from the bank, she accelerated. Kit
shafted again at the same time, and slowly and very reluctantly
it seemed, the butty tore herself out of the mud and weeds of the
bank. I was lost in admiration until another hearty bump from
the stern reminded me that I was supposed to be steering. As

the nose of the butty swung out into the cut, so of course did the stern swing into the kerb . . . a little point which I had overlooked. Vera was now well away and getting ready for the next corner and this time Kit came and stood in the hatches with me and told me exactly when to do things, and picked out landmarks on the bank for me to steer by.

She was very fond of this method, but some of her choices were very peculiar. Further up the cut beyond Leighton Buzzard, in the Jackdaw pound, are some more bad bends and here there was one famous spray of bramble, not more than eighteen inches long but hanging down into the water at a very critical spot. Kit always steered by it and I used to think it would be a bad day for all her trainees when the spray broke and fell into the water. It was rotten from the start, but funnily enough it lasted me out and was there to help me round on my last trip home in July.

With Mother McCrea and me having "instruction" and Vera "polish," we went on up as far as the "Fishery." This is a lock but it takes its name from the pub beside it. It is a very pleasant tie-up, open and yet near shops and a glass of beer and, best of all, a bath. On one side there is open common ground that runs up to Hemel Hempstead railway station two or three hundred yards away and on the other several rather nice houses with grounds running down to the towpath. We used to scrutinise them as closely as we could from where we were and decide which we'd live in when we retired.

You could generally get cake or buns from the baker on the bridge and, by going to the pub and ordering it, a bath as soon as the water had been heated up for you. There was only one other pub which offered baths to us on the round trip, but I hope their names are specially remembered by the Recording Angel for it was a treat which we appreciated beyond words. To be able to cover your whole body in water at the same time was wonderful to a degree . . . even if it did entail taking rags and Vim with you and half an hour's hard work before you could decently leave the bathroom "as you would wish to find it." It was well worth it and we would come out feeling brand new.

Especially after coaling in Coventry was a bath welcome, to remove coal-dust which would otherwise be in hair, nose, eyes and down your throat for the return journey home. The Public Baths in Coventry are marvellous. For ninepence (sixpence in peace-time, I believe) you are given a new cake of soap, which you can keep, a bath-towel which is lent to you, a large and spot-less cubicle, a huge bath of boiling water and civility and service. They even cleaned the bath after us ! which I should have been sorry to have to do for one of us at *any* price. . . .

Perhaps it was just luck, but it always seemed to be fine and a lovely sunset whenever I tied up at the "Fishery," which en-deared it to me more than ever. A little bit farther on the cut is very pretty and being "locking country" all the way it is always interesting. Though the locks are hard work, it is far more amusing than day-long stretches with no interruption, which happens farther up still.

Kit had an ingenious system which she put into operation every night. We took it in turns to have a "bath" night which simply meant a good all-over wash with two kettles of boiling water and the cabin to yourself. In order to achieve this the other person would go into the butty, when supper was over, and spend the evening either going over the events of the day and asking questions about any difficulty which had cropped up, or else just talking. (In my case the first generally degenerated into the second automatically.) If there was no pressing "homework" to be done we'd take our mending over, or sit and write letters and, once in every four nights, Kit would come over into the motor while her cabin was turned into a bathroom by the other trainee. It was a very good system and really enabled the washer to spread herself.

I had begun to be very fond of the cabin by now. I knew my way about, the short cuts and how to get the best out of it and it was pleasant to be able to sit about at the end of a hard day, without doing anything in particular. Even better was supper in bed, but I don't think Vera and I ever reached those heights of luxury. That came later when I had a butty cabin to myself and touched the pinnacles of comfort.

"The rolling English drunkard made the rolling English road," and at first glance it looks as if he made the English canal system, too, but the pioneer engineers of the eighteenth and early nineteenth centuries weren't drunk . . . far from it. To avoid as much as possible the expense of building locks, aqueducts and tunnels, the canal had to be cut through the most level ground they could find, even if it meant twisting and turning sometimes in an almost complete circle to avoid rising ground. They thereby made the subsequent life of generations of boaters a very much pleasanter one. Only those who have experienced it know how boring is a straight stretch of water without bend or curve. Thank heaven and the rolling English country, there are few such stretches on the Grand Union. For the most part the trip from London to Birmingham is as curly as a poodle's coat; there is always the possibility of adventure waiting just round the next corner. This explains too why the cut manages to meander through six counties on a journey which is only 112 miles by road.

One of the things that fogged me most on that first trip was never knowing where I was, geographically. Very few of the cut place-names bear any relation to the names you will find on the map. They are traditional and many of them are corruptions, due to the average boater's inability to read or write. For example, the seven locks at Marsworth are known as "Maffas," while the G.U. workshops at Bulbourne are referred to as "Boubon." I was unfamiliar with this part of Hertfordshire to begin with and I had no map with me; the trip did very little towards clarifying my mind.

The next day we travelled from the "Fishery" to "Cow Roast" . . . and I wonder how many people will know what places we went through or where we tied up that night? Here is a list of the locks: SLAUGHTERS (or SALTERS) BOTTOM, MIDDLE and TOP WINKWELL, SEWERAGE, BOTTOM SIDE, TOP SIDE, SWEEPS 2, BROADWATER, GAS 2, BUSHES, NORTHCHURCH, DODSWELL 2, COW ROAST. There are several clues here; Northchurch and Dodswell are both marked on my 3-1 inch map, there must be many people who

know the "Cow Roast" Inn, and practically the whole length can
be seen from the L.M.S., railway line; but would anybody who
didn't know this bit of country suspect that we travelled straight
through Berkhamsted, Broadwater lock being nearly beside
the railway station there.

This confusion lasted all the way to Birmingham; it
took me a trip or two and much map study before I got sorted
out.

Mother McCrea was wilting perceptibly by the next morning,
which was probably why we took the day fairly easily. It should
only take about four hours to do this stretch, but perhaps we
also had a "bad road," which is boat language for all the locks
against you. Kit always insisted on letting other boats through
if they were pressing behind us and though it was maddening to
have to give away a lock which was ready she was, of course,
perfectly right. We were only learning and were fearfully slow
and should have delayed the professional boaters hopelessly had
we insisted in keeping in front of them. They all knew Kit, of
course, and realised that she had half-wits with her and were
duly grateful for her consideration; they would often help us by
leaving a lock half ready behind them.

Boat people are like that; once they know you are to be trusted
and accepted as doing the same job as themselves under the same
conditions, they will go out of their way to give advice and help
whenever they can. I have known them stop for over an hour
to help my steerer and me with our snubber, which was wound
hopelessly round the propeller blades; in spite of our repeated
entreaties to them to go on and not bother because we knew they
were in a hurry, all they said at the end of their labours was:
"You're welcome." If you were idiotic enough to let them think
that you thought you knew as much as they did, then the word
would go round, and you might stay on the mud for the duration;
not one boat would come forward to help you. But I am glad to
say that people with such ideas were very rare. Most of us were
only too ready to acknowledge our incompetence and show gratitude for the experience of a lifetime, if they were kind enough to
offer it.

It was a funny feeling doing one's stuff in public, as it were.
The locks we had done so far had been very much in the country
with only a few passers-by, but going through "Berker" is very
different. Everybody is always interested in canal boats and loves

to see the lock being worked. Crowds would collect from seemingly nowhere, and dally while we sweated. I always tried to look as if I knew all about it; it was certainly one of the major comforts that very few of the onlookers knew *more* than me about how to manage a boat and, presumably, could not guess that my knowledge was practically nil! We were still something of a novelty; a crew of three women and no men, and once on the Oxford Canal where the women's boats did not go as a rule, I heard an old gentleman in his back garden exclaim as we went past: "Good heavens! an all-woman crew!" in tones of incredulous amazement.

Poor Mother McCrea had not slept at all the night before and was listening to Kit's instructions in a coma, so I scored by getting more than my rightful share of steering. I was beginning to enjoy it tremendously and to feel that satisfaction which comes only from gradually learning to master a Craft (with a capital C because I don't mean a boat, but a craft which entails the use of hand and brain, be it boating, carpentry or what you will). I was making the most awful mess of getting into the locks, of course, but so long as I remembered to go fairly slow there was no damage done to the boats and "just round the corner" there would be another lock where perhaps I should do better.

There is a great deal to be learned about the behaviour of water in locks. How it is affected by the incoming boat, how it will behave when the paddles are drawn, what are the dangers and how to avoid them. Truly, Kit and the other women trainers must have had nerves of steel to go through all this with one lot of trainees after another. We had none of us done this work or anything even faintly like it before, we were all grown women, unused to being told to do things like small children, and we had to run, jump, bend and pull and climb, in a way that most of us had left ten or fifteen years behind. But somehow or other the trainers did it, and one or two pairs of our boats could give the boaters a run that was not to be despised.

After supper Kit, Mother McCrea and I went down to the "Cow Roast" pub where we had beer all round and finally came home through a frosty moonlight laden with cabbage and apples, a present from the innkeeper and his wife.

Next day the fourth member of the party was in a very bad way; she still had not slept and, in addition, turned on a bilious attack. Vera and I began to bet on how long she would last out.

C

After the "Cow Roast" comes the Tring summit, a level stretch
with no locks, which takes about an hour to cross, and is the
moment when one always tries to have a meal. Vera and I had
our porridge and put our heads together over the invalid. She
was obviously very wretched and would be much better off at
home till she was well enough to re-join the boats, but it wasn't
our business to say so. We could, however, make it easy for her
to *go* home and with that end in view we worked like blacks all
day and got through the seven Marsworth locks and the five
that straggle after, as quickly as we could. Kit was pleased with
us and asked if we would like to tie-up rather early; she seemed
surprised at our passionate desire to go on to Leighton Buzzard.
It is a good bit farther and six more locks, but we were working
like machines and didn't notice the difference. It was a lovely
evening, too, I remember . . . Mother McCrea was now being
sick over the side of the butty.

When we did tie up it was getting dark but the invalid at once
disappeared into the town, while Vera and I cleared up and got
our supper. Around eight-thirty she came back and announced
to Kit that she had found a night's lodging, and a landlady who
would call her in time to start at seven next morning, so if Kit
did not mind "could she go and have a night in a proper bed?"
she thought the rest would bring her to life again. Kit thought
it was a good idea, so off she went. Vera and I looked at one
another but kept quiet until we were in our own cabin again.

After breakfast next day we went to Kit in a deputation and
humbly suggested leaving the patient behind till she was well
or sending her back to London from Leighton Station. Light
broke on Kit at last.

"Is THAT why you were so anxious to get on to Leighton?"
she asked. We owned up. If there had been a railway station
nearer we should have been very ready to tie-up when she suggested it. At this pregnant moment Mother McCrea appeared
down the towpath, still looking very wan but distinctly crisper
in her manner. Vera and I tactfully melted "below."

In five minutes it was settled. Her immediate needs packed up
and a cordial farewell all round, Mother McCrea passed down
the path out of our lives. I shall always think that we did her a
good turn because I do not think, even if she had been well, she
would ever have settled to the life. Lots of people did not and
it was nothing to be ashamed of. It was certainly an acquired

taste, but it did take guts to go back home and announce that you could not take it. It must have been bad enough not to like the life but to be feeling thoroughly ill on top of it must have been real misery.

Next day was a change from anything I had done yet. First of all Leighton lock, half a mile on from the tie-up and then the ill-famed Jackdaw pound with its S-bends and bad mud. Apart from this the country was lovely; a sparkling frosty morning and the open fields all round us. The birds were a great feature of the cut and I saw any amount that I had never seen before; herons and wild duck and little darting kingfishers, like green lightning against the copper of the autumn leaves. The berries in the hedges too were lovely, bramble and hips and haws and the sinister black of the privet, and dark purple elderberries that I insisted on cooking for our dinner, to Vera's horror. The mushrooms and toadstools were at their best then and we were very keen on trying out the edible ones. One of my happier memories is of Kit mounted on her bicycle, stance and all, lock-wheeling along the tow-path with her book on "Edible Fungi" open in her hand, periodically leaping off and shooting into a field to pick some ghastly-looking thing she had spotted from the path.

From Marsworth on the locks had been all downhill, which involves a different technique in entering them. So I was learning all over again and was indeed lucky in that, being now the only new trainee, Kit could give me her undivided attention which was an enormous help. And, of course, there was correspondingly more work to be done now that we were one short. Kit would make me do one particular thing over and over again till I began to get the hang of it and then would put me on to something else and make me repeat *that;* it was excellent practice and I shouldn't have had nearly so much to begin with if we had had another trainee as well.

Soon after the Jackdaw we came to three locks close together, Solebury or Stoke Hammond 3, whichever you prefer to call them. Then there is a shortish pound to Talbot's lock and after that a long one of an hour to Fenny Stratford where we tied up to collect tinned milk and for me to sign a form for my quota. We got condensed milk, too, to use in our morning cocoa and save the sugar ration; vegetables from Mrs. Vaughan at the pub and a fill up of all the water cans. Then we settled down to a long pound of four hours before the next lock.

Changing from one boat to another is a bit tricky. You can
easily get off the motor at a bridge-hole and wait for the butty
to come along and pick you up, but getting from the butty up
to the motor is not so simple. The only way to do it without
slowing down the boats, is to leap off at a bridge-hole and race on
to the next one before the motor gets there. It is obviously un-
wise to choose bridge-holes that are too far apart or it will be a
very weary body who stumbles panting on to the counter of the
motor ! There are two excellent bridges for the purpose in this
long pound, an hour from "Finney." That meant, for example,
that Kit and Vera would start off on the butty, with me ahead on
the motor; at bridge 84, Vera would hop off the butty and come
running up to bridge 85 a distance of only a hundred yards, where
she would get on the motor and take over from me. At the next
bridge-hole I would get off and wait for the butty to pick me up.
In this way we could take turns to be off duty and also break up
the long time without locks.

Time "off" was not so rosy as might be supposed. There
were always a hundred things waiting to be done in the cabin;
washing-up from the last meal or preparing for the next one,
making up the fire and perhaps finding there was no coal left in
the coal-box. This meant a trip, bucket and shovel in hand,
round the gunwale and under the topsheets into the back-end
to shovel some up from the permanent supply. Sometimes we
had time to sit down and read or write but not often; you would
remember that the outside brasses had not been cleaned that
day . . . and up you would jump again. But on a cold or wet day it
was heavenly to drop down out of the tearing wind and rain into
the warmth of the cabin, relax in front of the fire, change wet
clothes and have a hot drink. After steering for an hour or so I
used to find that my eyes were strained from constantly looking
ahead and it was a great relief to be able to focus on nearby
things for a bit.

Four hours from Finney comes "the pig-trough." This is
the irreverent nickname given to the aqueduct which carries he
canal over the river Ouse. High in the air it goes, on tall brick
pillars, a narrow towpath on one hand and on the other . . .
nothing, but a sheer drop to the valley below. It is an extraordinary feeling right up there, but I should love to be in the
valley some day and watch "narrow" boats floating through the
air above my head: that must be more extraordinary still. The

Cosgrove pig trough is only a short one; on the Shropshire Union Canal there is one of over a thousand feet, built by the great Thomas Telford, who was also responsible for the Menai Suspension Bridge and the Caledonian Canal and who was born, incredible as it may sound, three years before George the Third came to the throne.

Cosgrove itself is a very shallow, gentle little lock and is only remarkable, from the boat point of view, for an unpleasant bottleneck immediately before it where the cut is very narrow indeed and mud awaits the unwary; and also because it heralds the return of the uphill locks again. There is also a most attractive cottage by the lockside, which in summer is covered in wisteria, pale mauve and silver grey against the old orange bricks.

We could, and did, do more changes at Cosgrove in preparation for another two-hour pound to the bottom of Stoke Bruern 7, the first Northamptonshire village at which we stopped. These two long pounds are a welcome rest after the strenuous locking days which precede them, but we were always glad to have more locks to do with the chance of a gossip with oncoming boats or a dash into the store (which is inevitably there, at the lockside) to replenish the coffee tin or to get more bread.

Sometime during that day I had pulled a muscle in my middle which worried me a bit. It caught me when I was pulling up the paddles and I didn't much enjoy shinning up the lock-sides, in case it went back on me in mid-air so that I lost my footing and fell in. I would like to say here, that there is only one bad danger attached to falling into the cut. If you do it near the stern end of the motor there is a grave risk of being pulled into the propeller blades. One of the very first things Kit taught us was to put the motor into neutral *at once* if this ever happened. Apart from this, the only thing about an impromptu bathe was the impossibility of ever getting your clothes dry again. I am glad to say that, with one honourable exception which I shall come to later, I never did go in.

When I told Kit about the muscle, which I was forced to do to explain my slowness that day, she exclaimed:

"Well, you have timed that beautifully! Now you can go and see Sister Mary; she lives at the top of Stoke and we can call on her in the morning and get her to have a look at you."

I was not at all sure that I wanted to be looked at by Sister Mary and asked anxiously who she was.

"She is the boaters' Nurse," said Kit. "She lives in a little cottage at the top here and anyone who is ill goes and asks her help. When the boaters' wives have their babies, they always tie up here so that Sister Mary can come to them, and for ordinary illness they try to get up here before they have to knock off. If you see boats tied up here in the day-time you may be sure some-one is ill, or else it's a baby."

I thought I should have to go through with it and see what Sister Mary had to say. I had a horrible feeling, which I kept quiet about, that it might be my blessed kidney playing up and if that was the case it meant good-bye to the boats for me. Winding up paddles had been gruelling hard work for my weak abdominal muscles and my arms could not take all the strain yet, but every day I felt them getting harder and stronger and it would be cruel to have to give up. I went to bed feeling horribly apprehensive.

Stoke Bruern has the reputation of being one of the most beautiful villages in England but there is little of its charm to be seen from the bottom of the seven locks which climb the hill into the village. Not until the top is reached, and, even then, it keeps its best for those who take the trouble to leave the canal and wander through its lanes. I did not have a chance to do this till much later; all through the winter it was always too dark when we tied up to make a walk worth while.

From the top lock one gets a fairly good idea of what is in store. To the right a row of quiet mellow brick cottages with well whitened steps leading up to their doors, the faded green framework of the porches nearly hidden by the climbing roses. To the left, a low line of whitewash and thatch, and a barely legible inn sign swinging from the eaves . . . "The Boat"; just visible over the thatched roofs is the tower of the village church up on the hill; ahead, down the cut, a thickly wooded vista and the inevitable curve which hid the rest from view.

We had no sooner got into the top lock than Kit sent me off to Sister Mary, the first cottage on the right. Apprehensively I knocked.

"Come in, come in! I shan't be a moment," called a voice from somewhere above my head and I walked into the cleanest room I have ever been in in my life. Everything seemed to be white; the chairs were draped in it, and the muslin curtains were tied up with bandages. All round the walls were hung First Aid charts and diagrams of the human body. At that moment in floated Sister Mary, shooting her cuffs and beaming at me. I say "floated" because, with her white veil streaming behind, she did not look as if she was in need of any other form of propulsion. I was led next door into her sitting-room, which I took to be a mark of special favour, and a clean snowy sheet was spread on the sofa for me.

"But, Sister Mary, I *can't* lie on that . . . I'm filthy," I protested, but she would not listen and soon I was stretched in all my boat grease and dirt on that virgin surface. I was thankful that at least I had a clean vest on.

She prodded me and pummelled me and finally announced that there was nothing the matter with me, nothing serious, that is . . . only a pulled muscle.

"No paddles for three days," said Sister Mary firmly, "and feet up whenever you can."

Kit popped her head round the door at this point and caught the last remark. She was given minute instructions for seeing that I did as I was told and, with many thanks and a fond farewell on both sides, we dashed off to the boats again. I saw Sister Mary on several later occasions, but I never needed to consult her again. If I had, I should have done so with perfect confidence. She knows her stuff all right and knew very well what kind of strains we were up against. The boat people trust her implicitly; I have often heard them say: "I'll ask the nurse when we get to Stoke. She'll know, she'll tell me what to do."

Before we came out of the lock we checked the head-lights to make sure they were in working order for the tunnel that lies round the corner. If anything is wrong with the lights it means using the big oil lamp from the engine-room but I only remember having to do this on one occasion.

Blisworth tunnel is nearly two miles long, and when you enter it it is not possible to see the other end. This is partly due to being temporarily blind, coming out of the bright outside light, but even after this has worn off, it is some time before you can see a tiny pin-point of light ahead which is the other end of the tunnel. And sometimes it is the headlight of an oncoming boat that you mistake for the exit, but you can soon tell which it is.

Steering in a tunnel is not funny. I was always bad at it and on this first occasion, and for a long time afterwards, I was terrified into the bargain. One's natural tendency is to over-steer

violently. You cannot see a thing but feel you ought to be doing
something, so you steer from one side to the other, bumping
alarmingly and upsetting everything in the cabin, which you are
far too frenzied to be able to rectify. The first time I had Kit
with me, of course, and never have I been so comforted by
feeling her hand on the tiller and her complete calm in spite of
all the crashes. Unless the head-lights are amazingly strong, they
don't do more than reflect a very faint glow from the dripping
brickwork of the walls on one side or the other, and as soon as
you see a glow at all you know you are far too close to that side
and there will shortly be an ear-splitting crash . . . which there is.

If you have crashed with sufficient violence the boat will have
bounced off one wall and be heading for the other, a point I
overlooked until the stern crashed in its turn, and then the fore-
end hit the other wall and so on. I really have often been through
a tunnel like this, with my nerves at full stretch through the
bangs and bumps. How I hated them! but like everything
else I got better at them and didn't mind so much in the end.

Meeting boats was rather tricky; it was quite possible to pass
one another of course but you had to be careful, especially the
butty boats of each pair, which were strung out seventy feet
behind the motors and could quite easily get their two snubbers
entangled. The only comfort was the thought that it was extremely
unlikely that the other pair would be women as incompetent as
me; if they were boaters, which in all probability they were, then
they could be relied upon to get me out of the mess, if and
when it happened.

Taking the motor through a tunnel was much more restful
than being in charge of the butty. You could always slacken
speed if you felt a bump coming and, for reasons that I have
already explained, the motor responds more readily to the tiller.
The butty, on the other hand, can only go at whatever speed the
motor chooses and it doesn't matter how badly you are steering
and how violently you are bumping, it is impossible to slow
down or even to hold any communication with the motor. The
noise of the engine in the enclosed tunnel is all pervading, and
scream, shout or bellow as loudly as you may, you will not be
heard. This gave rise to a pet phobia of mine which haunted me
to the end. It started with Kit's habit of standing on the gunwale
to steer with us, in just the same way as she did down the open
cut. If the stern of the motor got too close to the wall even Kit

would have been squashed from where she stood, but she would only move to the other gunwale in an extreme crisis, and as a result I lived in a perpetual horror of scraping her off on the wall without knowing it! Even after I had left Kit and was steering on my own, I used to worry myself sick in tunnels in case someone from the butty had fallen in and I was none the wiser. Of course it never happened but something very like it did happen to a pair of the women's boats.

They were coming through empty, which meant that the butty was tied up close behind the motor, but there is not nearly so much strain as with a loaded boat. At the tunnel mouth the motor emerged into the daylight and the steerer looked round casually, to perceive with icy horror that she had lost her butty! The cross straps had slipped somewhere in the tunnel, she had no idea when, and the butty was somewhere inside. The story ended very fortunately as some other boats were following fairly closely and they, of course, picked up the butty, "gave her a snatch," and towed her through to be re-united with her well-nigh frantic steerer.

Very luckily for me I did not know that story on my first tunnel day; it was all quite bad enough without that. Before I had done with the cut I had a tunnel story of my own of which I am very proud, but that was months later.

There are certain things to be said on the credit side for tunnels. It is a wonderful opportunity to sing at the top of your voice—if, like me, you love singing but have not been blessed with the wherewithal to do it. In the tunnels I could bellow to my heart's content, no one could hear me and be hurt by it. Or alternatively, I would recite pages of poetry or long speeches from Shakespeare without risk of being thought mental; the closed-in walls gave tremendous resonance to the voice, too, so that I sounded simply magnificent . . . it also had the effect of taking my mind off all but the major crashes. Another good thing about tunnels was getting into them out of the rain, wind or snow, which was sometimes a great blessing; more often than not, though, we would go in in bright sunshine and, the English climate being as versatile as it is, emerge at the end of fifty minutes straight into a downpour for which we were not prepared. And lastly, one of the three people on the two boats could have a perfectly legitimate rest while we went through; the only possibilities to nag your conscience being cooking or "the

c*

inside brasses." If you were clever you would have already disposed of both.

It was funny, but after my first few days on the boats, after we had come back from Limehouse perhaps, I was never conscious of the water all round us as a hostile element and a source of danger. I think we got so used to it that we forgot all about it and if anyone fell in, as frequently they did, no one paid the slightest attention beyond cursing them for messing up the cabin with wet things. Accidents do happen and sometimes they are fatal ones but generally speaking there is very little real danger. While I was on the cut there were two fatal accidents which shocked and horrified everybody. In one case an elderly man lost his footing in the ice and fell into a lock. The lock-keeper and another man pulled him out at once but the ice-cold water had killed him. In the second, dreadful, case, a boater's young wife slipped while crossing the gates of an empty lock; she caught at the hand-rail as she fell but it gave way. She was also rescued without delay, but in spite of hours of artificial respiration she never came round. I heard that, in the opinion of the doctor who had worked unceasingly to try to save her, it was hopeless from the first as she had banged her head in falling, probably with the treacherous hand-rail. Her husband was left with two tiny children and a pair of boats which no man can run single-handed: I never heard what became of him. In both these cases the fatalities were due to abnormal circumstances which were not to be expected as part of the everyday risks.

On a much lower scale come the accidents due to handling ropes. The wise boater keeps his young children down in the cabin while working through locks. Ropes have a way of getting round a child's legs and then tightening up suddenly, which may result in a broken limb. There are minor accidents, too, of hands getting caught, knees or ankles crushed between boat and lock-side or windlasses flying backwards as the paddle runs down, so quickly that your hand has been caught half a dozen times by the whirling iron before you have time even to step back. But all these are calamities that do not befall the good boater, who believes that to be incautious is to be incompetent.

At the north end of the Blisworth tunnel the cut follows the railway for nine or ten miles, passing close to the busy station of Weedon and finally dividing at Norton Junction about a mile from the village of Long Buckby. Here one arm goes east to

Leicester and the other west to Warwick, Leamington and Birmingham. Just before the Junction are the seven Long Buckby locks, providing a welcome change after the three and a half-hour pound from Blisworth.

"Bugby" (as it is pronounced) provided a lot of excitements, all told. The farm where we went for fresh milk, the bridge-hole which was so narrow that we nearly always got stuck on the mud, the yard, on a bend, where there was a snow-white turkey, which so fascinated me that I invariably crashed the wall because I was looking at the turkey and not at the cut! And at the top lock, dear Mrs. Dawson who was so kind and always had jam tarts for us and, in the summer, as the height of achievement, would produce ice-cream if we would produce mugs to carry it away in.

A hundred yards farther on came the biggest thrill of all. Norton Junction Toll Office . . . it does not sound very exciting but to us it spelt LETTERS, the first since leaving the depot. We were gauged, too, to make sure we were still carrying the same amount of steel that we had started with, though what we could have done with it *en route* I cannot imagine. Coal was a different matter and I suppose it would have been possible to have sold a ton or two at dead of night and cooked the invoice accordingly; but no, going up and coming down we were gauged. Nobody minded. We were far too busy tearing open our precious letters and perhaps some angel relation had sent a cake or jam to eke out the rations. (I hear that the gauging place has been done away with now, and that it all happens at the top lock instead.)

There is a welcome straight half-hour after this before Braunston tunnel; just as well, for with all three of us reading letters from home the steering was only very sketchy. Once in the tunnel, only the lucky third person could go on reading; the other two standing in Stygian gloom had to bear their souls in patience for another forty minutes.

I don't remember if I had letters or not on this trip but I expect I did. I used to hear from the children, usually, when we got to Norton. By this stage of the journey I would have lost all account of time and not know if it was weeks or months or only days since I had left home.

We tied up at the top of the Braunston locks; the end of my tenth day as an aspiring "canal boatwoman."

I must have been improving considerably by now because

my very incomplete diary tells me that we went from Braunston to Warwick the next day; that stretch includes thirty-two locks, of which twenty are in two sets of ten each. In addition, from Knapton Junction on the locks are of a more modern design and the paddles are like nothing I had ever seen before. The old ratchet principle is scrapped and the "new design" are worked on a spiral thread, the whole thing being encased in concrete so that you cannot tell at a glance if the paddles are up or down, but have to go and peer through a small window, which is a horrible waste of time. On the other hand the actual locks are much tidier; concrete edges and neat steps instead of the loose gravel and grass banks of the more southern country. We had special big windlasses for these locks so that you did not have quite so many turns; even then there were quite enough. If I remember rightly, twenty turns was the minimum and about twenty-four the most. It varied with the size of the paddle, which in its turn was dependent on the depth of the lock. The first dozen turns were very hard; after that it would get easier, but I was always glad to get back to the old locks again; I am, in nearly everything, thoroughly conservative.

But before these novelties unfolded themselves we passed the "island" at Knapton Junction. Here the Coventry canal goes off to the east and we had to take a left-hand turn for Birmingham. There is a small grassy island in the middle of the cut with three lengths of water turning it into a triangle. Whatever you were doing "you always turned left at the triangle" which Kit rubbed in to such an extent that one almost tried to turn right, out of sheer nerves. And when the moment came, later, when there was no loading in London and we came up empty and had to turn RIGHT for Coventry and coal, the shock nearly sent me into a decline.

They are very pleasantly spread out, these thirty-two locks. After the first three, an hour's pound before Itchington 10, then, to help you to recover, another forty-five minutes before Radford 10. In addition, the pounds between the locks are so short that we could take the boats into several locks breasted-up. The first eight of Itchington can be done that way and the first four of Radford, with a great saving of labour.

I was not being spared that day though. Going into locks breasted-up was an entirely new technique for me and Kit made the most of it. It is not difficult but you have got to get used to the butty pulling you sideways, and allow for it when you steer. The boats go much more slowly, too, when they are tied together, but that is rather a good thing when you're learning as I was. It is not quite so frightening to steer fifty tons, two boats and three people into a downhill lock (with a sheer drop over the gates at the bottom!) if you feel that you are not capable of much speed.

Perhaps it sounds too obvious to mention but does anybody, unaccustomed to them, realise that boats have no method of braking? That reduction of speed is, therefore, a very gradual affair, and a sudden stop quite impossible? That the nearest approach to it is to put your engine into *reverse*, or "astern" to be correct, a much lengthier operation than applying the foot-brake of a car, and one that takes appreciably longer to have any effect on the speed of the boat. Individual engines do vary in this respect but the main point is worth driving home, I think, if the judgment and timing necessary in handling boats skilfully is to be fully appreciated.

Anyone who has watched the G.U. boats working through the locks near London will have been struck by the ease with which their steerers bring them into the lock, and have probably thought, "That doesn't look complicated; I'm sure I could do that." So they could . . . after a very great deal of practice. The boat-people have had their craft handed down to them, from father to son, since the first canal was opened in 1761 and they will tell you that they are still learning.

This little digression is to point out what we hopeful members of the Women's Training Scheme were trying to pack into *two* training trips, of approximately three weeks each. It is not surprising that, to start with, the boaters looked on with amused scorn at our efforts; nor, knowing them, is it to be wondered at that soon they were willing and anxious to pass their highly skilled knowledge on to us. As a race they are fundamentally kind and courteous in a way that puts to shame their educated brothers and sisters, for hardly any boater can read or write.

The great thing about the Warwick tie-up is the pub at the top lock, "The Cape of Good Hope." It keeps a brand of beer not to be found in the southern counties, of which I am particularly fond, it has an automatic piano which grinds out tunes for a penny, and some perfectly lovely china plates grouped round the walls of the bar. It also sports a settle, scrubbed wooden tables of a dazzling whiteness, and I am not at all sure that the floors aren't sanded. Altogether an enchanting place.

The fresh water-tap at the other side of the cut is a few feet only from the tie-up and produces a stream of that very soft Warwickshire water, so we always used to keep all our laundry for Warwick and at once get rid of any hard water we had left in our cans.

Just round the corner comes the marathon of locks, Hatton 21. The first few appear quite normal, the cut winding as usual so that the distant view is invisible, but after that . . . ! Before the glazing eyes of the new trainee appears a hill, a steep hill, and climbing the side of it the rest of the twenty-one locks are seen, their white balance beams marking the rise of the hill like the treads of a giant's staircase.

This really was an endurance test for the newcomer, and even Kit has been known to tie us up in the middle for food. In any event she always insisted on us having something to eat and drink before we started on Hatton. If they were "against" you the labour was of course doubled; with the locks against you, you have the prospect of two gate paddles to get the lock ready, plus two gate paddles to get the boats through, which is $2 \times 2 \times 21 \times 24$ turns with the windlass ! I make the answer 2,016 turns.

We shared it of course, and even the lock-wheeler had a relief after six or seven locks.

As a practice ground, though, it was perfect, to cure some fault that the other more widely spaced locks did not offer; not many people can possibly have emerged at the top of Hatton without knowing more than they did at the bottom.

After two or three hours of Hatton (according to whether fate had been kind in having the locks ready for us or not) we were more than ready for the three-hour pound to the last five locks before Birmingham, Knowle 5. After Hatton they appeared as chicken-feed.

From Knowle, another three hours brings you, in theory, to Tyseley where we unloaded. In theory only, for it may well be that the new trainee, puffed up with her Hatton successes, would fall foul of the mud on an attractive piece of the cut known graphically as "Muck Bend." This was worse going up than coming down the cut, because going up we were loaded and, much of the boat being under water, it is, therefore, much easier for it to nestle on the slime at the bottom. But all things being equal, it is curious how a bend may be easy one way and far more difficult from the opposite direction, or vice versa. I do not know why this should be so but it undoubtedly is.

All sorts of things may happen on "Muck Bend" and they usually did. You could rush head on into the bank without knowing there was a bank . . . under the water; you could take the corner too fine, which resulted in the motor tipping gently but inexorably to an angle of forty-five degrees; or you could get quietly entangled in mud which slowed you down to such an extent that the butty would rush up on you and in the general *melée* the snubber would coil itself enthusiastically round the propeller blades. In the first two cases there was no limit to the peculiar things of which the butty was capable on her own account, so that it will be seen that the combinations of possibilities were infinite. I tried them all in turn at a later date, but easily the best occasion was when I got the motor heavily embedded, and going so fast that the butty, coming up and past me, was able to give me "a snatch" and pull the MOTOR off the mud, an unorthodox but nevertheless brilliant operation for which I take full credit. . . .

After "Muck Bend" is safely over, the rest of the way seems very long and never ending and one goes through several miles of populated town before coming to the wharf at Tyseley . . . or so it appears. It feels cramped and shut in after the long stretches of open country, and the constant coming and going along the towpath, buses humping over the bridges, the clang of tram bells, all reminded me vividly of the London docks, now nine days behind me.

CHAPTER VII—BRUMMAGEM AND THE BOTTOM ROAD

As soon as we were tied up at Tyseley, Kit went off to the office for letters and to find out when we should unload. She returned with the information that we should not be done before Monday (it was now Saturday) and that we should have to go round to Castle Hill, another wharf a little farther on. It is only half an hour's run and perfectly straightforward, so Vera was given permission to go to her home near Coventry for the week-end.

This was the only chance I had yet had to live in the cabin on my own, and I really spread myself. The first thing Kit and I both did was to wash our hair, which was considerably easier with the cabin to oneself, but for all that I found it an awkward business, having to re-fill and re-boil fresh kettles with my hair dripping in rats' tails down my neck.

The moment I had been waiting for came at bed-time. Plenty of room, by boat standards, to undress, wash and even, as the last refinement, to brush my hair. And then I started to try out different ways of sleeping. I tried my head down the cabin and my feet up by the door, which had the advantage of an overhead light to read by, but I missed my fire and my ash-tray. The next night I tried with my head in the same place but my feet in the cupboard and liked it no better; by the time Vera got back on Monday I was quite content to return to my original position which I never afterwards changed, unless I had to.

On Sunday morning Kit and I took the boats round to Castle Hill which is very similar to the other Tyseley wharf; if anything a little quieter. I don't remember it very well as I never went there again and there was nothing conspicuous about it. In the evening we went to the pictures with one of the boater boys, who I will call Fred because it was not his name. He was one of the most good-natured lads I have ever met and unfailingly ready to give us a hand, lock-wheeling for us and helping us over the more difficult and wearisome patches. He worked with two other men, all of them unmarried, and with a reputation second to none for shifting up and down the cut in record time. They would take it in turns to work all through the night, and I don't suppose they took their clothes off between London and

Birmingham; as they could do the trip in two and a half days this is not quite as bad as it sounds.

But Fred was tremendously poshed up that night, to accompany us to the pictures. He sported a natty blue suit (and how on earth it *was* natty after being stowed away in a drawer in his cabin, *I* don't know), collar, tie and scarf, and was topped off wtth a great deal of highly odorous brilliantine which had turned his red head quite black. He walked outside us on the pavements and attempted to pay our bus fares like the gentleman he was; a good time being had by all (?) in the cinema, which was showing a particularly ghastly Hollywood musical if I remember rightly.

Fred has left the cut to go and drive a lorry. I hope he has prospered as he deserved; the cut was a more austere place without his effervescent good spirits and kindness.

Vera got back early on Monday very clean and sleek after a more or less continuous two days in the bath; during the afternoon they unloaded us, too late for us to make a further move that night. The boats take quite a bit of tidying up after unloading and I was glad to have another night's rest before we moved off. It seemed funny to see the boats high out of the water again, and of course, when it came to handling them the following day I felt a perfect fool and oversteered violently, forgetting how much quicker they can turn when empty. Kit had not had three years of trainees without being ready for this, so I did not get as much ticking-off as I had expected.

On Tuesday morning we let go at 8.30. It must either have been a very dark morning or else the locks cannot have been open before; this was far later than our usual hour of starting.

At 8.30, then, we embarked on what is known as "the bottom road": for what reason I have never discovered, unless it be that it clearly should have been called "the top road," running as it does north of Brum., and for miles and miles through the country to the north-east. It makes an enormous loop, with turnings to right and left off the main route, to include all the various collieries which abound here.

For interest's sake here is the "bottom road" route. (It is worth following it out on a large-scale map to get an idea of how it twists and turns and goes out of its way and in the opposite direction from our destination, which was Coventry.) Gravelly Hill, Minworth, Curdworth, Fazeley, Glascote, Polesworth,

Grendon, Atherstone, Nuneaton and Hawkesbury . . . the latter
being the Office where we got our loading orders.

But the two most outstanding things about the "bottom road"
from the boaters' point of view are its dirt and its single locks.

The dirt doesn't last all the way, admittedly, and there is some
lovely country later to make up, but the single locks are with
you to the end. There are thirty-two of them and they are only
wide enough to take one boat at a time. This means that at each
one the butty must be cast off, the motor put through the lock,
the lock emptied and the butty towed in by human energy, the
lock re-filled and the two boats re-united again. The towing
process is known as "bow-hauling," and is accomplished by means
of a line fastened on the stud at the fore-end of the butty, draped
over the shoulder, clasped in both hands and then simply PULL
and PULL again.

I felt very hard used when asked to turn myself into a beast
of burden in this way. It was fortunate that I had no foreknow-
ledge of a later trip when we had to bow-haul *loaded* butties from
Knapton Junction to Oxford, and got stuck in the too-narrow
locks into the bargain !

I felt more hardly used still when I discovered the dirt of the
rope I was holding. The whole of the towpath here is small
gravelly stones, permeated through and through with oil,
grease, soot and noisome vapours from the factories at the cut
side. That is at its best; at its worst it is black mud, through
which the rope drags and falls as the bow hauler creeps onwards.
It is no exaggeration to say that by the time we got out into
the open country, we had a black stripe over our backs and
shoulders, which penetrated right through to the skin, and which
stayed there till we could scrub it off in a bath. We used to tow
the ropes in the water for a mile or so, to clean them.

As we progressed and I saw whole families of small children
helping their "mums" to pull the butty, their boots leaking and
their clothes filthy, I could visualise what this meant in terms
of human wear and tear. The state of the cabins at the end of the
day . . . the condition of the kids' already threadbare clothes . . .
the strain on their immature bodies . . . the harm done to the
boater's pregnant wife . . . I felt that we had progressed not at
all since the scandal of child labour during the Industrial Revo-
lution. I asked passionately WHY were the boats sent round
this way when they could get to Coventry by going back the

way they had come and turning off at the Knapton island ? It was something to do with "saving water". . . the answer to every anomaly on the cut. The boaters got paid extra for the bottom road but even this inducement did not satisfy them and there was, not surprisingly, a lot of unrest on the subject.

I never did the bottom road again; on my next trip, just as we were due to start on it, the order went forth from the authorities: "No more Bottom Road" . . . but it had taken an unofficial sit-down strike to achieve it. After that everybody winded their boats at Tyseley and went back through Knowle and Hatton.

I remember very little of the rest of the bottom road except the lovely names Minworth, Curdworth, Bakery, Dog and Jacket, one unforgettable morning start, and the most humiliating experience I ever had.

I am not even sure where this latter took place, but it does not matter. Perhaps it was at the top of Atherstone that Kit told me to take the motor on to the top lock, while she stayed to give Vera a hand with bow-hauling the butty. Feeling very proud of myself I did all my stuff in the approved style and safely brought the motor out at the top where I tied her up, close to the gates, and went down the locks to get it ready again for the butty. As I pulled up the paddles there came an amused shout from the lock-keeper who had chosen that moment to appear:

"Hey ! You're losing your motor !"

I tore to the top gates in horror. It was quite true . . . my strap had slipped and the motor was chugging peacefully off on her own down the middle of the cut. I had left her in gear, idiotically, and she had slipped her moorings. I screamed to the lock-keeper:

"What on earth shall I do ?"

"Take the rake," he replied unsympathetically . . . and walked calmly off in the opposite direction.

I turned to the hedge at the towpath side, where the rake is nearly always to be found. It was there right enough, and with difficulty I heaved it off its pegs. These rakes are ten or twelve feet long, good solid wood with an end rather like an ordinary table fork at right angles to the shaft. They are used to remove "foreign bodies" from the bottom of the lock; the lock-keeper must have had his tongue well in his check when he suggested me using it; he must have known I could hardly lift it horizontally, let alone hold it at the extreme end in order to lunge it out

over the water to catch my errant boat. If she had been fairly
close I *might* have done it; as it was, she was some way away by
now, and to reach her I had to hold the unspeakable rake at the
extreme end, in which position I could barely lift it off the ground.
I abandoned it and watched the motor miserably, wondering how
soon Kit would materialise and see me looking and feeling the
fool I was.

It dawned gradually on me that she was not running straight;
bless her little heart ! she was heading for the opposite bank . . .
I was saved, if I was quick, from utter ignominy.

Over the lock gates I went, like a stag, into someone's vegetable
garden and down the other bank to head her off. I remember,
dimly, tearing through an orchard and bursting my way down
the bank to arrive panting on the fore-end of the boat. I had
never scrambled on more quickly; round the cratch and down the
top-planks I went, over the cabin top and alighted on the counter
in time to twirl the engine into astern before we were too badly
embedded in the soft earth of the bank. I backed her gingerly,
and oh, so slowly it seemed, till we were back where we ought
to have been, and was just unbending from my second effort at
tying up as Kit appeared with the butty. When I owned up she
laughed at me; I expect she knew what I had been through in
hurt pride without any further comment being necessary.

The morning start that I shall never forget was when we let go
from, I think, the Bakery. It was quite dark and very cold. A
few stars were showing in the black sky and to my left was a line
of willows, throwing so deep a shadow on the water that I
couldn't see where the bank and water met. Ahead I could see
nothing but blackness; I went very slowly indeed, groping my
way. I think Vera must have been on the butty with Kit, because
one of the outstanding things about that morning was the feeling
of perfect solitude and complete quiet, the only sound the popping
of the engine; not even the birds were awake yet. I stood and
breathed in the frosty air, and the smell of grass and trees and
very early morning.

In front I could see a small red light which seemed to be quite
near and moving from left to right. I glanced round, and back
at the little pin-point . . . good heavens, it was above my head,
above the cut ! That could only mean one thing; we were just
going under a bridge; the kindly lorry or cyclist, or whoever it
was, had saved me a nasty crash at the right moment. Under the

bridge the blackness was blacker still, and the engine rever-
berated like thunder, but at the other side the sky seemed lighter
and I put on a little speed.

Gradually I could pick out the line of the banks on either hand
and could begin to make out the water curving on ahead of the
boat. Away on my left a ridge of hills appeared in the distance,
the sky looked lighter over there; but then I did not realise what
was going to happen in a minute.

Everything was like a picture in monochrome; not a scrap of
colour anywhere; deepest black in the water beside my boat,
black trees and bushes, grey water ahead, grey fields beyond,
paler grey line of hills meeting pale grey sky . . . and as I watched,
sky and hills getting swiftly lighter and lighter, passing through
pearly grey and white to light itself, golden dazzling light as the
sun came up from behind the ridge.

"But look, the morn, in russet mantle clad, walks o'er the dew
of yon high eastward hill . . ."; as I remembered those beautiful
lines I lived them fully, instead of only hearing their music.

Shakespeare's dawn may have been "russet"; even if it was not
he may surely be forgiven for his choice of that exquisite word ?
My dawn was pure pale gold and was laying its Midas fingers on
all the country as I watched. Gone was the monochrome; colour
was in everything now. The grey of the distant hills had warmth
and depth, the fields and trees had brown and green shadows on
them; even the berries in the hedge turned to their accustomed
purple and red. The sun was blazing such a trail across the sky
that the naked eye couldn't look directly at it; far away to my
right the small pale stars were puffing out, swamped in the golden
flood, their night's work done. It was day.

I see from my diary that it was 31st October. Why, when we
decide to look at the sunrise, do we always choose the summer ?
Or is it only I who have made this mistake ? If so, it is one that
I shall never make again. Perhaps it could be summed up like
this: if it is a feast for the eyes you want, then choose the autumn
as I had it chosen for me; if a feast of scents and smells, then the
summer will give you what you seek. Whichever you choose it
will be a salutary experience, as I had that morning; to feel
an unmattering atom before the splendour of something not of
man's devising.

We took three days to get down to Hawkesbury for our loading
orders. There is a regular Piccadilly Circus outside the G.U.

Office there with the cut going off in three different directions;
one to Long Ford, one to London and one the way we had come,
from Bedworth.   There is a pub-cum-shop, a lock with a rise of
four inches, and a hairpin bend that caused much suffering to me
and my fellow trainees.   If we were lucky, there were also letters.

The shop was a sort of miniature Selfridge's.   There we could
buy rations, buns, paraffin for the stoves, boaters' pies, overalls
and underclothes.   There were also bread, tinned goods, jam and
treacle, ink, pencils and bootlaces; all packed into a shop no
bigger than a medium sized bathroom; truly, *multum in parvo*.

Kit came back with the news that we were to load at Long
Ford with coal for the A.B.C. Head Office in Camden Town, a
very long journey indeed as we usually got rid of our coal somewhere on the way back to Southall.   It was not often we went
farther than the G.U. depot; actually the A.B.C. was the farthest
anyone ever went.

Collecting our things from the shop we set off to Long Ford,
which is only about twenty minutes away, but it takes longer
on the way there, because it includes a rather amusing piece of
boat management which I think may be interesting to read
about.

The coal is loaded by chutes above the boats, and the cut is
not very wide here.   For this reason it is necessary to wind the
boats before getting as far as the chutes, and going the rest of the
way backwards, so that when you are loaded you are facing the
right way home.   The only place where the boats can be winded
is not very wide either, but an ingenious system has been worked
out to surmount this difficulty.

There is a telegraph pole on the towpath, conveniently placed
just opposite the wide bit of the cut.   Bringing the breasted-up
boats close in the path, one person jumps off the fore-end
with a cotton-line which is tied up to the fore-end stud of the
motor.   This she makes fast to the telegraph pole, while the
sterns of the boats are shafted round in the very limited space.   In
this way the boat is made to turn on a pivot, taking up much
less room than the more usual backwards and forwards method.
When she's nicely round, the line is thrown back again and the
person on the path gets another one chucked at her, this time
from the motor stern; with this in her hand she walks down the
path keeping a tightish pull on it to keep the motor well over, and
to counteract the pull from the breasted-up butty.

Not a lot of steering can be done in reverse, and of course the whole operation has been carried out with the boats tied together, which makes it even harder to steer effectively. The pair of them are thus conducted neatly down the cut till they are opposite the chutes, when the line is once more thrown back and the poor bank person has to walk about half a mile through the town till she can find a bridge to take her over to the other side of the cut again.

On this occasion I had to walk, but it paid a good dividend as I spotted a shop which sold the kind of coffee we liked and managed, too, to collar a boy selling evening papers.

When I got back to the boats they were singled out ready for loading in the morning; there were several other pairs tied up waiting, as well as ourselves. In view of this we had a "lie-in" next morning, which was extremely welcome. I don't suppose it was a very late one because the boats have to be got ready for loading coal just as they have for any other cargo; beams and stands out, sheets unrolled and all the rest of it.

The coal chutes are fascinating. The boat goes directly beneath the one which contains your special brand of coal, a trap-door opens, and the coal descends in a black avalanche, assisted on its downward journey by two men with shovels standing on the floor of the chute. There is another man shovelling in the hold of the boat to get the coal evenly distributed, and usually Kit joined in this operation herself. She was frightfully technical about how her boats were loaded and knew exactly how she wanted the weight disposed. There is a lot in this, of course; a badly loaded boat is fiendish to steer and many a time I have shovelled coal, and other cargo, too, in an effort to get rid of a fast-developing list. This applies specially to the butty where the steerer is quite certain to be trying to cook the dinner at the same time, and it is infuriating to have a boat that insists on climbing into the hedge if you leave her to light the Primus.

The time spent at night in re-shovelling was always time well spent; Kit, being Kit, got hers done once and for all, at the beginning, by superintending it herself and deciding how much was to go on the motor and how much on the butty.

The tonnage varied a good deal, some boats being slightly wider than others, and some boaters being anxious to take a heavier load and get paid more for it; on an average it was fifty tons between the pair of boats.

After the coal was arranged to Kit's liking we had to sheet up again, but with coal it is not always necessary to do more than the side-sheets. If the weather is likely to be fairly dry there will not be a lot of rain to get into the hold and the side-sheets are enough. Lots of boaters never sheeted with coal at all, but we nearly always did; once when we didn't I.hated the feeling that there was nothing between the coal and the water, and I think it looks untidy as well. But then I was not in the habit of keeping dog-kennels and chicken runs on top of the coal, both of which I have often seen done.

Throughout every trip the bicycle had to be carried with us. While intensive locking was going on, it lived on the cabin top of the motor, where it would be flung by the relieved lock-wheeler on discovering that the next lock, at least, was ready. When it was not in use it could go in the hold of an empty boat, but had to be tied to the top-planks once the boat was sheeted up. This was a most perilous-looking position; I could never understand why we didn't lose it. It was hitched on in such a way that the hand brake caught slightly on the top-plank, the rest of the cycle lying flat on the taut side-strings, and one turn only with the long end of one string was allowed round the frame, under the saddle. It always worked marvellously, even staying immovable in a crash.

We grabbed some dinner before starting off again at half-past two (triumphantly facing the right way round) and returned to Hawkesbury, where a slight argle-bargle ensued over me not doing as I was expected to do turning the difficult bend there.

I was steering the butty, and had I been clever (or even moderately intelligent) I should have caused the butty to run into the motor stern with a good bang which would have pushed the nose of the motor round the way we wanted to go. Instead, being only very foggy as to which way we *did* want to go, I carefully banged the wrong side of the motor and pushed her round into a thoroughly awkward position, from which it took all Kit's ingenuity to rescue us. I did not emerge from this unscathed, I might add.

In fact, from a rather irrelevant entry in my diary: "China tea," I am able to deduce that a blistering row took place; I almost certainly arguing black was white rather than be in the wrong, and Kit being justifiably enraged by idiocy, plus insubordination, we no doubt presented a particularly stimulating spectacle to watchers on the Hawkesbury bend.

Kit is a born teacher; she knows how to put her subject across and how to appeal to different kinds of temperaments. She knew when to lam into me and when to lay off (that it was usually "lamming" and not "laying" was my fault and not hers); after an exceptionally brisk round between us, I would be complimented on something that a mentally deficient child of two could have done better, and my ruffled feelings would be accordingly soothed. I don't know if this is good psychology or not; I do know that it is very effective, and I herewith salute the patience and self-control that made such compliments capable of utterance.

Failing a pleasantry of this nature she would think up something else equally soothing, and this is where the China tea comes in. It was a very special treat to us, as it was to most people during the war, and only came out on high days and holidays. That we should have had it on that particular day, therefore, is an indication of the magnitude of the row which preceded it. . . .

We tied up at Stretton that night, but I rather think that on the way there occurred the moment when I *placed* a perfectly good packet of cigarettes in the cut. Evidently not my good day.

We had a wonderful system of signals from one boat to the other; you could not hear without stopping the engine, so some kind of dumb show was essential. One of Kit's pets went like this: "Poop-poop," from the sackbut (very like "Mr. Toad") . . . motor steerer turns round . . . Kit is describing arcs in the air with her arm . . . motor person nods understanding . . . Kit is seen to be smoking an imaginary cigarette . . . more nods . . . more arcs in the air, followed by much pointing down the cut ahead of us . . . complete comprehension from motor steerer, who instantly searches the ticket drawer for Kit's cigarettes, which she has left behind when going back to the butty, and now wants putting off at the next bridge-hole for her to pick up as she passes.

So when I heard the "poop-poop" and read the ensuing message, I knew what was expected of me, but, perhaps to try to make up for my stupidity earlier in the day, I thought I would be extra clever and not wait for a bridge-hole, which I could see was going to be some time coming. I accordingly chose a bit of cut that looked both narrow and deep enough to take the motor in close, and with the precious packet in my hand and a smile of encouragement to a distraught Kit, I edged in closer and closer

till at last . . . yes, that was all right, I could reach . . . and I placed
the prize on a tuft of grass at the water's edge, only to see it
sink and disappear before my eyes. I have seldom felt a bigger
fool.

When we got to Stretton I rushed straight off to the pub and
bought a replacement with which to face Kit; the lesson, however,
was learnt and I always waited for a bridge in future.

By about this stage of my first trip my hands had become
agonisingly painful. It was pretty well hopeless to try to wear
gloves while working because our hands were constantly getting
wet with the ropes; in despair one shed them and worked with
bare hands, which was much easier. At the same time the wind
blew, and the rain rained, and the frost froze, all on top of one's
defenceless wet skin which didn't like it a bit, and retaliated by
developing such chaps as I did not know existed. We dried
them when we could but it was not easy to dry the towel that
dried the hands that stopped the chaps that saved the skin, etc.,
etc., the net result being that by this time my hands were swollen,
cracked and sometimes even bleeding. To bend my fingers
round a pen and write a letter in the evening was nearly impossible; if I did try I used to find my tongue sticking out with the
effort, like a five-year-old doing pot-hooks.

Darning I had given up completely; if I caught a thread on
my cheese-grater hands there would be a ladder, and to try to
slip my hand inside a sock to look for holes was like trying to
insert a hedgehog. This turned out to be only a temporary
inconvenience; on my next trip my skin got harder and I suffered
a good deal less and, later on still, I used always to sleep with my
hands smothered in grease and gloves on; several people did
that, and it made a lot of difference, though it took the first big
clothes-wash on leave to get our hands clean. The dirt and oil got
into all the cracks and chaps, so that it really would not come
out, however hard you scrubbed; anyway, scrubbing sore hands
is not one of life's pleasanter experiences.

While we were on a trip and had occasion to go into any
public place unassociated with the cut, tea-shop or bus, we used
to keep our hands in our pockets, we were so ashamed of them.
I remember Kit saying once: "Do you notice, when you go on
leave, how clean all the *men's* hands are?" That just about sums
it up.

We met a good many of the other women's crews from time

to time on the way down to the A.B.C., but it was some time before I got them all sorted out in my mind or could recognise them easily, which is why I have not mentioned them up to date; I do clearly remember, however, my first encounter with the crack performers among the women. They had been working together for some time and had got really very good indeed as a result; team-work counted for a lot. Kit always called them, collectively and in one word "Audreyevelynananne," so that it was weeks before I managed to disentangle them or give them individual personalities.

Into the bargain, the first time I met this triumvirate was in the Blisworth tunnel in total darkness. Kit was teaching me how to steer the butty rather more professionally than was my custom in a tunnel, when we saw that another pair was coming towards us. When at last their motor steerer came alongside us, and was illuminated for a second as she passed, by the head-lights from her own butty, Kit let out a shriek:

"It's 'AUDREYEVELYNANANNE'," and then to me: "Go down into my cabin *quick* and get my brass bowl; I want to show it to them !"

How she hoped to do this I did not stop to ask, but fell down the steps to get the bowl. This was a beautiful old mixing bowl of copper with a rounded bottom, which Kit had picked up in an antique shop and it was the pride and joy of her heart. (It finished this trip with us and then alas ! she took it home with her when she went on leave and we saw it no more.) I could quite understand that she wanted to show it off, it was a very handsome thing, but I felt the circumstances were hardly pro-pitious.

I was reckoning without Kit. As the other butty came up she started to yell at them, telling them that she'd got it at last, etc., so that in the split second when there was a glimmer of light from both our open cabin doors simultaneously, they were able to focus their eyes on the bowl, and let out suitable ejaculations of surprise and envy. The bowl did its best, too, glowing like a live coal in the dim light.

After this brief encounter it was not surprising that the next time I met this pair of boats I still felt that I did not, what you'd call "know them."

When we finally got back to the depot we did just pause long enough to collect letters, and then turned left as if we were

going down to the docks again.   The A.B.C. is nearly as far
as Limehouse; after we had unloaded it would have saved a lot
of time if we had been able to go straight on down to the dock, but
we were all due for leave so instead we had to turn round and
come back again.

We were tied up there for a couple of days being unloaded;
it was great fun with a lot of traffic going up and down constantly,
the most bewitching smell of freshly baked bread night and day,
a good choice of cinemas for the off-duty hours, and some very
excellent cheap eating places; I had my sister down one day to
see the boats.

A day or two before we got down to Camden Town I had
come across an announcement in an old newspaper that was
wrapped round some bread that Vera had bought.   It said that
"there were rumours concerning a likely successor to Archbishop
Temple"; it made me ponder, and when I got to Camden Town
I rang up a friend, who has always thought me mad anyhow,
and asked him the meaning of it.   He told me that the late
Archbishop of Canterbury had been buried a fortnight ago . . .
we had not even heard of his illness. . . .

That same night Kit and I went to the pictures; almost as soon
as we got there the News came on and the first thing to be flashed
on the screen was: "Result of elections in U.S.A . . . F.D.R. IN
AGAIN."   We gaped at one another in the darkness; we had
entirely forgotten that the elections were due at that time and
had not given a thought to the outcome.

I have mentioned these two incidents to show how completely
cut off we were from anything outside the actual job.   On a later
trip we did have a wireless, but if it hadn't been for that I doubt
if we should have heard about VE-day.   We hardly ever managed
to buy a paper, or if we did get one there was no time to
read it.

Have I made it plain what a wonderful job this was, what
a superb piece of escapism, while yet doing war-work?   There
was no time in a beginner's mind for anything but the work on
hand; so much learning left no energy or mental space for specu-
lation, no matter how important it may have seemed a month
before.   Not for us was the misery of listening to the news four
times a day and pondering the result of a reported battle; of
standing in queues for food; of doing all the housework without
domestic help; of trying to keep up one's personal appearance

on forty-eight coupons a year, and of all the other little fidgeting things that had got many housewives so completely down.

In case I sound very unpatriotic, I would point out that we *were* conscious that the war was still on, and that in our own line of country we were doing what we could to help win it. If in so doing we could also escape from it what more, short of victory, could anyone ask ?

I went home for a week's leave at the end of this trip feeling as if a tornado had blown through my body and mind, tearing away all the cobwebs with which I had been hung for years, and leaving me revitalised and vibrating with life and new hope.

My friends thought I looked very dirty; they were right, I was filthy; my hands were a disgrace and a tribulation, my hair looked as if the mice had been in it, and all my movements were big and clumsy and my table manners appalling. I had put on a lot of weight and my eyes had a great many new, and grimy, lines round them from being constantly screwed up and looking into the distance, and I suspect, though nobody was unkind enough to say it, that I was frightfully hearty.

What the outside world could not see were the pictures in my mind, which will always be there; the warmth in my heart which comes from feeling that you fit into something; the delight in using my whole body to do my job and not only my feet and hands; the comradeship that I had found, the comradeship of people all doing the same difficult work and sharing the same hardships; and finally, the pleasure of resting my tired body in the knowledge that soon I should be going back to start it all once more.

MY second trip began officially on 21st November; in reality it began in my mind long before the first one was over and, owing to unforeseen circumstances, it only started properly on 30th November.

During my leave I had turned my attention to my wardrobe and was now much more suitably clad. I had found out from practical experience what clothes I needed and which were the most comfortable and workable. I now had an oilskin which did not flap and a sou-wester (both borrowed, I must add), a pair of regulation Navy bell-bottoms which I had bought while we were hanging about in Camden Town; the first of three pairs, all of which were warm, comfortable and practicable and did *not* wrap themselves round my ankles and trip me up as I had anticipated.

I had done some good work on an old leather golf jacket of my father's, which on the first trip had been miles too big and very awkward. I removed the collar altogether, also the elastic round the bottom and had put a Zip right up the front; the sleeves I cut off just below the elbow, in shameless imitation of Kit's leather coat which I had noticed never got in her way when she was working. The result, though far from stylish, was excellent. Being a man's coat to start with, mine now came well down at the back, and my forearms and wrists were free of surplus material. I grew to be thankful for my leather coat which was nearly wind-proof and was loose enough to take layers and layers of jerseys under it.

From the Navy shop where I had got my trousers I also bought a sailor's guernsey of thick blue wool, coming nearly down to my knees, but under my trousers it didn't show and was divinely warm at all times. This subsequently had a large "G.U.-C.C." sewn across the chest (provided by the Company when we passed our test in proficiency at the end of our training). I had bully-ragged my sister into parting with her old navy ski-ing cap, the type that has a peak in front and a flap behind and which is every bit as practical on the water as it must be in the snow.

This was more or less the "uniform" which the Women's Training Scheme had evolved for itself; there was nothing provided for us in the way of clothes: we did get the extra "industrial ten" coupons a year, though they represented practically nothing in garments, a pair of men's heavy boots or shoes, for instance, taking nine of the ten straight off. Women's shoes were no use for the job in my opinion, being nothing like strong enough, and footwear was always a frightful drain on coupons.

All the old woollies I could find went with me this time and one or two oddments which I thought would improve the amenities in the cabin. Also a practical darning outfit and some cooking utensils without which I had been lost before.

I have gone into this clothes question at some length because people so often say: "What did you wear?" that I think it may be of interest. It wasn't elegant, this costume, but it was warm and it was workable and what we looked like was of no importance at all, so long as we could move quickly and easily.

Attired thus, then, I set off from home at 8 a.m. having been awake well before 6 that morning in anticipation. I had loved the rest, but I was longing to be back again.

I went to Hayes again and not Southall as I knew we should be taking the motor down later to pick up a new trainee, Vera having done her training and passed on to higher things. The motor could pick up my kit at the same time. Going down in the train from Paddington, I had a railwayman as a companion in the carriage; inspired no doubt by my somewhat unusual attire, he started to pump me as to my work and then sat open-mouthed when I told him. Apparently he had not heard of us and was fascinated by my glowing description.

Kit was already in residence when I got to the lay-by, so for some time we exchanged gossip and news before ordering our dinner at the canteen and then setting off to the "arrival bridge" to fetch the new trainee. Kit made me do the winding for practice; there were barges moored both sides of the cut which made it very complicated and I was glad it was not my "test." This took place at the end of our second trip and was conducted by Mr. Curtis in person; as it always took the form of going down and winding the boats at this spot it was not as alarming as it might have been. All the same I was glad I was not doing it now, and hoped that when I did I should not have barges in the way.

There was no sign of the new trainee but Kit came back from the station accompanied by the F.L.V. and a new recruit who was being shown the boats, as I had been. I watched jealously while she clambered easily all over the motor, and up and down the top-planks without turning a hair. The F.L.V. greeted me with enthusiasm but seemed to belong to another life, so much had happened in the last few weeks.

With many oaths about people who cannot stick to arrangements, we went back to have our dinner. In the middle of this the trainee walked in and all was forgiven her when it was discovered that she had come from the north and her connections had let her down. After she had fed we collected her kit from the store, where it had been waiting for her, and took her down to the lay-by to show her her new home.

It was my turn to do the courtesies to the newcomer as Vera had done them to me. I hope I was fairly kind to her. She was very young and had never been away from her home town before, so this was going to be a very big adventure. I will call her Ruth.

The inside of the cabin was not too bad, but the outside looked filthy after a week without attention. The two chimneys were red with rust, the brass round the portholes was dark green, and all the paintwork needed washing. When we went on leave we used to put all "movables" inside the cabins, which were locked in our absence. These included straps of value (most of them, that is), water cans, shafts if they would go in, windlasses and even the chimneys if they were very much decorated with brass, which Kit's were. Your boater has a jackdaw's eye for anything that shines and it was as well to remove temptation from his way.

During my leave I had acquired a perfectly gorgeous Primus made of chromium, which used to create a minor sensation wherever it went. I now tried out its usefulness and found with some surprise that it did all it ought to do, and boiled our tea-kettle for us in record time. After tea Kit sent me into Southall with her bicycle which needed attention; I tried at the same time to get my watch repaired and could not . . . an awful nuisance as Vera had removed her alarm clock and neither Ruth nor I had the time in any form. From now on Kit used to wake us every morning by leaning out of her cabin door and beating on our wall with her poker . . . brutal but effective.

Ruth embarked on letter-writing, as I think we all did when we first arrived, but this harmless sport was soon cut short by the light going out; evidently the battery had run down, and we had to finish the evening with the enormous lantern from the

IDLE WOMEN

by SUSAN WOOLFITT

1 The dustwrapper of the first edition of *Idle Women*, based on the photograph used in the newspaper advertisement seen by the author in September 1944 (*see* page 9). Evelyn Hunt is in the cabin watching Audrey.

2 The author in the late 1940s. 3 The Badge (*see* page 46).

4 Grand Union Canal Carrying Company boats at Bulls Bridge in the late 1930s, including No 53 *Hyperion* (*see* pages 135–152).

5 Sister Mary, still working at Stoke Bruerne in about 1961 (*see* pages 69–71).

6 *Bognor* and *Dodona* during the trip described on pages 197–9.

7 *Bognor* during the same trip.

8 Women boaters at Bulls Bridge. From left to right: Kit Gayford, Audrey, Mary, Frankie Campbell-Martin, Evelyn Hunt, and Anne. Audrey, Evelyn and Anne became a crack crew (*see* page 91).

9 Women boaters sheeting up after loading coal at Longford on the Coventry Canal: Cicely Ramsay on *Alcor* and Margery McPhee on *Alphons*.

10 Daphne French (at left) with trainees (left to right) Mary Andrew, Mrs Evans, and Susan Blood on *Capricorn* and *Cleopatra* at Marsworth, 1944.

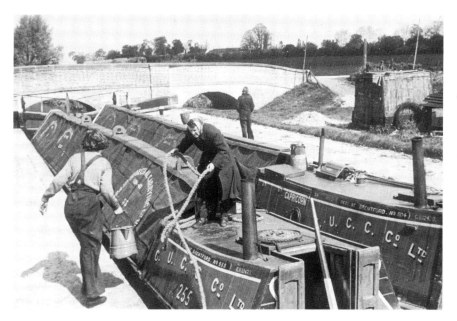

11 Left to right: trainees Mary Andrew, Mrs Evans and Susan Blood at Marsworth on *Capricorn* and *Cleopatra*, 1944.

12 Trainee steering *Alcor*.

13 Trainee steering *Alphons*.

14 Grand Union Canal Company policeman at Regent's Canal Dock, 1939 (*see* page 49).

15 Calling up boats at Regent's Canal Dock, 1939.

16 Mary Andrew on *Capricorn*, 1944.

17 Susan Blood on *Capricorn* at Marsworth, 1944.

18 The *James Brindley*, a cut-down wooden boat hired by the author from the Canal Cruising Company at Stone for a family holiday after the war.

engine-room. It gave a beautiful light, but as there was nowhere to hang it, it had to sit on the side-bed, which meant that all the illumination in the cabin was at knee-level; not conducive to the continuance of my "home-work" which I was studiously attempting to do.

Kit had a wonderful little "book of words" which she had compiled herself; it was a route book of the whole trip, with all the snags, tips, names of locks, shopping addresses, details of boat management, and a thousand and one other things which Kit had accumulated in her three years of experience. Her trainees were supposed to be *au fait* with it and I was in the throes of copying it out, because I have always been able to learn most easily that way, and I felt, too, that I should like one of my own. It was quite invaluable and was known reverently as THE BOOK.

I used to try to find out from Kit roughly how far she thought we would get on the next day's journey, and then go and study The Book before I went to bed. This slightly pompous procedure did make it far easier to learn the work, and also to get to know the way and the names of all the 152 locks. My Book used to live in the pocket of my leather coat and got so dog-eared and greasy and crumpled that it was practically illegible.

Next morning Ruth startled us by waking up with a thick red rash. Not knowing what this might portend, Kit took her off to the doctor in Hayes and I was left to get on with black-leading the chimneys and our stoves. They looked lovely when I'd done with them but alas ! *I* wanted a bath.

The others returned with the news that Ruth was all right, but was to stay in that day, so we ate at the canteen and spent the afternoon repairing the whipping and splicing of the side-strings, in butty and motor. Thus Ruth escaped being "shown Cowley," but made up for it by the intensity of her splicing instruction. After tea Kit and I cleaned ourselves up and went to pay a call upon a friend of Kit's brother, who had a converted Dutch barge on which he lived with his wife and family; it was tied up close to the lay-by and it only took us a few minutes to find her.

She looked immense lying there with her canvas rolled on the deck and her lee-boards tucked into her sides like great wings. Every bit of wood was scrubbed white and every bit of brass polished like gold, but even that did not prepare us for the in-

D

terior, which combined all the comfort of a luxury hotel with the attraction of a sea-going ship, on a very miniature scale. We spent a delightful evening and I made a date to go round on the following Friday and pick up a copy of A.P.H.'s *The Water Gipsies* which I was dying to re-read.

Back in our own boats Kit had a visit from one of the boater girls who was always a great friend of ours, and we ended by playing a round game of Kit's devising; all four of us in her cabin, having an uproarious time, egged on by Lil's roars of laughter at her own bad luck in the game, and her more than lurid language. We had boaters' pie, from the canteen, and cocoa all round. To bed at a late hour, with Ruth not quite sure what kind of a madhouse she had come to.

She had more or less recovered from the rash next morning, and was inclined to put it down to having slept in blankets for the first time in her life; she was very likely right. We got our orders before dinner and let go at noon on an uneventful trip down to the City Road lock in Islington, considerably farther than the first day of my last trip, and within an hour or two of the docks.

Being, by now, more accustomed to being dirty than Ruth was, I told her she could have her "bath night" after supper if she liked, and I would go over to Kit and do some more home-work, with which Kit was always ready to give help if we wanted it. This trivial decision of mine saved my life . . . literally.

Kit was on the side-bed when I arrived, cleaning her brasses. Inevitably I sat me on the cross-seat which was the only available space; equally inevitably we had soon forgotten The Book, and were talking about everything in the world, bar the boats. I was not expecting the lights to go out with utter suddenness and the contents of the cabin to come hurtling round my ears. Ducking instinctively, I called: "Are you all right?" though what I meant I don't know. I was conscious of masses of things happening but I did not know what any of them were; they would not stop long enough for me to find out. Everything was very dim, with that curious fluidity of noiseless sound and invisible motion that one experiences coming round from gas.

Getting no reply from Kit I raised my head to look for her, and suddenly my brain was pricked awake.

From the darkness inside the cabin the square of night sky through the open doors looked very light; it also looked as if it was going to tip over sideways, tilting to a fearful angle as I watched. I suppose my subconscious mind supplied the answer because I remember thinking: Well, if I *must*, I don't mind being blown to pieces, but to be sunk in the cut and drowned struggling in the cabin is quite another thing . . . and I raced my thoughts up the steps and out of the door.

Kit was standing braced on the path pulling at the tying-up strap; on the opposite side of the water an enormous building was wrapped in flames from top to bottom. I could see the windows hanging like twisted wire from their frames, and high, immensely long jets of water from the N.F.S. launches, already in action. I remembered that it was a factory and had been humming with life and work when I came over to the butty a few minutes ago, and I felt slightly sick.

Kit called and I saw her hair standing on end all over her head like a golliwog, while her face was covered in blood from the nose down. I jumped for the shore.

"Kit, what on earth's happened? Have you cut yourself?"

"I don't know . . . I'm all right. Get up the fore-end, I think the boats have broken loose" . . . then, as I was going, we both said together: "My God! the child!"

"Go and see if she's all right; get her into the butty and then come and see to the boats."

I ran back again and over the butty quicker than I have ever moved before. The motor cabin was in chaos but Ruth was all right; tastefully arrayed in her *négligé* she was standing looking utterly bewildered in the middle of the debris. It was then she came out with her classic line:

"What's happened? Has the Primus blown up?"

I am ashamed to say that I was too overwrought to laugh. I bawled at her, instead: "God, NO, it's a *rocket*!!" grabbed her and hustled her, just as she was, into the butty cabin.

Kit was on the fore-end of the butty by this time, and she threw me the snapped end of the tying-up strap which just reached, so that I was able to tie the boat up again.

"They've come unbreasted . . . look, the motor's swinging right out across the cut . . . go down and throw me a rope . . . quick . . . the short cotton-line will do."

For the first and last time I disobeyed Kit's orders. Instead of clambering over to the motor, I jumped back again into the butty which was beside me and with the long shaft managed to catch the motor before she swung out of reach. Kit soon had them re-breasted which was a relief, as a nasty idea had just struck me.

"Kit, for God's sake come down . . . we don't know what that building is and there may be another explosion at any minute."

She did come down, but only when she had finished securing the boats thoroughly. This was the unsuitable moment that I chose to fall into the cut; the only time I ever did.

When we had originally tied up (was it weeks ago?) I had noticed that the concrete kerb had a long bay cut into it; I think it was to enable the horses to get a drink. The boats stretched beyond this bay at both ends, but as a result of it they weren't touching the kerb the whole way along; straight into this treacherous gap I now walked. It was not at all deep, only coming to my knees (which is another reason why I think it was for the horses' benefit), but it would be hard to imagine anything more uncalled for at this precise moment. I lost my balance and sat down, losing a bedroom slipper as I went. It was a very precious pair of sheepskin slippers and most comfortable, and I was not going to lose it without a fight, so I started to feel for it in the mud at my feet.

At this moment Kit saw me and rushed up with a boater who was tied-up just in front of us. Between them they tried to do a lifesaving act, and were a little surprised and hurt when I got up from my kneeling position in the water to curse them and tell them to leave me alone. I did get my slipper, but it was no use after its bath and the pair had to be scrapped.

I now had one saturated shoe on and a sock on the other foot, but was quite beyond caring. With Amos' help we pulled both the boats back into the shelter of the lock steps, about thirty yards farther back, feeling that if there was another explosion we should be safer there.

From the moment when our lights had gone out till now was, I suppose, not more than three minutes at the outside; the fire was burning like a furnace over the water and fire-engine and ambulance bells were shrilling urgency from all the streets round us . . . we thanked Amos and went to view our cabins by the light of the fiercely burning factory.

The mess was indescribable. Readers can imagine for themselves what it was like. The floor a mass of broken china and glass, books, papers, food, all piled together and everything saturated with water and dust. The cabin top and path itself were thick with powdered glass and lumps of masonry from the surrounding buildings, Kit's doors had disappeared and it was quite dark inside. We found a torch and looked again; mixed up in the debris on the floor were at least twenty one-pound notes, our pay for the trip, some so filthy they were hardly recognisable.

"Kit, do wash your face and find out what you've done to it . . . it looks too awful. You may have been cut by flying glass," I insisted.

"I know," said Kit. "I must wash my face . . . no, I must pick up those notes . . ." she put her hand up and brought it away covered in blood . . . "I *must* wash my face . . . but the money's not mine . . . I must count it. . . ."

I suddenly became aware that we were both making pools on the step as we stood there gazing into the wrecked cabin and decided that seniority did not matter at a moment like this.

"Go on then and pick up the notes," I said, "and change your clothes if you can find any others. I think we all want tea and if the Primus is still with us I'm going to make some."

My cabin was just as bad as the butty but thank heaven the lights were all right, and the Primus in one piece. With Ruth's (dry) help I unearthed a tea-pot from the floor, three mugs still capable of holding liquid, and soon had a pot of hot tea ready. While the kettle was boiling I changed into dry things and tried to assess the damage.

Our doors had disappeared, too. As we were now directly under the lock gates and the rocket had, not unnaturally, brought out the local population, we were a little public, to put it mildly. Everything movable in the cabin was now heaped upon the floor; most of it was broken and a film of dust, dirt and glass lay over everything. It was a happy prospect that lay before us.

When the tea was ready I called to Kit. She came in minus her bloody face, but with her nose very obviously badly swollen and her eyes looking as if they had been hit for six. Her hair was still on end . . . when I commented on this she said it was solid with glass and plaster and wouldn't lie down. One of the minor pleasantries of blast, it seemed.

I have never enjoyed a cup of tea as I did that one. It warmed us all up and pulled us together like magic. We even began to laugh again about our chaotic cabins.

I think it was Kit who noticed the hole in the cabin wall, made by the bit of shell that had my name on it, but had been merci-

fully undelivered. The hole was a biggish one, in the wall immediately behind where my head would have been bound to be
if I had stayed in the cabin while Ruth was washing. On the
stove opposite still stood our black enamel kettle, in a direct line
with the hole, and also in line with another hole in the wall behind
the stove. The handle of the kettle had a furrow ploughed
straight through the length of it, the jagged metal curling over
on each side and showing the iron foundation. Hole, handle,
hole . . . whatever it was had been in a hurry. The only thing
missing from the chain of reconstruction was my head . . . I
finished my tea rather silently.

We went and viewed the damage in the holds afterwards. It
was pretty grim, but the thing that struck us most was the extent
of the damage achieved by blast alone. We had not had a direct
hit or anything like one, and yet the boats looked as though a
giant had torn them to bits in a rage.

Both the solidly built cratches were knocked down and lying
in the holds, the floorboards had been wrenched up, six of the
eight top-planks had disappeared completely, the side sheets
down both sides of the two boats had been ripped undone and
hung flapping down inside the holes, while most of their strings
had gone. The chimney from the motor exhaust was found in
the butty back-end, Kit's eight-gallon water can had vanished, as
had the iron motor tiller-handle, and over everything was a layer
of brick, plaster, dirt, dust and general filth.

It was a miserably depressing sight; we thought we should be
better employed going up on the road and finding out how bad
the damage was on land; Kit was anxious to inquire after some
other boats which she thought were tied up down the City Basin,
so we set out.

I had had no experience of London air-raids, having been
more than usually lucky to date, and it was with mixed feelings
that I walked through the streets of broken glass and saw the
efficiency of the Defence Services in action. I shall not easily
forget the roped-off street and the little crowd gathered round
the policeman on duty there. One girl of about fifteen was
frantically trying to get news from him, but the casualty list
wasn't yet known. In reply to a query she said: "My mum's in
there." There didn't seem to be anything at all to say in answer
to that.

Very thoughtfully we made our way home to our blitzed boats

and bed. With tarpaulins over the doorway we were not so badly off; the crowd had thinned and we were no longer of much interest to the sightseers. With difficulty we made our beds and got into them; then a rather curious thing happened. Ruth, at least fifteen years younger, instead of dropping into an exhausted sleep as I should have expected, suddenly went off into a passionate tirade against war, the war-makers, and the senseless futility of dropping bombs on civilians.

She was having an attack of nerves, I realised, so I let her talk herself out; a good half-hour she went on at her theme, and as she talked, raging and storming at the world and the mess it was in, my imagination gave a twist and I heard the voice of all the young people in every country storming at the older generation who had seen this thing coming and had done nothing to stop it. Ruth wasn't talking sense at all; it was the frightened child shouting defiance at the thing which frightens it and I answered her question as best I could, as I should have answered my own eight-year-old daughter's terrified ravings. Quite suddenly she stopped, said "Good-night," and went to sleep. But it was some time before I slept.

The excitements of the night did not prevent me waking at my usual hour but the "child" still slept, so I went over to the butty where Kit and I breakfasted together amongst the remains of the "home beautiful."

My hostess was a sorry sight; she had "two lovely black eyes," a very badly bruised knee and thigh, and the tip of her nose was a shambles. Apart from this nasty mess we were unhurt and, I think, fully appreciative of the miraculous escape we had all had. As soon as possible Kit telephoned the depot from the lock-keeper's office; it was not long before Mr. Curtis arrived over in person to visit the bomb-damage, and decide if the boats were safe to be loaded.

In the meantime Kit went to the local hospital to have possible bits of glass removed from her very painful nose; this gave rise to the rumour that met us in Birmingham when we finally arrived there, that Amos had been burnt to death and "Kitty, she's in 'orspital!"

To our bitter disappointment Mr. Curtis decided that it was not safe for us to try to load as we were; apart from the awful mess in the boats, he was afraid the seams might open under water with the weight of the cargo. We had hoped that we could

have loaded first and then been tidied up on our way back through
Southall; I think it had dawned on us by then that the mess was
not just a question of soap and water and scrubbing brushes,
but that we should have to have help from the carpenters,
plasterers and painters at the works, and quite a lot of accessories
renewed before we could finish the trip.

Sadly we winded and made for home, eating our dinner on
the way. I found life rather full as Kit could not climb comfort-
ably with her bruised leg and Ruth had not been on the boats
nearly long enough to be able to climb at all. Kit did a good bit
of steering; I did the rest, and all the running and clambering
necessary.

The only thing that cheered us on the way home was the
reaction, caused by our appearance, on the boats we met coming
down. They all started off by looking at us with the deepest
contempt as we got close and they were able to see the frightful
appearance we presented. "Just what you'd expect from the
woman trainees!" was the expression on one face after another,
but the change that came over them when I yelled out: "We're
not such bad boaters as we look, mate! We've met a ROCKET!"
was a joy to behold.

We arrived back in a blaze of glory which was quickly doused
when we heard next day that we should have to have "survivor's
leave," to give the men time to tidy up the boats. The stream
of sympathetic visitors to view the damage did nothing to
lighten our spirits, and my somewhat forced pleasantry, that
we ought to have a rocket painted on the nose of the boats
like a bomber had, was greeted with the hollowest of hollow
laughter.

Kit went up to the Office and came back with the news that
we were to have until Tuesday off (it was then Saturday), by
which time the hordes of workmen who had come and cast
their professional eyes upon our honourable wounds thought
that they could have the motor patched up temporarily, but the
butty would have to go altogether. She was a wooden boat and
had taken the count rather badly.

This was a bitter, bitter blow to Kit who had called her "home"
for over two years and was deeply attached to certain old-
fashioned peculiarities which were not to be found in the more
modern boats. She was not comforted by the news that she should
have a brand new butty, just off the stocks; it was a sad and

funereal procession that made its way buswards that evening for an enforced holiday.

It was not till I finally reached home that I realised how dog-tired I was and that the whole thing *had* been a strain.   At the time there had been so much to do and think about that I had not noticed it; at home the reaction set in, and I spent all Sunday in bed with a blazing fire. The warmth and rest were heavenly; when it was time for my early start on Tuesday morning I felt grand again.

At the lay-by I found Kit moving into her new butty, the *Pavo*. She looked very smart, with cream paint-work and the most brilliant red, white and blue outside. But the interior looked very cold after the darkness of the old *Uttoxeter*.

My motor was up on the slipway but they let me bring her back to the lay-by for the night: they had hardly touched her over the week-end and there was still a lot to be done. The next two days were very busy indeed, getting everything ready and doing all the whipping and splicing of the side and top-strings in the new butty. None of this is done for you and it does take time. We could transfer our old straps over, which was one good thing; getting a whole set of new ones ready is a long job.

Kit's leg was by no means right yet, and she went off for the night to let her doctor see it. Ruth re-joined us on Wednesday, and on Thursday we got fresh orders and were away . . . exactly a week since we had been blown up.

There was a wonderful little dairy on the way down to the docks which very kindly opened at 7 a.m. and the next morning produced no less that six pints of milk for us. This kind of thing was all very well in the winter and we appreciated it enormously, but in the summer it was agony to be offered six pints somewhere, knowing that it would be days before we should be able to get more fresh milk and yet sure that six pints at a time was quite certain to go sour on the boats. Sometimes we were offered more than our jug or can would hold, on a bicycle perhaps, and some way from the lock side. I used to get over that difficulty by drinking the surplus there and then in the shop, looked upon with surprise by the other shoppers and nearly choking myself with *ice-cold* milk straight out of the refrigerator.

We made the docks by dinner-time but there was nothing in the cargo line for us and Saturday morning produced only short loads as far as Marsworth; Kit didn't take these if she could avoid

D*

them as it meant branching off empty at Knapton and the trainees missing Hatton, and all the rest of the route up to Birmingham.

There is nothing more deadly than hanging about, whatever the job; hanging about at the docks waiting for a load was the worst of all. There was nothing to do *in* the dock, once you had swept, polished and black-leaded everything within reach and we couldn't go too far off in case something turned up. I organised a friend to tea on Saturday afternoon, a wise move as she turned up with tinned plums, drinking chocolate and some extra tea. Bless her heart, she was a friend of my old cruising-on-the-Broads days and she guessed that our food would be a bit more difficult than in those distant peace-time days of plenty.

Nothing happens on a Sunday in the docks. It is, as it should be, a day of rest and it is only when the load is safely on board that the boater works on, uninterrupted alike by the Commandments of Moses and the views of more up-to-date prophets. We used to lose all account of time while we were working; to hear church-bells suddenly was only to be woken to the fact that the bread was nearly finished and there was little hope of getting more that day.

Sometimes we managed to get to the end of our day's run in time to go to Evensong but we never stopped for a morning service; at least I never managed to, I don't know how other boats worked it. On this Sunday there was nothing to stop us and Kit and I went to eight o'clock service at the lovely church of St. Anne's, Limehouse.

This church was built in 1724 by Nicholas Hawksmoor, a pupil of Wren and collaborator with him in the building of Greenwich Hospital, and with Vanbrugh in building Blenheim Palace. Opinions vary as to its beauty but I find it entirely satisfying outside; the service was held in a side chapel but because of the darkness we could not see the main body of the interior as we should have liked.

Before dinner we did a round of "locals," in this part of the world very much worth getting to know and, later, I went up to get a bath and supper from my friend of yesterday.

This is only worth recording because of the sequel. Coming from Sloane Square to Aldgate East I missed the last bus which would take me down the Commercial Road to the Dock; there are, of course, no taxis in this part of London on a Sunday night so I started to walk. It is perfectly straightforward so long as you begin right. I took the wrong turning at the start, without knowing it; at the end of what seemed like hours I was beginning to get very worried. I could not see any of the landmarks that I knew should be there and there did not seem to be anyone to ask. Besides, I was doubtful about the wisdom of admitting to the first person I saw that I was lost . . . in Limehouse. It was quite dark and I felt that perhaps my silhouette, in bell-bottoms, didn't look very promising, but if I once opened my mouth to ask the way the game would be up; my voice would not match my trousers.

"The London policemen are wonderful"; don't I know it! Just as I was getting really desperate about what to do . . . I did not dare try to cut through side streets which all seemed to be so narrow that they presented yawning black tunnels to my feverish imaginings, and the thought of retracing my footsteps all the way to Aldgate East and beginning again simply made me want to cry . . . a copper came down the road on a motor-bike and, heaven reward the man, decided to turn round exactly where I stood. I yelled at him, and he brought his bike over to the kerb.

"Officer, where exactly am I?"

"Where are you? In the Bow Road. Isn't that where you want to be, then?"

"No, it certainly isn't. I want the Regent Canal Dock."

"Whew! you're a long way from there, miss!"

"Yes, I'm sure I am! Er, which is the best way to get back there? I mean, on foot, because I don't suppose I'll get a taxi out here, will I?"

"No, that you won't; not at this time of night. Well, now, let's see . . ." I waited breathless, with my eye on his pillion, ". . . you could go on a bit further and take the first turning to the right and cut through . . . but that's not a very nice way for you . . . wait a bit . . . go back about 'alf a mile and take the left and fork through . . . no, you can't go *that* way either" . . . would the penny *never* drop? " . . . I don't know I'm sure. Of course, I *could* take you on the back of my bike but I'm afraid you'd find it very rough, miss, you know . . . bumpy like . . . ?"

I laughed hysterically and, with difficulty, refrained from kissing the man. Instead I proceeded to pack him like a suit-case. I had my bath things, my hair-brush and comb, a tin of coffee and about three pounds of knitting wool that my friend had given me.

This went across his chest with his coat buttoned over it, one selection of toilet requisites found a home in one of his enormous side pockets, a further consignment going in the other; the coffee tin I wore as a chest protector myself, thereby leaving both my hands free to clasp round my deliverer's waist.

Pillion-riding was never a popular pastime of mine, but I skipped into position that night with the greatest alacrity, tucking my heels up out of the way of the wheels and adopting a bear-like hug round the somewhat distorted shape in front of me. We whizzed round corners at frightful angles and tore through the most doubtful-looking streets; I was exceedingly thankful that I was not finding my own way home.

He delivered me at the very gate of the dock and, after disentangling my possessions from his person, passed out of my life, but not out of my memory. The fatherly policeman at the gate wanted to know where on earth I had been and looked rather scandalised when I told him, until I pointed out that had it not been for his colleague I should still be wandering the streets. He bade me a tender good night but could not leave his post to help me down the ladder on the dock wall, an operation I found rather tricky, hung about as I was with bits and pieces. I did actually get into bed without waking Ruth or Kit.

Chapter ix—"ALL CHANGE HERE"

On Monday we were expecting a new trainee to join us. The only thing Kit knew about her was that she, too, was very young. I therefore suggested that, as I should be leaving fairly soon for the Christmas holidays, we should readjust the age groups a bit and that I should move to the butty with Kit and leave the two youngsters to the motor. She agreed to this, so I spent the morning rearranging myself in the *Pavo*. I hoped that I should come up to the high housekeeping standards prevailing therein and prepared to pull up my socks.

The new trainee materialised at dinner-time. Her name was Joan and by evening it was clear that she and Ruth were going to hit it off perfectly and have a wonderful time reading the *Filmgoers Weekly* in their spare moments, while the two old ladies in the butty wrestled with more advanced problems.

I had to find a new way of sleeping in Kit's cabin; she, like me, preferred the side-bed-with-head-opposite-the-stove position. I started off the first night with my feet in the cupboard and my head on the side-bed; Kit was too short to kick, thank heaven, but in spite of this I changed later to having my head in the cupboard.

This was painted bright blue inside, and was very much wider than my mattress, so that I had a space beside my pillow on which to put a candle for reading in bed. Thus illumined I would retire for the night into what Kit ribaldly referred to as the "Blue Grotto!" It was extremely comfortable, as was everything else about Kit's mode of living and I look back upon my two trips in the *Pavo* with gratitude as well as laughter.

One thing I found slightly startling to begin with. This was Kit's habit of talking in her sleep. I would wake to hear her saying with the utmost urgency in her voice: "Tiller in the other hand . . . no, no, the OTHER hand . . . quickly . . . that's right . . . now the other, HURRY UP . . . good . . . ease down, *ease down* . . . EASE DOWN, will you ! ! ! . . ." It used practically to get me out of bed to start with, until I got accustomed to it; I used to ask her at breakfast where she had been having trouble the night before, "was it Muck Turn, or only on going into a lock too fast ? "

This awful trip had already lasted a fortnight before we got our load, steel for Tyseley, on Tuesday, 5th December. I was getting rather frantic because the children's holidays were due to begin on 14th, and it did not look as if I should be able to finish the trip off. I rather wanted to get a day or two's break before they got back, if it was humanly possible, to turn myselt from a canal boatwoman into an ordinary mother again, and to open up the house.

We only got as far as the City lock that night, taking rathei a long time over the sheeting-up with the two new ones, and me not much more advanced than they. They told us when we got to City Road that only one life had been lost in the blaze of last week; after seeing it, it seemed almost unbelievable, but we never heard how many injured there were.

The general opinion seemed to be that the rocket had fallen into the cut and not on the ground at all. It is much the most tenable theory and explains how Kit came by her extraordinary bruises and bangs. The rocket falling into the water would cause a kind of tidal wave, first away from the rocket and then rushing back towards it. In the middle of the wave back, Kit must have jumped for the shore without realising that she was jumping a widening gap, and, falling short of the kerb, had come down with her face right on it. There is no other theory that I can see, to explain why she mis-jumped, even in the heat of the moment; she was far too experienced a performer to have missed it and in any case, urgency would surely tend to make one *over*-jump, not the reverse ? It would also explain our ropes all snapping.

This was the slowest trip I ever did. Misfortune seemed to dog our footsteps all the way. (It began in November and finally didn't end until January ! but I had gone home long before then.)

We spent one day behind barges all the time; on another, we came up with a pair of women's boats in difficulties, first through mud, and then developing engine trouble. We stopped and gave them a tow to safety; no mean feat on the part of our war-scarred motor, to pull three other boats and over 100 tons of cargo in addition to herself.

A little later the ice began, not badly but enough to slow things up a bit and make one very careful on the top-planks.

Kit was teaching me some rather more advanced boating by this time which I found fascinating, whether I could do it or not;

these tips were all invaluable when it came to the end of my training and going to join new boats.

After ice we had rain and, always, wind. We were all a little fed up and when poor Joan mistakenly upset a saucepan of porridge on to Kit's best carpet one day, the air became electric. I should have sworn at her and made her clear it up; Kit swore, instead, at me, and cleared it up herself, making the utterly deflated Joan a cup of cocoa with the other hand.

However sticky had been the day's progress, whether by reason of wind and rain and cold, or just all-round incompetence, with resulting ruffled feelings, the evenings when we were tied up made up for everything. Still at last, the noise of the engine silenced, the wind shut out, the rain beating harmlessly on the roof, the stove giving out a glorious warmth, a rattling good dinner inside you (even if it was the only one of the week) and weary limbs stretched lazily horizontal and no longer battling with the elements; a slight drowsiness and the knowledge that there was no more work till tomorrow; the shining brasses, and the books, and the wild berries in the copper jug, all adding to the charm of this minute home; enormous heavenly yawns, bed and a hot bottle; the little candle and an hour's reading for us both, interspersed with disjointed talk and finally, sleep.

The pleasure comes from the contrast with the day's hard work; you cannot have one without the other, and I think a lot of it, too, is derived from being filled right up with fresh air. I had never before experienced such deep content as those evenings gave me whether it was winter or summer; I doubt if I ever shall again.

My muscles were at last beginning to harden and I no longer felt as if my inside was dropping out when I wound up paddles. The relief this afforded was indescribable and I attacked the stiffest with abandon. It was a timely improvement, too, because neither of the youngsters had any muscles worth mentioning and were very slow with their drawing. In addition, from first to last, Ruth never achieved either jumping up or down from the boats in locks, which made more work for those who did. Poor child, she went through agony trying to brace herself up for it but it always defeated her.

The next excitement took place at the top of Bugby where we tied up one night. The bike had sprung a puncture, so Kit took it to a local shop before supper and said she would call back later.

In the meantime we had visitors in the shape of one of the other girls who came and drank cocoa with us; this made Kit very late in collecting the bicycle. Just as she was starting, there was a shout from the towpath and a very agitated female voice called out:

"Are you the lady that left the bicycle? '

"That's right," called back Kit, looking for her torch, "I'm so sorry I'm late. I'm just coming now."

"Oh! . . " said the voice in a wail, "there's been a *dreadful* accident . . ." Kit and I both reached for the first-aid box, automatically, " . . . your bicycle's been STOLEN ! ! ! "

"Oh, thank heaven !" said Kit, "is that all . . . I mean who's stolen it ? Wait a moment, I'll come." And she disappeared into the darkness.

She was a long time getting back and had a very odd story to tell. The man had finished the puncture and had left the bike leaning against the wall outside the shop for Kit to pick up. The next time he went outside he found to his horror it had gone; in its place was a brand new man's cycle, all chromium and gadgets *but with both tyres flat*.

I hope I have made it quite clear that Kit's bicycle was no prize-winner; it therefore did not take long for them to deduce that whoever had done the swap demanded only one thing: . . . sound tyres; anyone who was in such a hurry as that must be up to some mischief. Reluctantly, Kit went to the local to find the village policeman and make a statement.

Our bike was easy to describe. I have already done so but it now had a nearly new modern type saddle in place of the old one (a little innovation of mine) which would make it look, if possible, more peculiar than ever. The bobby said he'd do his best and Kit came home.

We lay in bed and cursed fate. There were a mass of locks ahead and to be without the bike at this juncture was disastrous. It meant that someone had got to *run* ahead to lock-wheel, a very exhausting pastime which I frankly detested, it was doubtful if the others would be at all up to it, and poor Kit evidently envisaged an athletic few days for herself.

We did not wait about to see what the day would produce, but let go at our normal time in the morning; we had only got as far as the Toll Office, just round the corner, when a phone message came through saying would we go back again and wait for the bike, which had been found and was being sent by lorry from Towcester? Would we?!

We couldn't wind, so had to go backwards to our night's tying-up place, and hung about there for some time before the bobby appeared on the path, triumphantly leading our lost treasure.

"This is yours, isn't it?" he called out and was answered by a concerted shout: "YES! Where *did* you find it!"

But he was not to be hurried. Laying "Matilda" gently down, he accepted an invitation to come in; removing his helmet and mopping his forehead, he announced dramatically;

"You may like to know, madam, that your bicycle was found in Towcester this morning in the possession of a couple of Jerries, wot wos using it to escape from Stafford gaol!"

If he wanted to create a sensation he certainly succeeded. We plied him with questions and finally got the whole story. It appears he had noticed that the chromium-plated bicycle had a wisp or two of straw caught in the spokes, which had suggested to his inquiring mind that the rider had hidden it at some time in a straw-stack. People who don't want to be seen can travel by night and hide up during the day; accordingly, our policeman had thought it worth while to circulate a description of the bike to the County Police, who had passed on the information over a wide radius.

So, when two sad and footsore Germans walked into Towcester, leading the very easily recognisable "Matilda" with her old frame, new seat and total absence of mudguards, and a lady's cycle into the bargain, it didn't take the constable on point duty a week to spot her . . . and them.

Our bobby added that he thought they were rather relieved to be caught again. Knowing the bike, I could well believe it.

We fed him on cocoa and compliments which I think he richly deserved, and further regaled him with a minute tour of the cabin which was the first he had ever been in. Just as he was going, he told us that the unhappy man who had been riding our bike rejoiced in the name of "Otto Blink," which quite finished us; the bicycle was renamed from that moment. When we next rode her (or him?), we discovered that the seat had gone up, at least four inches, a thing we'd never been able to do as it was rusted into the low position. Evidently the misery and despair of poor Otto had lent power to his arm: the vision thus conjured up positively made our hearts bleed for him.

The next day held a dense white mist in store for us. This necessitated Kit doing practically all the motor steering as she was the only one who knew the way properly, but by three o'clock she had decided that this wasn't doing *us* any good so we tied up at the top of Warwick.

It was not Kit's habit to laze away the idle hours however; we soon found ourselves engaged in an orgy of splicing and whipping and cleaning; as an interlude to these delightful sports, she called for a "solo on the mud-box from Mrs. W."

This meant that I had to give a demonstration to the other two of how to clean out the mud-box. In this was collected all the filth from the bottom of the cut, which is the function of the aforementioned little gadget. I was supposed to know how to do it, having watched Vera's solo performed for my benefit on my last trip.

It is not complicated, but it's a disgusting job. Herded into the engine-room the others watched with deep enjoyment while I, with the only scoop with which Nature has provided the human body, scooped mud out of the bottom of the box and flung it over the edge. When it has nearly all been cleared out and your fingernails are full of it and your arms slimy and stinking to the elbow, you re-screw the lid and the "solo" is over. I hope I gave them their money's worth.

We got to Birmingham in good time next day and as soon as we had got tied up and sorted out I went off to telephone home and find out if the children had arrived safely, my sister having arranged to meet them for me in London. My feelings can perhaps better be imagined than described, when I learnt that they had not turned up at all, my sister having waited three hours for the delayed train to arrive at Waterloo, only to find that the children were not on it.

Fumbling with a torch in a pitch dark phone-box, I found I had just got enough of the right kind of coins for another long distance call, and madly rang up the school—in Devonshire.

Certainly they were on the train when it left Devon. Yes, the Headmistress was quite certain that my small girl knew that she was going to Waterloo to be met by her aunt; she had been made to repeat the address and full instructions just before the train left. No, she could not imagine what could have happened (nor could I, and felt as if I were having a nightmare) but the train should not have been as late as that, being a special.

"A WHAT?" I screamed down the phone. (It was the first I had heard of a special.) Hadn't I had her letter telling me that the train had been changed at the last moment on account of the rush of schools all wanting to travel on the same one? She gave me the time of the special's arrival and with a sinking heart I realised that it had got in twenty minutes before my sister arrived at Waterloo.

I gave it up—what else could I do, in Birmingham—and went back to the boats.

Kit with great tact let me rave, cooked me an excellent supper and forebore from telling me I was a fool not to have put my sister into direct communication with the school, which I now realised, too late, was what I ought to have done. The *day* of the children's arrival had been changed once already, by a Board of Education order, and I had assumed that that was the finish of it, little dreaming that the Southern Railway were still capable of changing the actual train.

Armed with more small change I went out again after supper and phoned home once more. My sister answered! Yes, they had just got back; the children were all right, but she had had the most awful job finding them; would I like to talk to them? My infant came to the telephone and appeared to be in terrific form; she announced that she'd always wanted to have a "Real Adventure" and now she had had one! Swaying slightly I said: "Yes, darling. Now run along and get to bed as quick as you can!" It was after nine o'clock.

I wired the Headmistress and tottered home to bed.

Ever since I had first joined the boats Kit and I had been planning to have a Turkish bath; I had never had one, and she wanted to repeat the experience.

Next day looked as if we were really going to get it at last. We were unloaded by 3.30 in good time to get cleaned up and catch our bus. Just as we were ready a small boater boy dashed up panting, to announce that "Mr. Hambridge had got his face cut open somethink orful and would Kitty come at once please!"

"Kitty" flew, leaving me to follow with the first-aid box. The Hambridges were tied up a length or two in front of us and I found Ron in his butty cabin being mopped up by Kit, while his four-months-old son waved his legs on the side-bed, to the accompaniment of his father's groans. Mrs. Hambridge was in Brummagem doing the shopping.

As soon as Kit stopped mopping, Ron sat forward with his head practically in the fire and his face getting greener and greener. Having had some experience of chopped-about males, I know that they are usually far more squeamish than women; as I did not see how Kit and I would be able to pull Ron out of the fire once he had fallen in, I suggested briskly that he would do better to remove his head from the stove and have a drink.

Spirits he hadn't got, but he produced some tea, so black and stewed that it would have left whisky standing; while he took a pull at this "leperous distilment" I looked at the wound on his head.

It was a nasty deep jagged cut just above his eyebrow, but less than I had anticipated from the small boy's description and the basin of gore that stood prominently displayed on the cabin-top.

Kit and I looked at one another. "Turkish Bath" rose soundlessly on the air and died without being spoken.

"Well ? ' said Kit.

"Well," said I, "I think it's all right, don't you ? But I do think perhaps he ought to see a doctor in case it wants a stitch. It might leave a bad scar if it heals without being pulled together."

Ron being, rather surprisingly, quite amenable, we found one of the boater's wives who promised she would look after the baby, and marched Ron and his eye off to find medical assistance. We'd no idea how to set about it but finally asked the telephone exchange. They helpfully provided us with three numbers, all fairly close. We rang them up. The first one had died last week, the second had just moved and the third was plain OUT.

Keeping a firm grip on Ron we started to walk in search of a brass plate. I should never have believed it possible that there would be so many dentists, chiropodists and veterinary surgeons gathered together in so small an area, but it was so; after walking for at least three-quarters of an hour and asking several people, who all looked incredibly surprised to hear that we wanted anything so extraordinary as a *doctor*, we found one at home.

Triumphantly we led our captive in; triumphantly he emerged from the surgery three minutes later with a new dressing and no stitch necessary !

It was five mintues to five and the Baths shut at five o'clock. Speechlessly we looked at one another and turned into the nearest picture house, having sent Ron home to his wife.

It was "The Way Ahead," the only bright spot that day; that, and the chips that we bought and ate coming down the street on the way home, after the show was over.

It was at this time that the "no-bottom-road" controversy was raging. We were all ready to start but Kit as "steerer" was in a ticklish position.

There were a lot of pairs tied up waiting to hear the result of the dispute, and if we whistled off down the bottom road it would be nothing short of blacklegging. The boaters had good reason to trust Kit and believe that she was always ready to champion their rights; so, also, had the powers-that-be every reason to trust her integrity. And so we sat and waited for things to develop.

The message for which we had all been waiting came through while we were having dinner; at once the whole wharf became a scene of furious activity. Boaters yelling at their kids, wives untying the boats, the last can being hurriedly filled at the tap, and the stream of waiting boats was off.

We let them get ahead, knowing there would be a queue later at Knowle, and started ourselves after we had cleared up dinner.

A pair of women's boats came in just as we were leaving; the same pair we had towed off the mud, and on our way down to Knowle we met Daphne in mid-stream. A brief but poignant conversation took place between her and Kit as the two boats passed one another; apparently everybody was trying to swap round crews. When this happened the trainers usually got to-together on it, if a meeting was possible, trying to work out from their knowledge of us all, who would fit best with whom.

This was not only for the sake of the individuals, but also in order to produce the best results. Work like this is *very* specialised; you have to have the temperament to do it and be willing to put up with the very unusual living conditions. It is obvious that the output will be affected by conditions prevailing on the distaff side, and to this end the trainers would try to assist in a re-shuffle.

By now I had reluctantly decided that I must get home as soon as possible; I was going to try for it sometime during the following day which was a Sunday.

Tying up that night at Lapworth, we had a farewell drink all

round at the "Navigation" and an extra one to my "third trip."
It was horribly unsatisfactory to be leaving before the end of my
second trip, and, if circumstances permitted it, I wanted to come
back after Christmas and do a third, so that I should feel I was
properly finished off. It all depended on how many new trainees
were lined up by then waiting for Kit's ministrations.

It was arranged that I could leave my bedding on the butty
while I was away; then, if I didn't come back to Kit, she could
leave it in the store at Bull's Bridge, for me to pick up whenever
I rejoined. But everything else had to go with me, and a frightful
morning ensued during which I packed with one hand and dealt
with Knowle and Hatton with the other.

The diehard Kit chose Hatton as a suitable place to teach me
a complicated piece of technique to be used when bringing a
loaded motor into a lock. As we were not loaded at the time,
and my mind was fixed on possible trains, this was not a success.

The lock-keeper at the top of Hatton (there is another at the
bottom ten locks) did his best to be helpful about local transport;
being Sunday his good intentions brought forth nothing which
was of any use at all, so it was finally decided that I should be
pushed off in Leamington, which we ought to make by dinner-
time. From there it should be an easy trip to London, even on
the Sabbath.

There was a bit of time after Hatton and Warwick to
get my packing finished off and myself tidied up, before we
reached the bridge under the gasworks at Leamington, this being
the salubrious spot selected for my debarkation.

It really couldn't have been easier; nor could it have taken place
with less fuss. I had said good-bye to Kit, who was on the motor,
and as we went under the bridge-hole, she slowed down, just
long enough to allow me to jump off the butty and have my kit
bags thrown to me by Joan and Ruth.

The moment kitbags and I were safely ashore, the motor
speeded up and the boats went off round the corner leaving me
disconsolate on the path. I scrambled up the bank to the road; my
holidays had begun.

CHAPTER X—THE ICE AGE

EVERY moment of the Christmas holidays that could be spared from festivities, dentists, darning and expeditioning, had been devoted to drawing pictures of the boats for the young, and telling them in minute detail what we did from day to day.

They were thrilled beyond words with it all; with the disregard children have for anything but the personal—the war, the G.U., Kit, and everybody else had been swept aside and quite simply: "Mummy's boats" became a password. It must have been very difficult for them to visualise what I described, and they did not really get the hang of it till the Easter holidays, when I took them down to Bull's Bridge and we were entertained to tea in the *Pavo* by Kit; all the same, my letters became a much easier business once I had given them a verbal account.

Also during the holidays I had worked out an idea of Kit's which was an up-to-date version of "Snakes and Ladders" translated into "Snubbers and Top-planks." You went up the planks and down the snubbers according to the square you landed on; the board was richly embellished with the most frightful catastrophes and triumphant pieces of luck that can occur on the cut. I got an immense amount of fun out of making this, and was forced to play it unceasingly with the children till they went back to school. This palled on me, but it also showed me that the game would be very popular with the boaters, which was my hope, as I intended passing the game on to Kit when I rejoined her.

I heard that they had not finished the trip till after Christmas, but had had leave to go off for the holiday; further it was going to be impossible for me to do the third trip as I had hoped. As the Zero-hour approached, the most complicated planning went on, by letter and telephone, to get me back to the boats.

The new trip had started before I was ready to leave home, so I had to pick them up somewhere *en route;* as the day got nearer and nearer, so the possible meeting-places got narrowed down, till it finally became clear that there would be a golden opportunity when the boats went through Berkhamsted, where, as I have explained, the cut goes right past the station.

On Tuesday, 16th January, I caught the 1.55 from Euston and

spent most of the short journey with my head out of the window (to the annoyance and surprise of the other passengers), trying to spot "my" boats as the train went past the cut.

This I did not do, but arrived at "Berker" with some time in hand with which to get my stuff from the station, down the road, through the fence on to the towpath, and from there to the top lock of Sweeps 2 which was where I had arranged to meet the others.

There was no sign of them when I arrived, but I asked some other boats coming up where they were, and they said they weren't far behind. Leaving my kit with the lock-keeper I dashed to our very excellent little butcher and bought my week's meat ration (as instructed by Kit the previous night on the phone), and then set off to meet them.

I walked about a mile down the towpath before I saw Kit on Otto Blink, pedalling furiously up the path to meet me. We couldn't, however, get down to gossip till she had made ready the lock; the boats were not far off.

Joan had given up the unequal fight and decided that boating was not for her, but Ruth was still with us and for a third we now had Sheila who had come back for a refresher course after being away ill. I was in the *Pavo* again and as soon as we got up to Sweeps I heaved my stuff on board and got unpacked.

When I started to steer again next day I was horrified to find how much I had forgotten. All my judgment seemed to have gone and I had to think very hard indeed to remember the drill in locks. Four weeks is too long to be away from work.

The load was fifty five and a half tons, too, which is a lot, and made the steering worse. And finally, it was a new motor; at least new to me. The old *Battersea* had been docked to have her bomb-damage attended to and we had, instead, the *Ascot*. We tied at Leighton Buzzard that night and had a visit after supper from one of the women who had passed us earlier, and had bicycled back from Marsworth to have a chat with Kit.

From my Diary:

"18th Jan.: Let go at 8.20 and Sheila and I did the Jackdaw between us. I then snapped the eye off the snubber at the top of Stoke Hammond through forgetting to cast off the butty which *rushed* up on me as I stopped dead at the closed locked gates. Altogether a very bad affair. Received very moderate treatment considering all things. On to Finney where Ruth

got the snubber firmly round the blades as we went into the lock
we spent three hours trying to get it out, but finally had to cut
it and take to our spare. Blinding rain by this time and tearing
gale but we went doggedly on to the top of Cosgrove where we
tied at 7.15. Very dark and tired.

19th Jan.: Let go at 8.20 without a fire as the coal had run out.
Bitterly cold all along but bright sunshine at Stoke Bruern where
Sheila went in to see Sister Mary, who says she has cracked a bone
in her wrist. She came out splinted and slinged to the eyebrows
and is to do no more work. Came out of the tunnel into a blinding
snowstorm which continued for some time. Stopped at Stowe
Hill to put Sheila off to go home from Northampton. Attempted
(me) to breast up at the bottom of Bugby, made a hash of it, as
usual, and lost my temper—also as usual. Tied up at 6.30. Kit
to 'The Spotted Cow,' me having a bath night. Asleep before
she got back, verv tired.

20th Jan.: Let go at 8.45 in thick snow which developed into
a blizzard as we came out of Braunston tunnel. Kit decided to
go down Braunston and tie up at Nurser's yard, but by the time
we got to the bottom it had cleared up, so on we went. This led
to another 'incident,' still my fault, at the top of Itchington. I
was again asked to breast-up, this time in the bridge-hole by the
'Boat' and again made a hideous mess of it. Result, such heat
that we tied up then and there (' . . . no good going on when
you're overtired . . . ') though we had a good road down the
locks. To the pub with Ruth and worked it off in Guinness.
Found it very 'good for me'! Tied up actually at 4.30, but
spent some time clearing the ice and snow off the boats before
it had time to freeze on overnight.

21st Jan.: Let go at 8.30. Ice very thick and it would come into
the locks with us if we were breasted, so we had to go in singly.
Got to half-way up Hatton after a slow and rather hard day and
tied up at 6, beside the Griffiths."

The ice made an enormous difference to everything. If you
tied up at night with a strap that was needed next day, when
morning came, you would find that it was impossible to use it—
it was frozen as hard as the branch of a tree. The weather got
colder and colder and it was freezing all day long, so that the
ropes would stiffen between one lock and the next; the cotton-
line, which we used a great deal for locking, was like a steel hoop
with a coating of ice all over it and it stuck to your hands when

you picked it up. So did the shaft; the metal part at the end was really painful to handle, giving you a sensation like an electric shock.

It did not matter how carefully we swept down the night before; the remains of the snow and damp had frozen into a thin film of ice on all the sheets by next day. Walking down the top-planks was really tricky, and even Kit didn't expect us to hurry and was careful herself. We used to spread the ashes from the fire on the gunwale of the motor and on the edge of the butty hatches on which we had to walk and stand. I think it probably saved a good many accidents.

The cold only worried us really when we had a long pound to do, against driving snow, or, far worse, wind and sleet. Then it did go right through you and your feet would be like blocks of ice, standing steering for a long patch at a time. Working through the locks was nice and warm; I used to start off with all my wraps on and cast them off as the drawing of paddles got my circulation going. The locks themselves were quite incredible in the ice; I don't know where to begin to describe the effect it had on them.

Perhaps with the gates, as that was the first thing we came to.

At the bottom of Radford, I remember, Kit signalled to me on the butty to get off at the bridge just before the bottom lock and go and open the gates, while she hung about with the motor and jockeyed for a good position. At least that is what I thought she meant, and off I hopped, glad of the exercise. As I passed the motor she called to me that she had meant Ruth to go, while I had a little practice in holding back the butty. As I had already started she told me to "go on now and hurry up."

It was just as well it was I who had gone. I was a good bit stronger than Ruth, but could I move that gate? I pushed and shoved and rocked and banged and nothing had the slightest effect. Finally Kit had to tie the motor up and come and help me; even then it took us twenty minutes of concerted effort to get the gates shut so that we could empty the lock.

Lock gates have not got hinges as a door has, but are hung on the collar and pin principle. This joint naturally is wet and this was what we were now up against. The collar had frozen solid on to the pin on which it was supposed to turn, and the ice had got to be broken down by brute force before the gate would move.

This did get a little better later because the lock-keepers had tumbled to the difficulty and were keeping the gates very well greased so that they could not freeze up; to start with, though, the phenomenal cold had caught everyone on the hop and we had to evolve a new technique all round, to cope with it.

But I've jumped ahead. This little how-d'you-do on Radford was on the way back and I left my diary on the way up to Tyseley.

"*22nd Jan.*: Went off to get some bread and cigarettes after breakfast, and got back to find they had let go at 9, and had got one lock up. We took two hours to do the next ten locks, clearing the top at 11. Normally we should have let go at 8, and been up in an hour. Bad ice all the way until the gas-works" [not the Leamington ones; there are some more an hour from Tyseley] "where it let up a bit because of the outlet of boiling water into the cut. The light had nearly gone when we tied at Tyseley at 6.

23rd Jan.: Unloaded almost first thing after a fearful unsheeting of ice and snow covered sheets. They are frozen as stiff as boards in their taut position and are very hard to roll when we'd got them unlashed. Very cold on the hands, too, and most painful. Went up and winded and came back to bag the length under the shelter, which may save us from being snowed on tonight. Shopped and to the flicks with Kit. Bed very late.

24th Jan.: Rushed to the shops to get food in, in case we are iced-up which seems very likely now. It is bitterly cold and the ice in the cut is inches thick, one layer frozen on top of another as the boats push it out of their way and it slides underneath the untouched expanse to either side of the channel. Let go at 10.15, with Kit on the motor all the way to Knowle, and me having a morning cooking. Got to the top of Hatton at 4.30 (ice very bad all the way) and went down the first ten with the help of the lock-keeper, George from the workshops and three other men. Even then it took us two hours to do the ten and we tied up at 6.30, half-way down. George came in after supper for cocoa and stayed till 11 p.m. Ruth has decided to finish the trip and then chuck it. I think she is worried by the jumping up and down business and admittedly the weather conditions are rather strenuous, though personally I am glad to be seeing it at its worst. I shall miss her for all that. She is always cheerful and has no grain of malice in her character.

25th Jan.: Let go at 10.30, having waited for the men to tell us if we could go at all. Eventually it was the ice-breaker coming through that enabled us to make a start. Even following closely behind them the channel froze before we could make full use of it and it took us two hours and forty minutes to get to the bottom, clearing it at 1.10, with the assistance of George and the bottom lock-keeper. Warwick not bad, luckily, as we had no offer of help there. Then we assaulted Radford and the fun began. Helped by Jack Franks and his missus, who were behind us, we managed to creep through the first three taking three hours to do it !" [We used to allow three minutes for a lock, normally.] "Huge mountains of ice collecting in front of the motor as she went in having to be shifted with the shafts before we could get the butty in. 'Podging' from the top of the lock side with the long shaft is extremely hard work and it takes ages to get a lump (about the size of a billiard table), from one end of the lock to the other. We worked it in relays, one person passing the 'table top' to the next and finally to the motor where the last person, braced on the counter, shoved it outside with the broom. There was no bracing possible on the top of the wall though and punting along these huge lumps, some yards below you, was very tiring. Ruth kept us well supplied with tea. The Franks very kind and helpful and following close behind us. Finally stopped—just like that, without any need to tie-up—above the third lock, just through the bridge and opposite the lock-keeper's cottage. Very tired, and icy cold during the night. It is the draught from the back-end door that catches me in the back. Shall try putting the cross-seat across tomorrow, to protect myself a bit."

Most people will remember that in spite of the intense cold, one of the compensations about this Arctic spell was the hoar frost. On the cut it was beautiful. There was still a lot of snow to come; the sky of lowering grey made a perfect background for the white lacery of the frosted trees, every little bunch of twigs on the top-most branches standing out with the delicacy of a Chinese painting. It was loveliest when there was no sun to give colour to the scene; or in the evening when sometimes the sun was just sufficiently there to redden the sky with its setting glow, and throw a pink shadow on the snow.

And all the day long that wonderful muffled stillness from the thick blanket of the snow.

The quietness was emphasised by the fact that there was very little traffic now. (We heard afterwards that most of the boats had tied up at least a day before we did, but we were so determined not to let down the "weaker" sex by giving up first, that we actually went on longer than most of the others.)

Apart from ourselves there were only the Franks on Radford that morning, 27th Jan.   They were empty beer boats and, inevitably, in a hurry or I daresay they would have given up by then.

At 9.30 the ice-cutter came through and the Franks were off at once. We followed them immediately but even so the ice was already re-forming. The lock was perhaps fifty yards away and Franks went in, up and through without trouble. It was at the top that his motor stuck on the bend and for a long time he could not move either boat.

By that time we had got the gates shut and the lock emptied for ourselves and went in at once. Kit had been watching Jack Franks and saw that he had his butty stern tied to the nose of his motor, and was thus pushing the butty in ahead of him. It was the only way to do it with such a cruel drag of ice slowing the motor down.

We copied them, but in spite of this our butty and motor got jammed, half in and half out of the lock; then the fun really did begin.

Between them, the two boats had pushed an incredible amount of ice into the already overcrowded lock; the upper end of which was now piled high with "table-tops." All of it had to be moved before we could hope to get the boats in any farther; and, because there is only six inches of water to spare when two boats are in side by side, all the ice had to be turned on its side and so escorted through the bottle-neck out into the open cut.

It was really a most stimulating pastime and the fever of the chase got hold of us. We were much pitied by our friends for this trip, but, looking back, I would not have missed it for the world in spite of its exhaustion and difficulties. One of its more amusing aspects being that there was no known technique for dealing with the situation, so that Kit for once became almost as much of a learner as Ruth and I; anybody's guess was as good as another's and a new suggestion was adopted and put into practice with its originator issuing orders like a field-marshal.

We took it in turns to be up on the wall and down in the butty; I never decided which was the worst. On the wall you had at least got firm ground under your feet, but had the horrible strain of the weight of the long shaft, and the pushing business all going on so far below you. It came very heavy on the stomach muscles and to begin with we had no one to help us, the Franks family having got successfully away. On the other hand, in the butty, our problems were almost too close. It was impossible to get any purchase into your push from a standing position, without losing your balance and going over the hatches into the water, so it all had to be done kneeling down and there was only the broom to operate with. We did try the shovel but it presented too much resistance to the water, and made the job much heavier than it was to start with.

Moving huge blocks of ice is really much harder than perhaps it sounds, if you have not tried it. It is frightfully heavy, which I know I have said before, but it cannot be overemphasised if our predicament is to be really relished. And then they slip and slide in the water to a surprising degree, and float away from you when you least expect them to; so you have got to have the shaft well impaled in the middle of your block and not let it get too far away till you have safely passed it on to the next person, who in turn escorts it down to the butty person who puts the finishing touches to its exit.

We got into that lock inch by inch and it took us three and a half hours to do it. We were boiling hot by this time and triumphant with success; as soon as we were in, though, we discovered that we were dead beat and, at my instigation, knocked off for an hour and had a proper hot sit-down dinner.

Just as we had finished this (and *what* a good idea it had been), the lock-keeper appeared and we quickly enlisted his help. He said there was plenty of trouble farther up and had heard that boats were tying up all over the place. We still thought we would try to get on a bit; in any case we couldn't spend the ice-up *in* the lock. (There had once been an ice-up lasting ten weeks when all the boaters went ashore and got jobs in local factories.)

Once the bottom gates were shut we felt that our troubles would be over; nothing could possibly happen now which would be worse than what had happened during the morning. The lock was soon full and the top gates open. Bidding a fond fare-well to the lock-keeper we started off—approximately the length of the motor; then we stopped dead.

No power on earth would move the butty out of the lock. It didn't surprise us really after seeing Franks stuck in exactly the

same place, and he had had the benefit of the fresh channel made
by the ice-cutter. It was all as thick as ever by now, and the poor
old motor was not up to being an ice-cutter and shifting the
weight of the butty at the same time. We were a good bit lighter
than Franks who had his empty beer barrels to give him the
extra bit of weight he needed; our quite empty boats, surprisingly,
were our undoing.

The next hour was spent in getting the motor backwards into
the lock again with a view to getting back to where we had "tied
up" the night before. As we were now, we were not even on the
towpath side of the cut and were effectively blocking the way if
the ice-cutter should want to come down. All the same panto-
mime went on getting the motor back but we achieved it at last
and down we went to fight with the gates at the bottom, which
had frozen up again in the interval !

What followed was the most fantastic ordeal of all that chaotic
period.

The channel of the morning was by now quite solid again. We
had perforce to travel backwards, and did not dare to allow the
propeller blades to bang into the unbroken ice behind the stern.
We should certainly have smashed a coupling, if not worse, and
to have the engine incapacitated now would really have been the
end. We could look for no help till the ice age was over and we
were in an awful position where we were, with no drinking-
water and on the wrong side of the cut.

So backwards we had to go, breaking the ice by hand as we
went, and becoming quite hysterical before we had done. The
odds seemed so hopelessly against us; we felt like pygmies
pitting our pathetic little strength against the elements.

We got rather good at it but it took some working out: this
is what we finally evolved—and it took us over three hours to
do that fifty yards.

Putting the tiller right over as far as it would go, so that it was
locked and the steering unaffected by the position, we used it as a
bar to lean on. This was very necessary; without it I don't think
we could possibly have used enough strength to break and move
the ice. With Ruth running the engine for us, accelerating and
decelerating to order, Kit and I took it in turns to hang over the
tiller and with the short shaft harpoon the edge of the nearest
piece of ice, pushing down on it with all our weight until it broke

off, when we would push it under the ice at the side and get
ready to harpoon the next bit.

We found we could manage six lunges each; at the end of the
sixth the harpooner handed the shaft silently to the relief, and
moved to one side, to lean panting against the gunwale and to
rest until it was her turn again. We dare not stop in case we got
frozen in where we lay; thus with infinite slowness and labour we
made our way back to the lock-keeper's cottage and managed to
get in close to the bank where we downed tools with inexpressible
relief at 6.30—nine hours after we had let go and having accomplished . . . exactly nothing.

We ate a titanic meal and fell asleep as soon as the beds were
unrolled.

From my diary:

"*27th Jan.:* It froze hard all last night again and the cut is solid;
no sign of the channel we cut so laboriously yesterday. The local
kids are cycling on it ! No ice-breaker this morning and the lock-
keeper came back from phoning the office at Hatton to say that
everyone is packing up. Kit sent Ruth home (we are only fifty
yards down the lane from the bus into Leamington, thank heaven)
and then went and telephoned some friends who have asked us
both to stay for the week-end. Extremely kind of them to include
me, I must say; they have never even seen me (perhaps that's
why). Spent the p.m. having a terrific spring clean of all the
interior paintwork and only just got finished as Kit's friends
drove up to fetch us by car. From the ridiculous to the sublime !
We gave them tea and attempted to pack and clean up, but our
host—the tallest man I ever saw and how he gets into the cabin
at all, I don't know—insists that all we want is to be conveyed
swiftly away and given a bath. He is too right, and I almost love
him for the suggestion. We *are* conveyed swiftly away, and land
up at tea-time at an enormous house, near Kenilworth, where
they have a very comfortable flat. Huge and boiling bath is
prepared and we toss for who goes first. I win and sink forthwith
into the most heavenly bath I ever had or ever hope to have. Lie
and wallow and feel the stiffness and weariness oozing out of me
and am enveloped in warmth from head to foot. Have managed
to muster set of clean clothes and talc powder, and put on elaborate
"face" before I join the others at tea, much to Kit's annoyance as
she hasn't even *washed* so far ! Sink into deep armchair and am
plied with hot China tea and buttered toast. This is clearly a

dream; or have I overbalanced from the motor and see my life passing before my eyes as I drown ? I wouldn't know, but it's a beautiful death. Very late bed. Kit and I are sleeping in the sitting-room in front of the fire. I've got a bed but she, being so small, can fit on to the sofa, thank the Lord. Enormous black Labrador of six months elects to lie on my feet for the major part of the night, but this is merely reminiscent of Vera's mattress and I am undisturbed by it.

28*th Jan.*: Breakfast at 11, after which Kit said she must bike back to see if the boats were all right, fill up the lamp for the engine-room, etc. Walked into Kenilworth with my host and hostess to drink a pint at a lovely old pub. A beautiful morning with brilliant sunshine and sparkling frost. Lunch at 3, and spent the afternoon with some friends of the Ds. Very late bed again.

29*th Jan.*: Very hurried breakfast as the Ds. were off to London. After they had gone we did a good fairy act and did all the household chores for them before going back to Leamington. Had an hour to wait for our bus there, so sat like ladies and drank morning coffee. Lunch on the boats off the remains of the Ds.' porkpie. Spent afternoon chopping up wood for our stove. Lock-keeper very helpful and kind, lending us his sawing-horse and saw. Mrs. S., his wife, had produced some eggs for us and allows us to draw water from her scullery. She has two nice children. Ran the engine for a bit to warm her up. Not too soon as she was not easy to start. Very early bed.

30*th Jan.*: Normal life having stopped altogether, we celebrated by early morning tea and then breakfast in bed; by no means comfortable, this, but much warmer than getting up. We still have no coal and the wood is getting low. The irony of it ! We spend our lives carrying coal up and down the country and then have to go and get frozen up while we are empty. It wouldn't have happened normally; we should have had some over from the last trip, but Kit has had the very small stuff which chokes the stove for the last three or four trips and we've been using the remains of the D.S. nuts for the time before that, and hoping for some more of them each time. That's why we're caught like this. It has snowed heavily again and has all had to be shovelled off the cabin top and hatches. Went into Leamington to do the shopping and had an excellent lunch in well-warmed restaurant, enjoying *Thank You, Nelson !* which I miraculously managed to

E

pick up; only saw it reviewed on Sunday.   Kit joined me at 2.30,
and we went to the pictures and back to tea here.   George has
called in our absence, with the van from Hatton, and has left us
half cwt. of coal.   The S. children came into see the cabin and
played 'Snubbers and Top-planks' *ad nauseum*.   Mrs. S. is in
despair as her coal merchant has let her down and she hasn't got
a bit to cook on; we have lent her one of our Primuses and the oil
to run it.   They would otherwise have starved.

31*st Jan.:* The thaw has started and gone on all day but the ice
is still very thick.   We waited on tip-toe for the arrival of the ice-
breaker but it hasn't come, so we've spent the day doing odd
jobs, splicing, whipping, baling the butty, clearing out the stern
cupboard and giving the engine-room the most glorious spit
and polish.   Diesel oil on a rag gets all the dirt off, and it is now
a joy to behold.   Felt we must do something; the boats are awful
if you are prevented from normal working.   Our first batch of
forwarded letters from the Bridge, and a wire from school to say
that the children are 'well, happy and *good!*'   This is in reply to
one of mine, sent because I foresaw the most frightful hold-up of
mail and wanted to be sure that they'd settle in all right.   Have
written to them a lot but doubt if they have taken in the extraordinary conditions here."   [It later transpired that the only thing
that had interested them at all was the description of the S.
children playing 'Snubbers and Top-planks'; similarly the S.
children were immeasurably fascinated by my account of my
young !]

"1*st Feb.:* Snow completely gone but Mr. S. says the ice-
breaker won't be through here till dinner-time, so I went to
Leamington to stock up food again before we get cracking tomorrow.   Hitch-hiked in, shopped, and spent an hour with cups
of coffee and the morning paper.   After dinner we did all the
brasses; had to take Vim and wire-wool to the motor but she
looks nice now.   At 3.45, the ice-boat came down and off we
went into the lock.   Still rather the same technique of having to
move great chunks of ice out, but we got on all right, two-handed,
intending to make the bottom of Itchington at least.   Not so.   At
the top of Radford, only seven locks on, we found Ernie Lane
tied up with engine trouble and so placed that, with him on one
side and the ice on the other, we couldn't pass and had to tie up,
at 6.30, in the mouth of the lock.

2*nd Feb.:* Let go in a great hurry at 8.30, to let a pair through the lock. Started ourselves and later let Eli Nixon through, in return for which courtesy, Ben, his boy, left half Itchington ready for us. An altogether dreadful day of wind and rain and me unable to do a single thing right. On the mud, making a mess of breasting-up etc., etc., ETC. Felt like biting Kit (wonder what she felt about me ? !) most of the time, and was delighted to tie up at Stretton at 7. Went straight to bed after supper.

3rd Feb.: Let go at 8.30, and I took the motor nearly the whole way to Hawkesbury, about two hours of it, and felt much better than yesterday. A most heavenly day with a beautiful sunrise. Nearly all the snow has gone and the ice is now floating about in the water in an entirely harmless manner. Met Daphne and Margaret at Hawkesbury and heard all the gossip. Their trainees have walked out and they are waiting for a reinforcement from the Ministry. After we'd moved round to Sutton Stop, we spent the afternoon mending the cratch of the motor and 'decontaminating the tenement'; in other words cleaning up the motor cabin which had got flooded in Hillmorton yesterday. It was filthy and soaking wet, and Ruth is supposed to be coming back the day after tomorrow. Got it looking wonderful with an oily rag; all the paint-work has come up creamy white, which no one could have suspected. Had a slap-up tea and tried to work out a new edition of 'Round Trip,' Kit's other boat game. Letters and bed. We are loading at Newdigate and unloading at 'Hayes cocoa,' next to the lay-by. Thank the Lord it's D.S. this time, too."

This really was the end of the "ice age." The thaw persisted though it took some time to get the cut quite free of ice. It looked funny to see it still floating about in the water when there was no vestige of snow anywhere and the sun was shining brilliantly.

It was Wednesday before we got our load; by that time we were thoroughly "browned off" having been iced up for five and a half days and then having to hang about for a further three when we got to Hawkesbury. But they had to lead us in strict rotation, and the boats that were ahead of us in the ice were still waiting to be loaded when we arrived.

We had long ago got through all the odd jobs we could possibly think of to keep us occupied; there was nothing for it but to keep going to the pictures, and one night I took Ruth into Birmingham to see the show at the Rep., which was "Toad of Toad Hall," very well done.

Nothing very eventful happened on the first part of the way
home. I pulled a muscle in my ribs which was a beastly nuisance
and slowed me up; in spite of this I managed to do the Braunston
tunnel in twenty-five minutes which pleased me very much, but
was really due to the lights behaving quite superbly, so that I
whistled straight through without wasting time banging from side
to side. I did the Blisworth tunnel, too, and emerged into deepest
night at the other end, breaking all records at this moment by
breasting-up almost perfectly for the first time, though I could
hardly see anything. Kit was so surprised that she never got over
it and I have not yet lived it down.

At Northchurch, disaster overtook us. Some little time before
that the gears had started to behave oddly and going into the lock
at Northchurch (with Kit on the motor I am glad to say), they
refused to engage at all. There was nothing for it but to pull the
boats back, out of the way, and phone the fitter. It was beyond
us to locate or mend the trouble, we knew.

Kit came back from phoning fitter and Ministry, to say that
the R.V. wished to speak to me as soon as we got back to the
Bridge. We couldn't imagine what he had to say that did not
concern Kit, as my trainer, as well; she had intelligently found
out that it was nothing personal. I was always afraid that something would go wrong with the children, though I need not
have bothered because nothing ever did.

If the engine had to die on us it was very considerate of it to do
it at Northchurch which is a nice tie-up in itself, and in addition is
near shops, church and some friends of mine who have a house
on the Tring summit. There was still no sign of the fitter by
lunch-time on Sunday, so I phoned my friends who came over
and had tea with us and then took me back with them for the
night.

I got back early on Monday but again we spent the whole day
waiting for the fitter. He had arrived on Sunday and had pronounced judgment on the engine. The gear-box had worn out
and we had to have a new one but he'd got some broken down
"beers" which claimed his first attention, so it was not until
Tuesday that our new gear-box arrived. We towed the motor
into the full lock and tied her up there, so that the men could
lift the heavy gear-box in easily from the lock-side.

This little excitement over, away we went again, and should
have been whistling along quite happily had not I, in a fit of

absentmindedness, put the motor most horribly on to the mud in the King's Langley pound, where the bends are tricky. It took some time, a lot of hard work, and the assistance of a Green Line bus-driver who happened to be passing, to get us off. In spite of all this, Kit told us, when we tied up, that it had been "very, very good going" so perhaps we were learning a little about team-work after all.

The next morning at Black Jack I gave myself and everybody else a nasty fright. I still don't think it was my fault, but Kit has other views on the subject. . . .

Just before we got to the lock we met a lock-wheeler coming along the path towards us. I called out to him and asked if the lock was ready for us. I do not think he can possibly have mis-understood, as this was what one always wanted to know from a lock-wheeler and the information was often volunteered before one had time to ask. At any rate I understood him to say that it was all right, so went batting along quite happily.

The lock lies round a corner and as we turned it the rising sun was directly in my eyes, dazzling me completely. I could just make out the outline of the lock but that was all, so I slowed down (thank God I did), to take the motor in; the fore-end, it must be remembered, was seventy feet ahead of my eyes. When there was about two yards to go before her nose went in, I realised to my utter horror that the gates were *shut*. I was on the point of charg-ing the top gates of the empty lock with a pair of loaded boats. I don't think I have ever been so frightened in my life. It was certainly far worse than the rocket.

Easing the motor down and frantically changing into reverse and then accelerating again, I had a vision of the gates unable to stand up to the onslaught, and the motor going straight through them and falling into the empty lock below. I prayed that Ruth would realise what was happening and take the butty into the bank which might act as a brake to me; I had no time to shriek at her and she wouldn't have heard me if I had. I was far too pre-occupied in selecting a suitable place for the bang which was now a certainty.

Bang we did, with a sickening shock and the motor lurching form side to side, but the gates held. I threw off the towing-rope and prepared to try to check the butty which I now saw was charging up on me, Ruth not having realised what was going on. The motor had rocketed over to the other side of the gates and

was now lying across them which did something to stop the
butty's headlong career, but Ruth was evidently so appalled by
what she saw that she left the towing-line streaming in the water
instead of pulling it in. I am not in the least blaming her: I know I
should have done no better myself in such a crisis.

I yelled but without the slightest effect, and the inevitable
happened. Bump-bump-bump from the engine . . . the tiller
jumping madly in its socket . . . and the engine cut out. Of
course, the towing-line was twisted viciously round the propeller
blades. By this time Kit had appeared from the depths of the
cabin but alas, too late to pull in the tow-rope. It was not, however, too late for her to express her feelings and a veil had better
be drawn over the next few minutes. The upshot of it was, that I
should not take things for granted and, just because I met a lock-
wheeler, assume that the lock was ready. A larger veil will be
needed to cover the interval of time it took us to get as much as
we could find of the towing-rope out of the blades, and to sort
ourselves out from the oncoming pair. I shall always think that
what really happened was that the other boats took much longer
than their lock-wheeler estimated in getting up to the lock, so
that instead of being through it and thus leaving it ready for us,
we actually arrived first. And of course the whole thing would
not have mattered a tinker's cuss if the sun had not got into my
eyes and blinded me until it was too late. However, the incident
taught me a very valuable lesson and after that I always went into
locks, even when I could see them easily, with the slowest possible speed, especially down-hill ones. I have never thrown off
the horror of plunging over the gates.

We actually spent the rest of the day getting out bits of tow-
rope at intervals and the motor steered very oddly.

When we got to "the cocoa," which is how the boaters always
describe the Nestlé's factory, they started to unload us at once,
and when I had done my bit of helping to get the boats ready I
went off to phone the Ministry.

I found the idea was for me to join two other women on G.U.
boats and be hired out to another firm which operated from Tam-
worth. We should be the first pair to do this, and if it proved a
success there would be others transferred to S. E. Barlow, who
had work for more boats than he actually possessed. I was to be
allowed to go off for the school holidays all right, and
as I had no plans for joining any other boats there did not seem

to be anything against the scheme. I told the R.V. that I would talk it over with Miss Gayford and let him know the next day. The others were actually in the lay-by waiting for the third member of the crew and proved to be Sheila (recovered from her cracked wrist), and Jennifer, who had been a trainer's mate and would be the skipper or "steerer."

We talked it over and I decided to go. To celebrate the decision we tidied ourselves and rushed up to town to see a show, getting back much too late after a long day.

I went up to the lay-by in the morning and saw Jennifer and the new boats and then phoned the Ministry, clinching the arrangement.

Daphne was up there, too, and I offered to go down to the arrival bridge with her and pick up her new trainee; this piece of generosity was inspired by my desire to get another shot at winding in readiness for my test, which I knew I should have to take before starting off on the new trip. The practice was much needed; I did the winding abominably and nearly cut Daphne's head off on the bridge as she shafted me round, but she was not a trainer for nothing and was used to saving herself from sudden death at the hands of incompetents !

My new boats were called, gorgeously, *Hyperion* and *Nebulæ* but this piece of scintillation did not compensate for the feeling of desolation with which I looked forward to going out into the wide, wide world. I had been with Kit and on (more or less) the same pair of boats for nearly two and a half months and the idea of anything else seemed strange and rather alarming; it was with a good deal of misgiving that I packed up and moved out of the *Pavo* by 8 o'clock next morning.

Jennifer was still "fitting out" so I went home for the weekend. When I got there, in a depressed state of mind, and turned on the water main for my bath, three separate bursts started to pour down the stairs. So the ice age had the ace of trumps after all.

Chapter xi—THE OXFORD CUT

THE *Hyperion* and *Nebulæ* were not new boats, but they had been done up inside and out before being hired to Mr. Barlow and every strap, rope, cotton-line and other impedimenta was brand new; it took us some time to get all this stowed away and ready for use.

It was the custom for the steerer to choose where she lived and the others sorted themselves out afterwards. Jennifer decided on the motor to herself, as many people did; Sheila and I had the butty. I so much preferred living on the butty that I would rather have shared it than live by myself on the motor. The door at the far end of a butty leads into a boarded-off and covered-in bit of the hold known as the back end; it is an invaluable place for oilskins, vegetables, paraffin cans and saucepans and I would give up any amount of privacy for the sake of getting all these unpleasant objects stowed away out of sight and for a chance to make the cabin look attractive. I mind violently what my surroundings are like and, long ago, decided that any form of camping need not necessarily be more professional simply because it is uncomfortable.

I, therefore, attacked the *Nebulæ* with gusto; with all the workmen busy putting the finishing touches to her, it was easy to organise small matters of personal preference, such as two shelves in the lockers, a shelf over my bed to hold my candle, and more shelves in the back end. A lot of this was copied from Kit's butties, but I lifted her ideas without shame. She had been longer on the cut than anyone else and had worked out the simplest way to be comfortable, on which point we had the same ideas.

Anything I had done was going to be an improvement to be shared by all, so no one minded in the least; Sheila herself had some very bright ideas for adding to the common weal and by the time we had finished, the butty looked good and was very comfortable to live in.

Mr. Barlow came down to the lay-by one day to see how we were getting on, and to establish personal contact with us, I think. He was then, and at all other times that I had any dealings with him, the most pleasant and reasonable employer one could hope to have.

Swept, garnished and, figuratively speaking, with flags flying, we started off on 21st February, just before dinner. We were all very delighted with Mr. Barlow who had promised to give us a load to Oxford if he possibly could. The G.U. doesn't go there, and we all wanted to see as much of every canal as we could as long as the job lasted. In the meantime we were going off to the docks to load for the G.U. and should only really become "Barlow girls" when we had unloaded in Birmingham and were reloaded with Barlow coal.

We should not have been quite so pleased with ourselves if we had been able to see what was in store for us. We made the dock at midday on Thursday and got no load till the following Wednesday. For five and a half days we kicked our heels in Limehouse, never able to go off properly because we never knew when they would start on us. I have already given some idea of how deadly the boats can be with no work to do; we were boiling with suppressed fury by the time our load did come in from the river.

In the interval I had managed to have my rib strapped up, which was indeed something to be thankful for, and we had all spent a riotous evening at the "Prospect of Whitby," a very well-known pub on the banks of the Thames. One might almost be allowed to give it the far pleasanter name of "inn," dating as it does from the times when the word "pub" was unknown—and certainly unsung. "The Prospect" has associations with the past as far back as Mr. Pepys, and both Thackeray and Dickens knew it.

I hope to visit it and inspect it properly one day; the night we went there the Dutch Navy had also mustered in some force, and their hospitality was such, that I haven't anything like such a clear impression of "The Prospect" as I could wish. . . .

We had as many visitors as we could collect, to pass the time, but it still dragged heavily. Jennifer and Sheila went home once or twice but I stayed where I was, preferring the butty to my dripping pipes at home. I think I must be about the only woman who has ever spent the night alone on a boat in the Regent Canal Dock; it was very comforting to think of the ring of policemen at every entrance, guarding my slumber for me. I spent one afternoon with Kit, who took pity on me and asked me over (she was on leave) and I visited a good many friends.

When our load at last materialised it was American rubber; a

E*

lovely load of neaf flat bags like squashed pillows, just not too heavy for us to lift and rearrange if the need arose.

We half-sheeted and popped off, delighted to be on the move again at last. Alas for our hopes: just beyond the Mile End lock we discovered with consternation that instead of the stream of water that should have been pumping itself out of the side of the boat from the water-cooling system, there was a cloud of very hot-looking steam. There was only one thing to do when that happened and we did it. We stopped the engine at once and shafted the boats over to the side of the cut where they were out of the way of other traffic.

Rather cleverly, and quite innocently, the spot we had selected to tie up was beside an N.F.S. post; it was a matter of moments only before we had a band of ardent helpers, all much better mechanics than we were, although they were not used to heavy oil engines. It did not take long to locate the trouble; in a fit of fun on the part of one of the fitters we had been sent out without a filter in our mid-box, and were now properly choked up. Jennifer went and phoned the Bridge and Sheila and I cleared out as much as we could. It was lovely, slimy, grey mud and smelt awful.

The position we were in was a trifle public, being immediately under a road bridge and providing a delightful view to anybody who cared to stop and look over. Apparently every single passer-by had the desire to inspect us at close quarters, for soon the bridge was black with people and we decided we should have to move.

Accordingly we got busy with shafts, only to realise with sinking hearts that we had not only got mud inside the engine, but were embedded *in* it as well. Without the power of the motor it was impossible to pull the boats off, so we had to settle down to a night of it.

It was not so bad while it was light, but when we turned the lights on inside the cabin it was money for jam for the crowd on the bridge. They could see straight in and took every advantage of their position. We pulled the slide over—to be greeted with cries of "Shame!" They could still manage a glimpse through the doors and a running commentary went on if we so much as moved a hand inside. We shut the doors; more loud cries from the bridge. It then became so hot in the cabin that we were nearly suffocated. Even with the back-end door open it was far too hot, and there was no possible means of making the stove go out quickly; we could only not make it up, and wait for it to die a natural death.

While doing this we decided on bed, with the lights out and the doors open, and got in as quick as we could. Disappointed, the crowd trickled away but not before we had had several invitations from the sky, to all of which we preserved an aloof and chilly silence. It was heavenly to get the doors open and to feel the fresh air again but our triumph was short-lived. The sirens started, the bombs and rockets bumped away with enthusiasm and, to cap everything, there was a pitter-patter on the cabin top which was worse than any bomb—RATS. We hastily shut everything up again; hermetically sealed we slept uneasily and uncomfortably and when I awoke in the morning I was somewhat startled to see that Sheila, still asleep, was tightly clasping the fish-slice, evidently intending to do battle with the rats if they managed to penetrate our defences.

That was quite one of the worst nights I ever spent. Thank heaven, the fitter came early in the morning with our missing filter, and we got away by 10.30, and were back in the lay-by by 6.45.

There were one or two calamities on the way up Tyseley, but for the most part we went along smoothly enough and the weather was lovely. At Leighton we had to tie up and wait for Mr. Barlow's fitter to come and readjust our motor tiller for us; I am afraid it was I who was responsible for wrecking it, but I cannot pretend I am sorry because it was the means of my introduction to the painter in the boat-yard at Leighton who afterwards painted the most lovely dipper for me, which I still have.

Jennifer went over to the yard with the motor and came back with a new dipper, and that started me off. Hers was a beauty, with roses all over it and I instantly decided that I must have one too; I went in and saw Frank before we left and ordered one. It wasn't really an extravagance because we only had one dipper to each boat, and in it we washed the potatoes, the dishes, our clothes and our feet, which did not strike me as even sanitary. There was certainly room for another.

One night we tied up at a pub near Cosgrove, about which we had all heard a lot, but had never visited. We never went again because it was the most appalling tie-up; thick mud so that we couldn't get the boats close in but had to have a shore-plank, and the bank was thickly planted with willow and brambles so that the person who jumped off with the cotton-line had a jungle to scratch her way through before we were tied up. Through the jungle, too, we all had to make our way in order to visit the pub, which we decided to do before having supper.

That was a happy decision; when we got to the pub and had ordered our beer, someone had the bright idea of asking if they had any food; sometimes the pubs would produce sausage rolls or rolls and cheese. We were definitely in luck; a large twenty-first birthday party was in progress in another room, with an excellent buffet supper. We were taken in and introduced to the celebrants who were sufficiently mellow to think the intrusion rather fun, and willingly agreed to our being fed on the remains of their supper. They asked us to stay but, feeling that the supper would taste far better without the necessity to make polite conversation to one another, we thanked them and retired to the bar again with our windfall, and spent a very pleasant evening by ourselves with our feet up, a good meal and some excellent beer.

From my diary:

"*6th March:* Let go at 7.45, but I 'lay in' till we'd started and then richly atoned for it by doing the flues as we went along. A very busy, hard day and not a lot of locks ready. Did High House bend abominably and also came round my own pet corner, after Weedon, in the quickset hedge as usual. Have never been round it in the water that I can remember! Got to Norton panting for our letters, to be told that they had just been given to Eli Nixon (WHY?) to bring down to us. As we had just met Eli at the bottom of Bugby without a word being said about letters, we were all furious. No mail for another week now, unless they can get a message through and stop Eli at Finney.

7th March: Let go at 7.15 but in spite of expectations had a bad road. Also, no cigarettes to be had anywhere which doesn't add to the sweetness of my temper. Finally secured some at 'The Blue Lias' on Itchington and then lock-wheeled Radford so that I could go and call on the Ss., and leave a book for the children. Mrs. S. gave me eggs and home-killed bacon and will have some more eggs for us on the way down. Hope that Kit hasn't come up the cut by then and scooped the lot. Tied up at the top of Warwick; 'Cape of Good Hope,' and early bed.

8th March: Had about six of Hatton to get ready, after letting go at 7.20; after that a good road. Oiled at the works and had the fenders put right by George. The *Hyperion* has always smoked, he says, so there doesn't seem to be anything more to do about the black fumes that come from the engine exhaust whenever we accelerate fully. Tied at Tyseley at 5.30, and had tea with Meriel and co.—who are in. Lost my cigarettes and lighter while on the motor, heaven knows where. They are not in the bilge but a very great deal of thick black oil is. Cleaned up, rang up the Bs., and went out to supper and to have a bath with them, on an endless bus. Enjoyed it very much, but bus even more endless coming back and only took me as far as Acocks Green, from whence I had to walk. Very late bed and Sheila not at all well for the third day. She has eaten a mildewed boaters' pie from—I won't say where. Jennifer has the digestion of an ostrich and hasn't suffered, while I, remembering Kit's words of wisdom about this particular shop, took one look at mine and pitched it over the side.

9th March: Started to unsheet at 7.30, and when we had done the butty, had breakfast while they unloaded us. Shopped and all had lunch with Miranda and crew—who had just got in. Did laundry; very necessary. Sheila and Jennifer off to bath and night with friends, while Miranda came and had supper with me, bringing it with her in the shape of fish and chips. Lovely pottering evening on my own and read very late."

The next night we were at the top of Warwick with Miranda tied with us, and the following morning we had a nice lazy time because we knew we could not clear Hillmorton locks by one o'clock, which is the time they close on Sundays.

We were just getting ready to start and had made the first lock ready, when a pair of "Jossers" came round the corner from Hatton. I signalled to them to slow down as we were just going to use the lock, but they paid not the slightest attention and came right on. This got my goat (we knew that the next twenty locks were ready for us and naturally didn't want the Jossers to get them), so I untied very rapidly and started the engine. Jennifer was ahead lock-wheeling and Sheila was in the cabin getting dressed.

A howl of rage went up from the Jossers when they heard our engine start, and we both rushed into the mouth of the lock together. The gates were still shut and we were tightly jammed, so I yelled to Jennifer to come and help me give battle, and begged Sheila to put in an appearance so that they would not think we were two-handed; if we had been, they would have been able to expect the right of way as quicker workers.

Jennifer hurled herself into the fray with relish and the most fearful battle ensued. We told each other the most crushing home truths we could think of, touched on the doubtful domestic habits of one another's forebears, the state of the boats and the rights of the case. They sneered at us and called us so-and-so and so-and-so trainees who didn't know the first thing about boats, while Jennifer put up a magnificent show, giving quite as good as she got. Miranda and her lot were listening open-mouthed by this time, lined up on the bank; Jennifer having argued the situation into a deadlock at last went off to get the lock-keeper to arbitrate.

He proved to be quite useless, with no authority whatever, so when we had exhausted our vocabularies we gave in, and told them they could have OUR lock "just to show that there was *still some goodwill on the cut*" (this was Jennifer's line); I must admit there hadn't been much sign of it up to that moment, but it saved our face.

I was still on the motor and I told the man that if he wanted the lock he would have to back a bit, so that I could get out and let him in. That started him off again and complete deadlock again seemed to have been reached. He point blank refused to move his boat an inch, so I said, "All right . . . we'll stay as we are till you do. There's nothing else to be done . . ." and started to go down into the cabin. Then the penny dropped and, cursing like one o'clock, he reluctantly moved his motor about three inches back.

It was enough to let me reverse, which I did at once and we had the pleasure of seeing them going into our lock.

A most exhausting but very exhilarating day ensued. We stuck on their tails as close as we possibly could; I do not think we had ever worked faster or produced better team-work than we did that day. At every lock one of us was there lock-wheeling while they went through; we propped ourselves against the wall and yawned loudly, we looked ostentatiously at our watches all the time, we passed loud remarks to one another so that they could hear; and the moment they were out of a lock we worked like fiends so that we should be waiting there for them to get out of the next one.

This is very undermining, as we meant it to be ! By the time we had got to the bottom of Itchington it was beginning to tell on them, and by the top the children were being given instructions to "shut the gate for the lady, Alfie." We rejoiced but said nothing, and at the top they went ahead and we thought we had seen the last of them. (This, by the way, was the family who had six children under nine years old.)

But we had not seen the last of them. Coming round the bad Oxford bends we came on them again—tightly fixed in the mud !

It is not often you see a boater on the mud, though we were often there and always felt it a deep disgrace. Picture then the feelings of "the so-and-so and so-and-so trainees" when they rounded the corner and saw the enemy delivered into their hands, in all the full flush of their shame and humiliation. Picture also the feelings of the enemy, if your imagination is lurid enough.

With the voice of a dove, dripping with honey and solicitude, Jennifer called to them, asking in what way they would like us to help them most ? Hardly able to articulate for fury, the boater told her what he wanted done, while his wife kept up a moan about the butty being too heavily loaded. We all agreed with the deepest sympathy that it was *very* hard to avoid the mud, with as much load on as that, and Jennifer went forward to give her help.

The whole situation suddenly became considerably eased by Jennifer losing her balance and nearly falling in, only being saved by the boater catching her by the seat of her skirt as she went. After this we all got very matey indeed, and when we had successfully got them off the mud they let us through.

From that day on that particular pair of Jossers were always firm allies of ours. In case anyone should think that we lowered ourselves by such an unseemly brawl, I would like to say that it was nothing but a trial of strength. They were out to do us down and they knew it. If we had taken it lying down they would, rightly I think, have despised us for ever. They got no more than they deserved and they respected us for it for ever after. They are a queer crowd, the boat people, and they can't be treated quite the same in some ways as other people. Their whole life is a fight for existence and the things they understand best are: strength, skill, giving a helping hand, and at the same time putting over the fastest of fast ones on a fellow who is not as quick as they are. Once you have got their trust they will place implicit

faith in you, but it takes a bit of getting. If they decide to dislike
you then heaven help you, for they won't . . . ever.

We found Kit with two new trainees when we got to Hawkesbury. She was down at Long Ford and as we were also bound for
there we tied up (after a good deal of difficulty which Kit eventually got us out of) in the next length, and she came and had
supper with me as the other two were both out.

In the morning I phoned the Ministry and asked what would
happen if I had to go home for the holidays and leave the others
two-handed ? This now seemed very likely as we had taken
so much longer than we ought to get as far as this. The result
of the conversation was that the Hawkesbury G.U. manager
came round in the afternoon and we talked the matter over. It
was finally decided that I should get as far as Oxford with them,
which I very much wanted to do anyway, and then leave from
there. It would be all right for them to be two-handed once the
boats were empty, and on the way back they would know the
route, too, which we none of us did at present.

I finished off the day going to the pictures on my own, and
then came home to find that Kit was still awake and prepared
for some more chatter. The others were away for the night so
I had the luxury of the butty to myself again.

Next day I went into Coventry early and met Sheila by arrangement and we went off to Stratford-on-Avon for the day. I showed
it to her very thoroughly, which I think she enjoyed, and we
ended up at the Coventry Hippodrome at a performance of
"Desert Rats" . . . "prior to London."

When we got back we found that we had been loaded during
the day; Jennifer had dealt with everything herself. This sort
of thing always seemed to be happening; none of the people in
charge of loading operations ever appeared to have the faintest
idea what was coming next. We either waited five days or else
missed the moment altogether. For this reason, amongst others,
we never all left the boats at the same time.

Two days later occurred the historic moment when we turned
RIGHT at the Knapton island for the first time in our history:
ten minutes later we were turning left into the unknown reaches
of the Oxford Canal.

Our first impressions of it were mixed. It is very lovely; the
cut winding through green fields and hedgerows with gentle
hills rising to the south east: one of these was topped with a wind-

mill which we found kept appearing and disappearing all day long till we wondered if we were going round in circles. A glance at the map, which by now I had with me, showed that we were travelling due south, but in a series of loops which must have trebled the distance to our next landmark which was the nine locks at Knapton.

The island is called Knapton Junction and the locks are called Knapton 9; it is fair to assume they are fairly close together yet it took us three hours to cover the distance between island and locks. We were travelling very slowly . . . not more than three miles an hour I should say, but we did not have any hold-ups on the mud so it is safe to estimate that we covered nine miles of canal, where the proverbial crow would have had but two or three at the most.

The cut was frightfully narrow compared with the G.U.; it was also very muddy which made the going slow, but we arrived at the bottom of the locks at midday.

All went well at the first lock. They were single ones, we had been warned, and that, of course, meant bow-hauling the butty as we had on the bottom road; this time, though, she was a loaded butty and the canal was very shallow as well as muddy, so it was not at all the same as before.

At the second lock the trouble really began. We *could not* get the butty in. Pull as we might she seemed bent on staying put and not one inch could we move her. We tried tying her to the motor above the lock and then starting the motor off but that had no effect either.

We got desperate. There were many more locks we knew, and our chances of getting to Oxford seemed small if they were all going to be like this. Further, we could not even turn round and go back. Straining every nerve we managed at last to shift the butty's position a trifle; I suppose that must have done the trick because after that she went in all right. We had spent an hour over the two first locks cf the Oxford canal.

A sit-down dinner was voted a necessity so we knocked off for an hour and then started the assault on the remaining seven. Contrary to expectations, the first six were all quite easy to get into (compared with the second that is), and we breathed again, thinking our troubles were over.

At the ninth and last, the butty dug in her heels again and refused to move. There was not an inch of clearance between her sides and the lock walls and it really looked quite hopeless. We did all the usual drill, over and over again, but she simply would not budge. As the final straw, the motor broke down above the top of the lock, evidently to signify her disapproval of the whole affair. So now we had not even got that doubtful help. At this point the lock-keeper put in an appearance and announced that we *must* get the butty in; he seemed a little hurt at the reception that this remark got from us. It was the absolute end to be told this, after our positively frantic efforts; the implication seemed to be that we had spent the afternoon making daisy-chains, without a care in the world. I am afraid he got his head taken right off and must have wished he'd never been born, when three furious women yelled in chorus: "We know that . . . BUT WILL YOU TELL US HOW ? ? ?"

There was a small bridge at the bottom of the lock and on this the rural population were now gathered to watch the fun. They all seemed to be farm labourers, and hefty-looking men at that, with a good sprinkling of Italian prisoners from the neighbouring farms, so we enlisted their help, got them down on to the tow-path and made them pull.

The Italians were enormously tickled by the whole thing. We could not make them understand a word but it was not really necessary. By now it was painfully obvious what was wanted, and they rallied round with much spitting on the hands and beaming smiles, nodding their encouragement and chattering like parakeets.

We tied the long cotton-line on to the stud at the fore-end of the butty, led it up over the top gates, arranged the Italians in a row under it and gave the word to—PULL. The inevitable happened; the line snapped and the men fell over backwards but the butty remained placidly where she was.

Our next bright idea was to try to tighten up the rigging chains inside the butty hold. They were buried deep in coal which we had to shovel out of the way before we could get at them. This was a ghastly performance, made worse by the feeling that it wouldn't do any good in the end. It didn't; we gave it up. Jennifer got on to her bike and went to phone the fitter to come and look at the engine, and we called it a day.

The lock-keeper did not improve the situation by keeping on about us blocking up the way for other traffic (none of which we had so far seen a sniff of), how we "didn't ought to have been sent with our big boats" and we "*must* get the butty in." We felt no love for him at all, and sadly missed the familiar lock-keepers on the G.U. who always seemed to be full of bright ideas. (This was less than justice to the Knapton lock-keeper, really. He couldn't help, because such a thing had never before arisen. The boats on the Oxford are narrower than ours; only an inch or two perhaps but enough to make all the difference. In addition, the walls of the locks had bulged inwards slightly as a result of the very hard frosts and that, plus the width of our G.U. boats, was really the trouble. I am sure the G.U. lock-keepers would not have been any brighter because there really was no solution.)

In the morning we waited and waited for the fitter who, when he did come, turned out to be George from Hatton. This made us feel a lot better and we poured out all our woes to him while he readjusted some loose bolts which was all that was the matter with the engine.

The lock-keeper, in the meantime, had thrown up the sponge and telephoned to the Oxford Canal authorities asking what we should all do next. They immediately sent down some engineers, who got to work with pulley block and tackle and three thicknesses of line. This was too much for the butty who reluctantly unglued herself from the mud and slowly but surely entered the lock, to the accompaniment of rousing cheers from every side.

The engineers did not go till they had seen us safely out at the top, but this went off all right and we were soon on our way down the eleven mile pound to Fenny Compton, leaving Knapton with no regrets whatever. We were, however, comforted by the thought that we had been trying with our three pairs of arms to do what it had taken pulley, tackle and three lines to accomplish.

We did not see another pair of boats till we got to the locks at Claydon. It was only one boat that we found then, tied-up there before us; and history flicked back fifty years or so. One horse-boat called *The Friendship*, her steerer an erect, thin, old man with the piercing blue eyes that are sometimes seen in boater families, and his name proudly painted on his cabin side: "Jos. Skinner"—one of the last of the "Number Ones."

A "Number One" is a man who owns his own boat instead of working for a company. There are very few of them left now; like all other individual effort in this "free" country of ours it is being stamped out and strangled by the doubtful advantages offered to the company employee. It is one of the minor tragedies that are going on all the time. Mr. Skinner was a good example

of the man who is his own master. Brisk, jovial and with an
ease of manner that I had not met on the cut before, we found him
and his "missus" delightful. They were very intrigued by us,
having heard of the women working but not, I think, having
met any of us before.

We told the story of the Knapton locks over again; the Skinners
were filled with gloomy prognostication about our luck farther
on, and we went to bed wondering what on earth was going to
happen next.

Sheila and I were feverishly trying to make a log-book as we
went along but it was not at all easy. There were not nearly so
many lock-keepers as we had been used to, and, other than the
Skinners, we only met one other pair of boats of whom we could
ask the names of the locks.

This really *was* a pair, being the "Mum and Dad" of one of
the G.U. boys. I had had a chat with him at Hawkesbury; when
he heard we were off to Oxford he told me to keep an eye open
for the old people whom he did not often see. They were delighted
to see us, though the expression on their faces as they saw our
unfamiliar red, white and blue paint was comic. They looked as
though they thought we had strayed on to the wrong cut by
mistake. But they were helpful, too, and told us where we could
get fresh water and what were the bad bends to look out for. It
was with regret that we bade them good-bye and went on into
the unknown.

In spite of all the prophecies we got on perfectly well in all
the other locks. The rest were down-hill ones which I believe
made a difference to us, though why this should be so I never
discovered.

The next day was Sunday, a lovely warm spring day. It was
very pleasant to wind our way, almost lazily, through the sunny
Oxfordshire meadows, the hills clad with fine trees in their fresh
new greenery and a glimpse from time to time of a little village
nestling in the gentle valley. We passed some beautiful houses
enclosed in parkland, standing high and looking out over the
pastureland below; the kind of houses you see advertised in
Country Life and lick your lips over. . . .

It was evening when we got to Banbury and found *The Friendship* already tied up there. Mr. and Mrs. Skinner greeted us with
enthusiasm and told us they had not expected to see us nearly so
soon, which we took to be a compliment. They had started long

before us in the morning, but with our double load we had only
been an hour behind them all day; with great courtesy they somehow implied that our engine had nothing whatever to do with our
speedy arrival but that our "boatmanship," if there is such a
word, had evidently been superb.

A compliment from boaters, even such a roundabout one as
this, was a very treasured occasion. We were always conscious
of our inferiority in the face of such craftsmen as these people are,
and to have a pat on the back from them really did produce a glow
of pleasure. We could be quite sure, moreover, that it was not
in the nature of an idly flung bouquet; they are not courtiers,
these people, but honest men, appreciative of skill when they
see it but silent when they do not. It was not very often that we
earned praise from them; when we did it meant a lot.

The highest praise I ever heard bestowed on us women by a
boater was when Fred (our cinema escort) was talking one
day of the performance of "Audreyevelynananne."

"They passed us at the bottom of Stoke," said Fred with
feeling, "and b . . . r me if it didn't take us three trips to catch
'em !"

We were locked-up at Banbury. That is to say, the lock was
padlocked for the night (it had probably shut at midday; many
of them did). Otherwise we might have gone on, but as it was
we were delighted to tie up and have a look at Banbury. I
should have liked a much longer look than was possible that night;
perhaps one day I shall go back there and be able to explore it
at leisure; I might even be lucky enough to find *The Friendship*
tied up there for the night.

Banbury will forever be associated in my mind with my brass
knob. Going to get water that night, I saw through the broken-
down fence a perfectly good rubbish dump which would obviously pay for closer inspection. Leaving my can on the path,
I climbed through the hole and found a glorious collection of
junk thrown out by the inhabitants of Banbury.

Fairly near the top of the pile I spotted the remains of an old
iron bedstead with, what joy ! . . . its knobs and rails still there.
Some boater had missed this all right. I did not take long to
remove a knob and rail and rush back to the boat with my find,
but it was a trip or two before I had the nerve to fix the knob in
position beside the cabin door, boater style. A row of brass
knobs inside the door signifies prosperity; obviously only a tradi-

tion now, when so many of the boats belong to the companies
and individual prosperity is very much more evened out than it
used to be. Also, we could hardly come into this category with
our wartime effort, but a knob or two did make the boats look
nice, and I feel completely for the boaters who like to have brass
everywhere they can find a corner for it.

The rail never got used; by the time I joined new boats I had
lost it and my new steerer had an extra one which she gave me.
Hers was a stair rod which was much more satisfactory, being
solid; you can buy them in bundles for a few pence at any junk
shop, which I did not know when I scrambled through the hole
in the fence at Banbury.

One of the features of the Oxford cut which fascinated us is
the wooden bridges which lead the farm lanes over the water.
They are hinged on one bank and by undoing a large iron pin
and pressing with all one's weight on the balance beam, the whole
bridge rises into the air to allow the boats to pass underneath.
The only snag being that you have to go on sitting on the beam
or the bridge will not stay up. Nobody seems to have thought of
any method of keeping it up when it is once open except this
one.

There was a nasty moment when I was sitting on one of these
beams and the boats were practically under the bridge; I suddenly
saw a small child on the bank getting perilously near to the water
and instinctively started up to run and catch hold of him. At
once the bridge started to fall so there was nothing for it but to
hurl myself back on to the end of the beam again and leave the
boy to his fate. It was that or letting the bridge fall on to the oncoming boats, with heaven knows what damage, and I felt that
of the two alternatives an impromptu bath for the child was the
better. Luckily he did not go in so all was well but I have seldom
felt so helpless, sitting there doing nothing.

On Tuesday we had a visitor. This was a young Canadian
airman who, with some companions, had been following our
progress for some miles on a bicycle. At length his friends drifted
away, but he went doggedly on down the path with us and
started to lend a hand with the gates. We asked him if he would
like to come on the boats for a bit of the way.

I have never seen a man move faster. He and his bike were on
the boat in a flash and he spent the rest of the day with us, only
leaving us as we got to Oxford itself because he had not got his

full uniform on and was not allowed to appear in public without all the trappings.

He was extremely helpful by the time we had finished with him, bow-hauling for us and checking the butty to the manner born. All the time he kept shaking his head and saying the folks at home would be just tickled to death when he told them about this. Seeing that "home" was the vast Canadian continent of space and speed I could well believe they would, and I suggested to him that he would certainly be able to go home and say that he had travelled by the slowest method known to man.

He was intrigued by the whole thing and thoroughly enjoyed himself. He was a nice boy and won my heart by producing "Sweet Caps" which he insisted on leaving with me, and a good supply of Canadian chocolate. How generous those boys were; they seemed ready to give away anything they had on them.

We had a bit of a job finding the place where we were supposed to unload our coal. Nobody seemed to have heard of it and we didn't know a thing except the name. Finally a man working in a factory yard registered intelligence, and we located our wharf soon after.

It was too late for us to be unloaded that night, so Sheila and I washed ourselves and went off into the town in search of food. This necessitated asking a very disagreeable foreman for the key to the yard so that we could get in again. He seemed to think it was quite unheard of for us to want to go out (as I daresay it was, for the boaters always stick to the boats), but we were in no mood to be regimented by any foreman alive and insisted that the gate should be left open for us. We had a search to find anyone who would feed us at the rather late hour that we turned up; neither of us knew Oxford well. My previous experience of it was confined to motoring through and meals at the "Mitre" or the "Randolph," at neither of which, even in wartime, did I feel I had the nerve to present myself dressed in bell-bottoms and only superficially clean.

When we did find a haven it was a very good one; the waitress took us under her wing and gave us double helpings of everything, which was warmly welcome as we had done no shopping for the last five days, since leaving Hawkesbury, and were distinctly hungry.

I need hardly add that we lost our way going home, having forgotten to ask the bus conductress the name of the stop where

we had got on, which was a precaution it was always wise to
take in a strange town, but we usually forgot. All we knew that
we were tied up somewhere behind Worcester College; all the
local inhabitants we asked seemed to be entirely ignorant of the
presence of a canal in the city at all so we ended by simply asking
for Worcester which they *did* seem to know, surprisingly.

We were very late back and I had my packing to do, for I was
leaving Jennifer and Sheila in the morning.   It was 20th March,
I was very tired and the holidays were due to start shortly.

I don't remember another leave that was as welcome as this
one was. I think the ice age had been both long and tiring and
I had not had much break in between. This trip had been trying,
too, having lasted nearly five weeks in all, but I had enjoyed
seeing the Oxford cut, and was sorry to say good-bye to the other
two with whom I knew I should not be sharing again. I joined
the "city men's train" at Oxford next day and was in London by
ten o'clock . . . a journey it had taken us ten days to do in the
reverse order !

CHAPTER XII—G.U. AGAIN

THE very moment I had put the two children on to the school train at the end of the Easter holidays, I went round to the Ministry to find out what work there was for me.

There didn't seem to me to be much point in continuing to work for Barlow when the only employment I could hope for was spare-wheeling when someone fell out. There was still only the one pair working on the Oxford but plenty of pairs on the G.U. who might need an understudy.

I put this to the Ministry and they agreed with me; mainly, I think, because there was actually a G.U. pair wanting a third at that moment. They were both people I knew; one was Margaret who had been Daphne's mate for a long time, and the other was my namesake, Susan. (We were the only two on the cut of that name and I foresaw difficulties ahead when we were on one pair of boats.) They were both waiting to make up crews and run their own boats; either the boats were not ready for them, or the other people were out on a trip so that they could not start. We calculated that we could fit in one trip together to suit everyone.

I had to be transferred back again to the G.U., a complication that the M.O.W.T. dealt with for me; besides that there was nothing for me to do but get ready as soon as I possibly could, and join the others at the lay-by. As far as I remember I had two days to convert myself from a matron to a canal boatwoman. Of course I did it, and this is how I started off on what was to prove one of the nicest trips I ever did. It was the end of April; the weather was getting warm and summerlike, the others were extremely competent, I think we all got on very well together, and I was going back to the familiar G.U. route again. Life looked very pleasant.

There was nobody at home when I arrived at the lay-by and nosed out my new boats, the *Bognor* and the *Dodona*. "All was locked and barred" but I found Elizabeth, who had taken my place on the Oxford pair, and she gave me all the gossip. Finally Margaret turned up with the keys and we got our stuff inside and went off to lunch.

She and I were to share the *Dodona*, to my great delight, being, as I am, a butty "fan." After dinner I took stock of my fourth new home. I am going to describe the *Dodona* at some length because I did three trips on her and came to love her very dearly.

She had belonged to one of the women, who had left after several years' service, and who had done the interior decorations herself. All the bottom part of the paintwork was dark blue; side-bed, drawers, etc., while the rest was white; not cream, as in the other boats, but plain white. It made her look very nautical, and to begin with I found the colour scheme a bit cold but later when I had her to myself and was able to import a good many of my own possessions, she looked ripping. By that time I had had various leaks puttied up and some more shelves put in and she was very comfortable indeed. But she was all right on this first trip, being essentially a dry boat which means much in one's daily life.

Boats vary very much in this respect ; it is something to do with condensation. The *Pavo* was awful; I used to have a steady drip down my neck in the "Blue Grotto," which had nothing to do with whether it was raining or not. The *Dodona* had had a damp course (or whatever the technical term is !) put in, and she was beautifully dry in consequence. The initial drips were only the result of her having been lying up for some weeks and getting too dry. The cabin-tops and sides have to be kept swabbed down every day in the hot weather to prevent the seams opening. You will see the boat people doing this every night as soon as they tie up.

The *Dodona* had a very good stove too; these also vary and some will draw and others will not. Ours was a good drawer and had a steel rail round the top, to prevent the pans slipping off, and a steel hob, all of which had been very well kept. This meant that it was far easier to go on keeping it well and I used to take the emery paper up automatically, whenever I had a spare second, a trick I had learnt from Kit. (I might almost say "picked up," rather than "learnt," because she was never known to sit doing nothing for a single minute. Long after I had left her, and used to go in and visit her, I would find myself reaching for the black-lead brush or the Brasso even while I was being offered tea in one of the best cups as befitted my status as a visitor). It was actually very necessary, too, to keep the steel polished, as the slightest drop of moisture, be it rain or the back-lash from a wet rope, would rust it at once; there were few things that were more depressing than a shower of rain just when we had taken special trouble with the stove, black-lead and all.

There was plenty of room underneath the stove and a big bookcase and the table-top was in good condition; all things that one set great store by.

While I was settling myself in, Kit came tearing down the lay-by on Otto Blink. She was supposed to be unloading at a place she did not know and was asking all the boaters in turn where it was. Opinions seemed to vary but she chose the most prevalent one and after a few words with me, rushed away again to pick up her trainees at the next bridge-hole and conduct them to their destination. When I had got more or less settled, I made myself a cup of tea and then went off to see if I could locate Kit.

I had an awful job finding her; it was a tiny little arm off the cut to Brentford and I passed it several times thinking it could not possibly be right, as it looked too small to take the boats under its low bridge. I eventually scaled a wall and found the boats nestling coyly in the back-water and completely hidden from the main cut. No wonder Kit had not known where it was.

We had a pleasant and reminiscent evening (no doubt I was cleaning the stove throughout); when I went home it had started to pour with rain and that night I slept under a ground-sheet, feeling strongly that there was still room for improvements in the *Dodona*.

The morning brought forth Susan, and an imaginary call to stand-by for a visit from the B.B.C. Imaginary, because nothing came of it but we hung about all morning waiting. As we had no orders we all decided to go up to town in the evening and play according to our taste; the plans finally arranged, we started to tidy ourselves up; just then the orders came through for us to proceed to Brentford, at once, to load aluminium for a short load to the bottom of Marsworth. We set off at 5 on an uneventful run, but it was interesting because I had never been there before.

It was a lovely evening I remember, full of belated sunshine after the rain. On the way down Susan's sister materialised at a lock side and came the rest of the way with us.

The only excitement happened after we had arrived. We were winding, and the stern of the motor was nice and close to what the boaters call a "wire 'ole," or weir, when the engine got stuck in reverse, which was rather alarming. Closer and closer we got, with Susan still trying to get it back into ahead but it was no use and just before we plunged to a watery grave she had to stop the engine altogether. We were, luckily, close enough to the wharfside to be able to jump off and get the boat under control with a cotton-line and one of the many boaters, who had watched the scene with deepest interest, came and fixed the gear for us.

We had to go down below the lock to load, so we were bright and early in the morning and had the boats ready for loading by 8 but as so often proved the case, nothing happened till 9.30. Any men who had anything to do with loading or unloading seemed to spend their entire time having a meal of some kind. It was not only maddening; it used to make me wonder why all these innumerable breaks were allowed to take place if we were really fighting the war as whole-heartedly as was given out.

By the time we were finished loading and had sheeted up we were all three starving; the larder producing nothing, we sallied forth into Brentford to find food, landing up after a long search at the British Restaurant from which we emerged, pleasantly full, into a blinding snow and sleet storm. The English weather is delightfully versatile.

It was bitterly cold again and I think we were all glad of the exercise provided by the locks on the way back to the Bridge. It froze hard in the night and we let go in the morning to a white world again: but at least there was a sun to cheer us up.

A day of perfect organisation, that was. When we got to Cowley I telephoned to a young relative and arranged for her to meet us at a more or less specified time at Croxley Green, where there is an Underground station very close to the lock. I had small hopes that she would arrive but behold, I met her quite happily as I cycled down the towpath, having constituted myself lock-wheeler for that express purpose. We had a magnificent tied-up, cooked Sunday dinner that day for which Margaret was responsible. Roast, two vegetables, and lemon pancakes: all cooked as we went along, be it remembered.

We got to the Fishery in time to put my visitor on to a good train back to town and ourselves went and had a drink before bed. Alas, no baths as it was Sunday. It was another lovely evening and much warmer.

We allowed ourselves a little respite in the morning as we hadn't far to go, and did not start before 8.15, getting to the bottom of Marsworth by tea-time. The men must have had theirs because for a miracle they started to unload us at once but had not time for more than half the butty before they knocked off.

Next day they were a man short and, as she had nothing much else to do, Margaret offered to help by slipping the crane slings under the aluminium; she was surprised and gratified to be paid 4s. 10d. for this service in place of the missing man. We got away at noon, but nine locks farther on we had an accident which held us up for a couple of days.

Coming out of the lock too much to one side, I felt the motor hit something under water, and the engine cut out. We pulled the floorboards up and discovered what we had feared, a coupling had smashed. I think it was a big boulder I had hit but never found out for sure.

This was absolutely sickening; it wasn't a job we could do ourselves as we were not allowed to carry even the smallest spare parts; why this was so I could never make out. It meant phoning for a fitter. Susan came back to say that all the men at Tring were away ill and we should have to wait till the Bridge could send someone up. Acute depression set in and, not feeling myself to be very popular, I volunteered to bike into Leighton and collect some food. I am very glad I did; next door to the butcher that we usually patronised in Leighton there is a junk shop and, as I turned away from the butcher's front door, my eye was caught by a lovely brass cooking pot hanging in the window . . . the only snag being that the shop was shut.

I rushed back into the butcher's and told a piteous tale about not being able to come back again which so upset them that they very kindly told me where the proprietress lived, and I went off to dig her out. The only person I could find was her daughter-in-law who "didn't know anything about the shop."

By now I was determined to have the bowl. I told the wilting daughter-in-law that the price was on the label; as the butcher had the keys of the shop, could he not get it out of the window for me and I would pay him? It worked; she gave me her blessing and I rushed back to the shop again, terrified that they would be shut by this time. But it was all right. They were only just putting the shutters up and I cycled back to the boats with my beautiful bowl.

Its inauguration nearly killed the others. Susan, because she adores brass and copper, and Margaret because she did nothing but hit her head on it where I had hung it on a hook in the cabin.

I am sure they both felt, too, that it was most unfair that I should commit a crime that slowed the whole trip up and win a prize for it. But they were far too pleasant to say anything about this.

Next day we hung about till we were nearly in despair but no fitter appeared, so Margaret and I went off to Leighton to the pictures; on the way I called at the boat-yard and ordered a miniature water-can to be painted for me, and also told Frank that I would like the background of my dipper, which he had not yet started, to be dark blue to match the *Dodona*. Need I add that when we got back we found the fitter had been, and mended us?

There didn't seem to be anything to stop us now and we got going early next morning. That is to say we got up early, because, after breakfast when it came to starting the engine, we couldn't make her move at all. We took it in turns, we worked in different pairs swinging all the time, we rested, we tried again; nothing was the slightest use.

You are really up against it with these C.I. engines. There is not the same variety of things to try that there is with a car . . . unless you know all about them which we hadn't the time to learn. You cannot clean plugs or flood carburetters or jiggle about with the choke as you can in a car. You just have to go on swinging and swinging, till you are very nearly dead. (The engine is fifty times heavier to swing too; just after I came off the cut for good I had occasion one day to swing our little Standard at home and, without thinking, I put all I had got into it with the result that she very nearly left the ground altogether in front! That is only a very slight exaggeration, but it does give a very vivid example of what I mean about the difference between the two types of engine.)

Well, there we were, worn out with swinging and not a cough could we get out of the *Bognor*. Two pairs of boats came through the lock and both the steerers came and put all their masculine beef into the job, and *still* she wouldn't start.

For two and a half hours we went on trying before we gave the engine best; then Susan phoned the fitter again, but this time Tring produced a man, who arrived very soon. I rejoice to record that *he* couldn't do anything with it either; it was not till he was reduced to using a strictly forbidden trick which we didn't know about, that she at last came to life.

Result: instead of starting at 7, as we had planned, it was 11

before we got away. "Lovely lazy life," people say. Yes, so it
is . . . at the wrong moments.

We worked hard all day to make up and did a pretty good run,
getting to the bottom of Stoke by the evening; within easy reach
of Hawkesbury for the next day. We were unloaded, of course,
and that does make a huge difference. It only takes two people to
run the boats empty, one to steer and one to lock-wheel so that
the third is resting and that, worked in turns, saves energy quite
a bit. Not that the "resting" one is having a nap with her feet
up; far from it. She is cooking, producing endless cups of tea
for the "workers," and doing a general tidy-up in the cabins.
And of course she has her part to play in every lock.

I have said very little about the business of working through
locks because it is rather technical. But it is in locks that the
teamwork of the crew (or the lack of it) becomes apparent. If
each person knows exactly what she has to do the pair of them
will always be in the right place at the right moment and so not
a second is wasted. (I am assuming that the third member of the
party is ahead lock-wheeling.) Perhaps a page from "The Book"
will give some idea of it all.

WORK IN DOWN-HILL LOCKS

MOTOR

Shut gate and drop paddle.
Go to draw.
Stand on bottom gates in
   centre.
Kick open butty gate.
Push open motor gate.
Run back and jump down on
   motor cabin-top.

BUTTY

Take out tiller handle.
Jump off with strap.
Check on stump.
Lift strap over gate.
Shut gate and drop paddles.
Draw bottom paddle.
Put on thumb string.
Replace strap on cabin-top.
Go on motor and, after sill is visible,
   take boats back.
Go back to butty and tighten thumb
   string.
Back to motor and put her in gear as
   gate opens.
Accelerate when gate is open.
Back to butty and loose off thumb string
   as towing-rope is picked up.
Replace tiller handle.

I have put it in two parallel columns to show that
both lots of work are going on simultaneously. It will also be
seen that the butty steerer has much the bigger job but even so

she very often found a moment to rush below and have a look at her cooking or to see if the kettle was boiling over. And "The Book" makes no mention of refilling water cans or wringing a couple of lettuces out of the lock-keeper or, worst of all, in the summer evenings, removing the interested public from the gates and paddles before you could get the work done.

Going into up-hill locks the butty person has to jump off *with* the checking strap and run up a small flight of steps provided in the wall of the lock, flicking the strap over the balance beam as she goes, so that it is quite clear of any obstruction when she checks. This was the moment the Great British Public loved to choose to hang over the balance beam in a row, watching the butty come into the lock below them. The rather rushed butty person, to put it mildly, would be aware of the row of heads above her as she jumped for the steps, and wonder how on earth she was going to get along the gate in time to check the butty from crashing the top-gates. This used to get me down to such an extent that I finally evolved a line that worked miracles. As I jumped I used to roar in stentorian tones: "IF YOU DON'T MOVE YOU'LL ALL GET YOUR HEADS CUT OFF WITH THE ROPE!" It was very gratifying to observe the speed with which they shifted, leaving the gate clear for me.

The next day is engraved on my memory, and for a wonder not because of disaster but because of success. From the bottom of the three locks at Hillmorton there is a four hours' flat run to Hawkesbury and on this particular day we had a pair of boaters' boats on our tails the whole way. Susan was on the motor nearly the whole time. She was an excellent steerer in a crisis like this because she takes more risks than anyone I know but *always* gets away with it. Margaret and I were on the butty, steering her that day, because it does save a little time in whipping round corners if the butty is coming along at the right angle instead of having to be dragged round.

The other pair never got close enough for us to have to offer to let them through but they were uncomfortably close for all that and we fairly batted down the cut, losing them round a corner, only to see them reappear before we had got round the next one. I shall never forget our feelings when we suddenly heard our motor slow down at a most critical moment and discovered that Susan was pointing with compassion to a brood of baby ducklings which she thought would have got swamped by our wash if we had gone by at full lick !

We won the race and had managed to tie up, stop the engine and arrange ourselves lollingly against the cabin side by the time Jack turned the corner and saw us. We all had a drink in the shop-cum-pub to celebrate.

Margaret possessed a wireless which was very lucky indeed; the date was 5th May, 1945.

We spent most of that day listening in whenever we could, which was fairly often because there was nothing to do but move round to the Newdigate arm. Our orders were for Hayes cocoa again, but when we got to Sutton Stop we found a mass of boats waiting to load and were told we hadn't a hope before Tuesday; it was then Saturday. We held a council together and it was decided that the other two would stay where they were and I would go home for the week-end. As soon as V-day was declared we knew we should have two days' holiday; everything on the cut was shutting down and even if we had wanted to go on working we could not have done so.

On Monday, 7th May, I was due to go back, and spent an agonising day waiting for the news to break so that I need not go. Not that I didn't want to go back to the boats; merely that I could think of nothing worse than having to spend two days' holiday, and such a holiday, down the Newdigate arm, which is scarcely more than a ditch, narrow and malodorous, with coal and cinders on the one hand, and rats in the muddy bank on the other. Nor did I think that I really wanted to be in Coventry either; on an occasion like that your instinct is to be amongst friends with whom you have shared the bad times, and to celebrate the peace together.

Although the evening papers were full of headlines there was still nothing definite by the time I was due at Euston for the 4.25 and I trailed miserably through the station to find my train. Suddenly the loudspeaker said in imperious accents: "Here is an important announcement !"

Everybody in the whole station stopped dead as if instantaneously petrified. The voice went on:

"The 4.9 for Northampton will leave from Platform 6 and NOT from Platform 7 as stated on the indicator."

There was—or it felt as if there was—a sort of howl of fury from everyone on the station, including myself; deliverance

F

had really seemed to be at hand and now there was nothing for
it but to go back to Coventry, which I duly did. When I got
back to where I had left the boats there wasn't a sign of them,
but an obliging boater next door said they had moved round to
Hawkesbury, "loaded you this morning, they did." This meant
a walk of half a mile down the towpath carrying my bag and
wearing a very uncomfortable pair of heavy boots that my
husband had had in the Home Guard. It was also boiling hot.

When I got to Hawkesbury, passing a bean-field in full bloom
on the way which partially restored me, the others took one look
at my draggled form and said in chorus: "Whatever HAVE
you come back for? Don't you know the war's nearly over and
it will be V-day tomorrow?" I could cheerfully have bitten
them both.

Instead we all had supper and planned what to do if and when
the news came through. Susan did not much mind; Margaret
was determined to go to London; I was determined not to stay
where I was. We were the only women's boats tied up there so
we could do what we liked without having to find out what
other people wanted to do.

By the time the news did come through, the wireless battery
had practically run down which lent a nightmare quality to
everything. We only dared to turn it on for a second at a time,
judge by the tone of the voice what the news was, and hastily
switch it off again.

We still hadn't decided anything; Margaret was more than ever
determined to go to London, hitch-hiking in all probability, or
failing that she had an urge to get into the middle of a large crowd
and dance, in the streets for choice. Susan and I begged her to
go, and have a lovely time. The only thing quite certain was that
we did not want to be there too.

In the morning I had a brainwave and suggested that we should
all hitch-hike to Stratford-on-Avon and spend our two days
there. It took a little while to woo Margaret away from her
dancing idea but she finally decided that she would come too.
We put everything we could into the cabins, asked a boater
friend to keep an eye on the rest for us, locked up and set off
with enough food to keep us from starvation if we could not
get anything else.

The thing of most importance now was to get to Stratford in
time to hear Mr. Churchill's broadcast at 3 o'clock. We only

just did it. First there was a walk of a mile or more to the main Coventry road. Then we found there were no buses and had to wait some minutes before we found a car which answered our flagging. He took us to the outskirts of Coventry and almost at once we found another lift to Kenilworth. There our luck changed and we waited for what seemed hours till a large lorry came by. To our joy they were N.F.S. men who were going right to Stratford; we piled into the back and covered the remaining distance at breakneck speed, rattling about in the back of the lorry, with nothing to hold on to, like peas in a pod. But no one minded.

We really had a wonderful two days there. Margaret did not get her dancing I am afraid, but there were other compensations and I do not think she regretted it. We found a bed for the night (a real bed) with one of the theatre staff and his wife, old friends of mine; we went to the theatre twice; we took our lunch on the river next day and ate it lazily, tied up under a tree beside the buttercup fields; and we listened to the King's speech, relayed through the theatre during the evening performance. We did the sights of Stratford (with me as a sort of Cook's man, for the second time), and we ate a great many ices and behaved altogether exactly like trippers and found it very enjoyable. We hitch-hiked back again on the second night, equally successfully, and were ready to start work again early on the Thursday morning.

The weather was simply heavenly as everyone will remember. It was hotter than I had known it since I had been on the cut; long days of sun and blue sky and enough breeze as we went along to keep us from feeling stifled; the fields were sheets of gold buttercups and pink clover, the cattle gathered in the shadows of the trees with swishing tails, or coming down to the edge of the water to drink as we came by. There were many young, leggy foals in the fields who would look at us with great surprise and then toss up their heels and race off to their mothers when we got too near them. Sometimes we would come up with a family of swans, mother and father in front, with the babies in an agitated line behind them; but best of all were the moorhen chicks, scuttling in and out of the reeds like tiny jet-black snowballs at the approach of our noisy engine.

One of the things that used to fascinate me most was seeing all the little gardens, up and down the cut, changing with the seasons.

One got to know the route very well and I would look forward to what I knew lay round the next corner, wondering what they had decided to put in the spring beds and what they would presently bed out for full summer. When I started everything had been asters, chrysanthemums, and Michaelmas daisies; after that the gardens had been dug and the plants lifted and stored, or cut down for the winter that presently laid its white blanket of snow over everything. With the trees bare one could see the houses themselves and wonder who were the people who lived in them and what they thought of the constant traffic of the boats. With the snow came snow-men, and I used to see them and be glad that I knew now which houses had children in them.

Then the bulbs; daffodils and crocus and narcissi; hyacinths and jonquils and tulips, leading into the spring flowers and renewed activity in every garden. Polyanthus and anemones and forget-me-nots and lilac, giving way to the showy laburnum, red may, scarlet poppies and lupins of every colour under the sun. In the evenings one could watch the owners digging, raking, hoeing; making seed-beds, sowing, watering, thinning out, tying up the climbing plants, pruning rose bushes, nailing up the ramblers till at last they would be sitting there in their deck-chairs with the garden in full bloom all round them. It made a lovely pattern through the year, as far removed from war or thoughts of violence as one could conceive.

The cut itself changed very much. Now in May the hedges were white and the air heavy with the scent of hawthorn; in the reeds at the water's edge tall yellow flags appeared and tiny water forget-me-nots; water lilies opened their saffron flowers to the sun and the grass grew tall on the towpath.

I was in shorts by now; the wood of the boat used to feel hot against my bare legs as I steered and the small hairs on my arms were turning white against the brown of my skin. Sometimes when I got ahead lock-wheeling I would take off my heavy boots and socks and dabble my feet in the water. We were working twelve and thirteen hours a day now that the evenings were longer, and we were all getting more like gipsies every day. My muscles were colossal by now and I was ashamed of myself in the holidays. I had to let out all the sleeves of my dresses to get my bulging biceps through. In spite of the hard work I had put on two stone since I started in October, had a huge appetite and had never felt fitter in my life.

When we arrived at Broadwater (Berkhamsted) on the way back, we were locked up with several other pairs including Daphne who was coming up. From her we found out that Kit was farther down, at the Fishery, with two of her old trainees, no new ones having been forthcoming. One of these was supposed to be making the third with Susan and me at the end of our present trip, so it looked as though we should have a longish wait for her to get back. In addition, the other one was supposed to be going on Margaret's new boats, to work for Barlow. Another wait there. I had a bright idea and as soon as we had tidied up the boats I got on to the bike and went off to find Kit.

When I arrived at the Fishery I found her in bed and on the verge of sleep although it was only about nine-thirty. With some difficulty I managed to convey, through the mists, that it would be a good plan if Rene and I did a swap in mid-stream when we met next day, I to go on up again with Kit and Iris, who was going to be my colleague on Susan's boats later, and Rene to go back with Margaret who would then not have to wait for her. I was sorry not to be finishing the trip with Susan and Margaret but I did not want to hang about and waste my limited time when I might be working.

All this complicated reasoning was too much for Kit who was fighting a losing battle with sleep; she asked me to find out if this fitted in with Daphne's plans; if it did that was O.K. by her. After saying which, she slept. Knowing my Kit, I wasted no more time but biked back to my own boats where I found the entire party having supper in the cabin of the *Dodona*. I was famished and very tired by now; over supper I expounded the plan to Daphne who thought it a good one as it would save wastage of labour which was the great thing. And so it was settled.

When the party had removed itself from the cabin I had to think a bit about packing, though I needed only to take the bare necessities; the rest could stay in the butty and wait for me on my next trip. I was already very nearly asleep but Margaret and I went on talking for hours, I cannot imagine why.

The two pairs in front delayed us a bit in the morning, which gave me time to pull myself together and I was all ready by the time we met Kit, just above Top Side. I was going to be in the motor with Iris so, when we met, we tied the stern of the *Dodona* to the stern of Kit's motor and effected the swap with the very minimum of delay and excitement. I don't suppose it took more than three minutes for Rene and I to change homes. There is much to be said for a kit-bag as an article of luggage.

Dodona and *Battersea* waved a lingering farewell to each other, and I turned and headed for the lock I had only left ten minutes before. Several lock-keepers that day looked as though they thought they were seeing things when I reappeared working the locks in the opposite direction to the day before. They always note subconsciously, if not actually on paper, who is going where and passing when, and their faces were so really funny when they saw me that I had to put them out of their misery by explaining.

We tied up at Leighton that night and went to the nearest pub in celebration of my birthday which I had forgotten till the evening!

We set off in spanking style next day and had a very good run to the bottom of Stoke Bruern, where two blows befell us with lightning rapidity. Kit was ahead lock-wheeling and Iris and I were conducting the boats very happily up the first two locks, when she managed to let go her windlass while she was drawing the side-ponds and the next thing I knew was that a bright-green Iris was holding a hand which looked as though it had been bitten by a puff-adder. The handle of the windlass must have hit the back of her hand half a dozen times before she could move away. It hurts like the very devil when this happens, and you are lucky if you get away with no bones broken.

I finished drawing for her, of course, and we moved rather slowly out of the lock, as Iris had only one hand she could use and was still very shaky.

When we got to the next lock Kit came to me and said there was a message for me to ring up my home, which I could fortunately do from the lock-keeper's little hut. The result of this phone call was that I should have to go home as soon as possible and leave the others to get on as best they could, and Iris with only one hand. I began to wonder if my bright idea had been as bright as I thought.

There was no possible means of getting to anywhere from where we were then so Kit arranged to go on as far as Gayton Arm End which is close to the station of Blisworth. From there I could get a fast train in the morning and be home by lunch-time. There was no desperate hurry now; it was too late for me to do anything. Kit gave me a wonderful breakfast in the butty next morning and I caught the 8.15 to London.

I was away a week and then rejoined the boats at Tyseley. It was Whitsun week-end and there was a lock-up so no one was able to move. The public holidays are used to carry out repairs on the locks; in this particular case they were putting a new gate in at Knowle, not before it was needed I might add. Only one gate at this particular lock had been capable of being opened; the other was permanently shut and it meant a lot of manœuvring to get the boats in.

When the message came through that Knowle was in working order again, all the boats started off together in a long brightly painted line. We hung about a bit and left at tea-time; when we got within sight of the top lock there were still a lot of pairs waiting to get down.

Kit decided to breast-up in the bridge-hole, about fifty yards before the lock. (It is much easier to control the boats, when you are waiting, if they are in one unit.) Unfortunately this was one of the very few bridge-holes on the entire canal where there is not room for two boats to pass. It was just sheer bad luck that none of us knew this; we might so easily have tried to meet other boats, at some former time, and learnt the lesson that way, but none of us had, so on we careered, full tilt, to our doom.

The motor was ahead, of course, and in came the butty beside her, perfect breasting-up but also perfect demonstration of jamming. Those two boats were fixed in between the two walls of the arch tighter than any cork in any bottle. It took a little time for the seriousness of the situation to sink in. After we had tried to back the butty and then to move the motor forward without the slightest effect, we stopped and thought again.

The next step was to take the iron bars, which we always carried for tying up, and try to prise the boats apart with leverage. Kit was particularly good and efficient at this form of sport and it usually worked, but not today. Then we tried a complicated system of lines and pulley blocks, using the wedged butty as a lever to move the motor. This also was a flop. Most of our endeavours were taking place under the interested eye of the assembled boats, the owners giving every sort of conflicting advice. They even came and pulled.

Eventually a boy on a pair of "Josser" boats, I think it was, announced that the only thing to do was to "give us a bang."

So saying he loosed off his butty and came backwards towards us. When he had got into a good position he revved up his engine as hard as he could and gave our motor a fearful welt on the nose with his stern. The fenders on both boats saved them from damage and the "Josser" was proved right. With a protesting creak the motor was driven backwards out of her death-grapple and we found that both our boats were free.

This little entertainment had taken upwards of an hour, during which time we had all snatched supper; when we got to the bottom of the five locks, in our turn, we only went on as far as "The Black Boy," a minute pub with a profusion of bachelor's buttons in its front garden. I had often before wanted to tie up here, it always looked so pretty, but the chance had never occurred. We went and bought very excellent cider and drank it on benches in the garden, the daisies at our feet, the water and fields of clover and sorrel lighted by the setting sun, spread before us. Complete peace after the day's work.

We had a very good run next day; it measures about twenty-seven miles on the map, not counting the bends, and must be more in fact; there are forty-six locks in this stretch from Knowle to Knapton, where we tied up after a twelve-hour day. It was a new tie up which Kit wanted to try, one of the boaters having told her about it. I am bitterly regretful that I never had a chance to do it again; it was simply lovely.

There is a short piece of straight cut just before the island at Knapton; on either side a grass verge separates the water from the thick hawthorn hedge, but on the side where we were the ground falls away, so that there is a beautiful view of the distant fields and hills over the hedge; like the previous night the whole landscape was gilded by the evening sun.

It was obviously too lovely to be inside on such a night and we took our supper out of the cabin and ate it sitting on the grass. It was a perfect evening, warm, windless and utterly peaceful; the grass was cool to our tired legs, there was no sign of any other living thing except the gentle cows in the field and the birds twittering in the trees; I have never tasted a supper so good as mine that night.

By the end of it we all felt as fresh as paint again; this was just as well in view of what happened. After supper Kit and I set out to view the ruined church that we had so many times seen as we passed by, and only now had a chance to look at. It lay two or three fields away and had always looked as though it would repay a visit; and so indeed it did.

The first thing we discovered when we got close, was that it was not ruined as we had supposed but it was locked up. We peered through the windows which were very dirty so that the view was not good, but what we saw made us long for more. The walls inside were covered in a pale terra cotta wash, most unusual for England. We went to the nearest cottage and asked for the keys.

Inside it was better than we had thought. The church was nearly empty and was obviously not in use. I don't remember any stained glass at all, and certainly no sign of any draperies, curtains or frontal which only too often make hideous what they set out to beautify. Everything was dusty, cobwebby and practically without colour but for the pale warmth of the walls, against which cream stone and bleached woodwork uttered the fittingness of their simplicity, unsmothered by the conventional church furnishings.

We penetrated up into the tower where Kit found a bell which caused her great excitement, mixed with disappointment that she had nothing whatever with her with which to take a rubbing. (I believe she went back on a later trip and got one.) When we had exhausted the possibilities of the church, we took the keys back and asked the man to whom we gave them something about its history.

It was, he said, the parish church of Flecknoe and although never used now it was still the mother church of the locality and a new incumbent was forced to have his induction there. This amused me, when I visualised all the *hoi polloi* of the neighbourhood picking their way through the fields to church; there was no sign of a road and hardly a track for the farm carts. I think that is one of the greatest charms of Flecknoe church, its situation right in the middle of the open fields with only a couple of cottages to keep it company.

While returning the keys Kit had spotted what she thought was the remains of the old Grand Junction Canal which existed before the G.U. joined several companies together and built a new one. It was nothing but a depression in the ground but the way it wound from side made us quite sure that it had been a canal at one time. We started off to trace it to its union with the cut we knew, at Nurser's yard.

F*

Sometimes it was as clear as if it had been still filled with water, at others we could scarcely make out where it went next; the fever of the chase was on us by now and on we went, regardless of the time. At one moment we scaled a high bank and crossed the main railway in an effort to see farther off; this succeeded and we were hot on the trail again, but by now it had become a point of honour to walk every inch of the way beside the cut, even if it swept away to right or left for half a mile and returned to within a few yards of where we were standing . . . we were quite mad.

Well, we did it and very interesting it was. I should think we must have walked about four miles before we came to Nurser's yard and our hunt was over. From there it took us perhaps five minutes to walk round the corner to where our boats lay. What an enormous saving of time the new cut had effected; at least an hour for every pair of boats both up to Birmingham and back. The moon was out when we got home and my watch said eleven o'clock before I blew out my candle. And this on top of a twelve-hour day !

One point I would like to make and this seems a suitable place to do it. Whether a day seemed long or not was not really a matter of hours spent in working; rather it depended on whether the work had gone easily and well, or if it had been one long fight from start to finish . . . every lock to get ready, hanging about for others to come through first, being chased all day, meeting boats in awkward bridge-holes, snapping ropes . . . all these things made one feel tired and sick of the day far sooner than twelve hours spent working steadily and well, without undue haste but never losing a moment needlessly. I suppose this is the same with any job, but it perhaps does not mean quite so much in efficiency, in a job where the hours are set. When we had a good day we felt capable of going on and on, and the only things to stop us doing so were if the light went, in the autumn and winter, or if we were "locked-up."

This would happen when there had been enough water drained from the summit level; the lock was then padlocked and the water would be pumped back again. Some locks always locked at seven at night. If you could clear one that you knew did this, before seven, you might have three hours more work ahead of you. In the summer when the water was low the locks were known to shut as early as three in the afternoon.

As an example of what I have just said about good and bad

days I remember one day when we started (I don't mean "got up" but actually let go) at seven and tied up at eleven; on another we started at five and tied up at nine. The working time was the same in each case, seventeen hours, but the first day was absolute misery from start to finish, while the second one (though I admit I was glad to sit down at the end of it) was quite easy in comparison. On both these days we were two-handed, Susan and I, without a third to lock-wheel for us, so that it was really working all the time without a break.

When we got our orders at Hawkesbury we found we were due to go for loading to Griff Colliery, about six miles north of Coventry. It was renowned for having one of the lowest bridge-holes on the cut; before we started we took down the cratch of the motor completely, but left the butty cratch and hoped we should be all right. This may sound very peculiar to take one down and leave the other up but there is a reason for it. The weight of the engine in the motor causes her stern to be much lower in the water than the butty stern and correspondingly the bows are much higher; it was more than likely that the butty would go through, cratch and all, because she rode level in the water; we were too optimistic about this as it turned out but it was worth risking, as taking down a cratch and putting it up again is a very lengthy job; the sheets are nailed in position and the nails have to be prised out and the sheets removed before you can get at the wooden structure underneath.

The first bit of the journey is really the "bottom road" in reverse; after five miles there is a sharp left-hand turn under a very low bridge into the smaller arm of water. Ah! thought I, this is it, we shall *just* do it; thank goodness we didn't bother with the butty cratch. (Kit was ahead on the motor, so I could not ask her.) We now wound down the narrowest little water-way I had yet been on; the butty seemed almost to touch the banks on either side and the whole stretch was densely wooded which made it seem smaller and narrower still. The trees met over our heads and the sunlight came through in spots and patches of light amidst the pale greenness of the "tunnel." The boats seemed much too big and I remember I felt as though we were trespassing there with our great panting engine. A more perfect Lover's Lane it would be impossible to imagine.

After much too short an interval of this idyll another bridge loomed ahead. That it was a bridge was obvious because we could see a boy on a bicycle crossing it, but it certainly did not look like one otherwise. It looked, from the cut, exactly like a large drain hole and to imagine the boats would go through it seemed quite fantastic. I had been wrong before, then; clearly this was the famous Griff bridge. Kit slowed the engine down completely before she got to it and we moved almost imperceptibly down the water towards this absurd little half-circle of brickwork which blocked our way. I think if I had stood on the cabin top I could have pulled myself on to the road, it was so low.

Very slowly indeed Kit steered the motor into the arch; it was at once plain that the butty cratch would have to come down if I was to follow her. With the motor right in the bridge-hole so that she could come to no harm, Kit stopped her moving altogether by the simple expedient of putting her hands on the bridge coping above her head and thus applying the brakes; then she came back on to the butty armed to the teeth with hammers and pincers and we all got to work.

"You'll have to take everything off the cabin top," said Kit when we had done the cratch, "and you'll probably have to take the tiller out as well and steer with your hands on the walls. And for goodness' sake crouch down and don't get your head knocked off!"

The whole thing was just like a dream in its unreality. I was irresistibly reminded of poor Alice looking hopelessly through the tiny little door into the wonderful garden beyond and wishing the White Rabbit was there to help her get through. It seemed equally hopeless for us to imagine that we could ever conduct our enormous boats through this miniature archway; even with the cratches down they still blocked up the entire entrance so that nothing whatever could be seen of the cut the other side.

Kit could not get back on to the motor by the usual passage but had to wriggle off the butty fore-end . . . which was still clear of the bridge . . . on to the broken kerb at the water's edge and so to her counter again. Very slowly she accelerated and I whipped everything off the cabin top, making a fine clutter in the hatches. The cabin was now the highest part of the boat; down came the chimney, the water can, mop, windlass, even the spare straps that were lying up there and finally the tiller came out and was parked in the cabin. And then I crouched; sitting on my heels in the hatches I pushed on the walls first one side and then the other to save the butty from rubbing, and so we got through and the dream faded into reality.

It was a fantastic experience to go under that tiny bridge, and one that will soon be a memory only; the lowness is caused by subsidence and very shortly something will have to be done about it and this extraordinary freak will have to go. In spite of the labour involved in taking down cratches it will be a pity; it is very picturesque with the ferns growing round the entrance and the wet walls trickling inside, cool and grotto-like.

Coming back loaded we were perfectly all right, of course; the weight of the cargo kept us down in the water so that the trouble did not arise.

Nothing of outstanding interest happened on the way home. I had some tiddlers in a jam-jar on the cabin roof and spent my whole life upsetting them and scooping the gasping survivors back into the jar again, to the disgust of my co-steerers; Iris bought a puppy at Finney, a not altogether wise move as he *had* to be tied up most of the day to survive at all and took a very dim view of it. Also he was in no way house-trained and made the cabin a doubtful haven at the end of the day; my tiddlers were far less trouble than their cabin-top companion. I merited, endured and survived a searing frontal attack from Kit on the subject of my "boatmanship" which was as unexpected as it was warranted. And lastly and most exciting of all, I collected my little painted can from Frank at Leighton. It was, and is, a little pet, most beautifully decorated with bands of roses, and multi-coloured stripes on its minute spout. It will be a real tragedy if this "boat painting" is allowed to die out; it is a most delightful craft and I think it is a pity it cannot be extended to other professions. How much mellower the Civil Servant might become if his dreary office could be embellished with a traditional design of fluttering forms and red tape. . . .

At Alperton where we unloaded there was a pair of boats tied just ahead of us with a small boy of six and a tiny baby; this baby was causing his mother a lot of worry and when we arrived "Kitty" was asked if she would mind going and having a look at him. Kit asked me to go, too, as I might be expected to know something about babies. *Anyone* could have told that the baby was desperately ill, I think. I have never seen one who looked so alarming. He was about ten months old, an age when a baby takes a keen interest in his surroundings, yet that baby's face registered absolutely nothing when we tried to attract his attention; he could barely hold his head up and, though he was a finely made little chap, his skin was clay-coloured. His mother said that he could keep nothing down and had not had a proper feed for several days; they had taken him to a doctor farther up the cut but had not been able to tie up and let the doctor go on attending him, with the result that the medicine provided had done no good; they had got down to Alperton as quickly as they could to find more advice, with the baby growing weaker all the time.

It sounded to me like gastro-enteritis and I knew that he should see a good doctor without a moment's delay; to contemplate the family going on working with the child in that condition would be madness and could only have one ending. Clearly they wanted immediate help and moral support, which Kit at once provided. In less time than it takes to tell, she, the mother and the baby had departed in search of a doctor's surgery (it was half-past eight in the morning) and Iris and I were left in charge of the boats to deal with the unloading.

In this we had the help of the baby's father, an example of the natural good manners of the boat people. Without a word being said or fuss of any kind, Mr. "Peaselum" came and worked on our boats with us as if they were his own, heaving the heavy planks about, shovelling the coal into the grab and tidying us up when we were empty; taking the place of our steerer, who was helping his wife. They were not back by dinner-time and Mr. Peaselum's face was getting more and more drawn with anxiety, so Iris and I organised mugs of cocoa and slabs of bread and treacle all round to cheer the party up a bit. I am afraid this had more effect on the small boy than on his father, who kept saying in sepulchral tones that he "knewed the child 'ad the mark of death on 'im, three days ago."

Poor chap ! he adored his baby and would obviously have gone through fire and water to do him any good; this is where the real curse of illiteracy becomes apparent. He was up against something unknown and had not the faintest idea how to proceed in the face of such a disaster. He only knew the cut; the ways of land dwellers were a closed book and to go to a hospital and demand treatment for the child was quite beyond his comprehension. All that he could understand was that he had to go on working without interruption; he could not possibly think clearly enough to know that this was a moment when nothing on earth mattered in comparison with the child's life.

While we were waiting for the party to get back I had a conversation with the small boy that went something like this :

ME: "How old are you ?"

S.B. : "I'm gonna be seven."

ME: "That's the same age as my little boy. What's your name ?"

S.B.: " Mauricewilliampeaselum."

ME (stunned, but persevering): "*What* a long name ! Do you go to school, Maurice ?"

M.W.P.: "Naow !"

ME: "Why not ?" (I knew that there were schools provided at various points which the children can attend spasmodically, but took "naow" to mean that Maurice did not go even to them.)

M.W.P.: "Don' like school."

ME: "I don't think anyone does very much but it's rather nice to be able to read, don't you think ?"

M.W.P.: "Dunno. *You* can't read ?"

ME: "Yes, I can. You see I went to school although I didn't like it much."

M.W.P. (in a *very* different tone of voice): "Go on ! You *can't* ! Can your mate read ?"

ME: "Yes; she went to school, too."

M.W.P.: "Well, I can write, then."

ME (slightly dazed): "*Can* you ? What can you write ?" (Exit Maurice William "Peaselum" to his cabin to return with a very dirty envelope on the back of which were a dozen letters of the alphabet, in pencil.)

M.W.P.: "There ! I done all those."

ME: "Jolly good, old chap. Do you know what they all are ?"

M.W.P.: "Naow ! but I can write !"

ME: "Yes, but if you went to school you might find out what they're all called and then you could read as well. Would you like me to write your name for you on this paper ?"

M.W.P.: "Yus, please. My uncle at Leighton, he can write his name."

With some difficulty I then wrote the magic words on his envelope. With difficulty because I was not at all sure how his particular brand of "Maurice" might be spelt and because he was still calling himself "Peaselum." It was not until much later I discovered that their name was Peaseland.

By this time, Maurice was breathing heavily into my ear and his excitement and interest in this superhuman woman was clear. I followed this success up with the name of his butty and his motor, which I wrote first and then bade him compare with the lettering on the side of the boat. Having proved to his satisfaction that I was of unearthly brilliance, we embarked on a list of the names of a string of barges which tactfully chose this moment to come past. He was beside himself with pleasure by now and I was made to write every single word that appeared on the barge sides and on the tug which was pulling them. I pointed out to him that if he learnt to recognise the names I had written down he would be able to know the barges when he next met them, and that was what reading was.

I believe this "reading" lesson could have gone on for hours; he was absolutely fascinated and ready to learn anything I could teach him. What a joy he would have been to an overworked and harassed teacher! On my next trip I found some tiny twopenny books with pictures of everyday things and their names printed clearly beneath, a selection of which I gave to Maurice when next I met him. I said they were for him "because he could nearly read" and he went pink with pleasure at this quite untrue statement.

Kit and Mrs. Peaseland returned after dinner, without the baby. They had been to a local hospital where the authorities were willing to take him, but as Alperton was a hopeless place for the family to be tied up indefinitely, Kit had organised them over to Brentford where the tie up is a recognised one. There the hospital had taken one look at the baby and moved another child out so that he could have a bed. I never got to the bottom of what he was suffering from, but before she left him Mrs. Peaseland had to sign a form saying she was willing for them to operate if necessary. What the poor soul would have done without Kit to see her through this it is hard to imagine. Kit was able to explain to her that it was only a formality, to the hospital almoner that "Mrs. Peaseland, her mark" was all that could be expected, and to arrange for the parents to telephone for news of the baby at special hours and to visit him when allowed, and generally to soothe them down and give them an explanation that they could understand of what was being done for the child, and to reassure them that he would be properly cared for and made well.

I did not hear the happy ending to this story until two trips later when Eli Nixon told me the "Peaselums" were working again and that the baby was all right. A few days after this I met them at the top of Denham lock and yelled to Mrs. "Peaselum" as soon as she was within earshot.

I shall never forget the look she gave me, and what happened next. Without a word she dived into the butty cabin and emerged a second later with Master Geoffrey "Peaselum," fat, bouncing and brown in her arms! He was full of chuckles now and was made to wave to me as we slid past one another. As they disappeared, I saw his mother prop him on the cabin top, tied on to the chimney, where he sat in the sunshine kicking his fat legs and looking the picture of health. I was on other boats by then so I didn't witness the meeting between the "Peaselums" and Kit, but judging by the expression on the mother's face when she saw me (who had done nothing on that awful morning), they were not behind with their gratitude. I am sure that Kit's quick action and help saved that baby at a moment when his grip on life was very feeble indeed.

After unloading we got back to the lay-by the same evening and I moved my stuff into the *Dodona*. Susan was there waiting for me but a fresh complication arose because Iris was due for leave after her two training trips, so rather than wait any more Susan and I decided to do a trip two-handed without her. I spent the night in the *Dodona* and got her straight; then because it was Saturday and we should have no orders before Monday, I went home for the week-end to get cleaned up and collect some personal bits and pieces for the "home beautiful," as Kit used to call it; the first time I had had a boat entirely to myself. It was a positively heavenly thought. . . . I was looking forward immensely to my next trip while I was at home selecting what I should take with me. One of the things I had to bring was my bicycle; *very* much hung about I returned to Southall on Monday morning, bound for the *Dodona* and trip Number Seven.

CHAPTER XIII—TWO-HANDED

ARRIVED at Southall station with two kit-bags, one containing clean clothes and the other household furnishings, plus a bicycle, it became necessary to do a little readjusting. With one kit-bag on the carrier and the other laid across the handle-bars I set forth to cycle to the depot, a thing I should have dreaded to contemplate six months ago. Not for nothing had I been trained on Otto Blink and the switchback towpaths of the Midlands; with ease and confidence I threaded myself and my bulky belongings through the maze of Southall traffic and arrived at the Bridge.

Here I found Susan already busy; she was, in fact, sheeting-in my butty back-end for me, a necessary job but one which I had expected to have to do for myself. We spent a delightful day getting straight; for me this meant putting into practice all the things I had spent the week-end planning, always a pleasant pastime. One of the things that I enjoyed doing most was fixing brass knobs and catches on to all my cupboard doors; the difference this made to the cabin was quite remarkable. I had brought some more cushions from home and during the day-time they lay on the side-bed and helped to "dress" the cabin; at night the top one had a pillow-case put on and the others went underneath.

My brass bowl was shining beautifully by now and I used to have that on the side-bed too, right down at the far end where it didn't get in the way, and I always tried to keep it filled with flowers. This was not hard. It was the beginning of June by now and the wild flowers up the cut were very plentiful. One of the things which always worried me about the cabins was having no pictures; it is nearly impossible to hang anything however small, because the sides slope and there is no space big enough. However, I was lucky in still having some of those wonderful pre-war postcard size reproductions left and I brought a selection with me which, by means of drawing-pins, could be varied as the spirit moved me. I only had two or three up at a time; one that never changed was Lenbach's "Shepherd Boy." He lay in the sunshine with his bare legs and outflung arm, the butterflies and the harebells beside him, over my table-cupboard where I could look at him as I lay in bed.

Susan produced a solid brass rod to hang over my stove, with acorn ends which unscrewed; I hung a curtain a foot deep round the space beneath the stove, which hid the loathsome bucket and added a touch of colour to my blue and white; I arranged my spills in something less hideous than a jam-jar, on the shelf above my pillow, and had my candle in a short silver candlestick. It was all very classy; what was far more important, it was extremely comfortable and workable.

Nearly always the communal cooking used to be done in the butty; partly because you can cook and steer the butty at the same time and partly because it is a bigger cabin to eat the results in. Susan and I decided to stick to this, which really meant that I became responsible for the catering. She used to have her butter and tea ration to herself and look after her own bread so that she was independent at breakfast; for tea-time or supper she would bring her butter into me and we would take it in turns to use the tea but we did not have to argue over this because I much prefer coffee; we lived a sort of "Jack Sprat" existence and it worked very well. Sometimes Susan would do the cooking while I was on the motor, she often helped me to do potatoes and we always washed up together.

There were two wide shelves fixed in the back-end on which to keep the saucepans and the frying-pan, the potatoes and other vegetables and behind the door was a hook for our oilskins. It was lovely to be able to get all these unsightly objects out of the way; and having the door wide open in the hot weather gave me a through draught which was more than welcome; when we were loaded there was a curtain of tarpaulin which could be dropped between the back-end and the cargo, to keep the coal out of the cabin. If it wasn't coal there was no need to bother with the curtain but in either case I did not get so much air when loaded because of the top-sheets over the hold.

Susan and I were delighted to find that we had been paid "waiting money" for the week-end; it was in great good spirits that we let go at six o'clock that night to make an empty run up to Coventry. It did seem very peculiar to be going up unloaded but we were not arguing . . . it meant a far easier run for us with only one boat to steer.

We tied up at Uxbridge at the "Swan and Bottle," only two hours from the lay-by but it was late enough and besides, the "Swan" keeps excellent cider and, usually, potato crisps.

After pub and supper we did a little gentle splicing in the hold, and were presently joined by one of the boaters, Jack Kent by name, and somehow the conversation turned to Turk's heads and Jack offered to show us how to do one. We had longed to be able to number this amongst our accomplishments and watched with bated breath, but alas, Jack only managed to do one. He said it was all a question of how you began, which I could well believe, and it is extraordinary how easy it is to begin wrong. I got a knotting book out of my cabin to try to muddle out the answer, but Jack would have none of it . . . indeed he could not for he couldn't read a line of it and refused to look at the picture ! In the middle of this his missus arrived, and the conversation took a different turn to the question of what it was best to feed babies on. A curious picture we must have presented, Jack seated on one of the beams worrying away at his Turk's head while Mrs. Kent and I leaned on the gunwale together, passionately discussing the rearing of infants, our remarks being interrupted from time to time by bewildered mutterings from Jack about "that there twist which didn't ought to be" and shakings of the head. It was quite dark by now so I am surprised he could even see the twist.

At a later date I got my book and a length of line and taught myself how to do a Turk's head, so that the next time I met the Kents I was able to show Jack how to avoid his "twist"; it was a glorious moment to be able to teach a boater anything. Actually, in this respect, they are quite extraordinary; even if it is something to do with the management of the boats, in which they are the undisputed experts, they will admire and even imitate something which they think is an improvement. I may say the occasions when this happened were rare in the extreme but I can recall one or two, and remember how struck I was by their attitude of being ready to learn. They will tell you they are "still learning" (old men who were born on the boats); it was generally said to comfort us when we were in a bad jam, but it is absolutely true; they *are* still learning, in that their minds are quite open and ready to receive a new method of doing something if they think it is an improvement on their own method.

In order to be near the pub we had left the next length, closer to the lock, free and the Kents had come up and tied there which was an error of judgment for which I was solely responsible. It meant that in the morning we had them immediately ahead of us and a bad road all day. It was not as bad as it might have been, as we were empty and one of us could lock-wheel; we did nineteen locks and then tied up for forty-five minutes to have our dinner. We used to have a sitting-down dinner very often, when we were working two-handed like this; we found that it paid a good dividend in restored strength and an ability to go on longer at night; when we were loaded it was almost essential; otherwise it meant standing for seventeen hours on end.

We got as far as Northchurch that night which was forty-two locks nearer Coventry, but were very much helped on our way by the most enchanting smell of fish at Sweeps 2, which on investigation proved to be the local fish and chips starting up. Need I say that I joined the queue and that the contents of my newspaper parcel were eagerly devoured as we worked up the remaining locks to Northchurch?

The next day will long stay in my memory; it was a treat. We started off all right with a good road up to the Tring summit where we tied up for a second (or so we thought), while I rushed up the garden to deliver a message to my friend who lived there. Unfortunately I found they were away and only one member of the family at home and she, not unnaturally, in bed, it being only eight o'clock in the morning. She must have loathed me, dashing in full of heartiness and fresh air at that hour, dressed in heavy boots and no doubt very far from clean, but she cloaked her feelings admirably and offered me a drink, which I refused, asking instead if I might grab some of the lovely mass of honeysuckle that was growing over the porch.

Thus laden I dashed back to the boats and calamity. I regret to say that owing to us chattering and not paying attention to what we were doing, the next thing we knew was that the motor was climbing the right-hand bank of the cut and tilting to the most appalling angle I ever saw. Why she didn't go right over I cannot to this day imagine. We were absolutely paralysed and simply stood and watched while she went farther and farther over towards the water. I think Susan did just have the strength to ease the motor down; apart from that there didn't seem to be anything to do until she had finished tilting.

We came to and viewed the possibilities. The stern was too far out in the cut for us to be able to get ashore from there so I started off down the top-planks. It will give some faint idea of the angle when I say that I could not *walk* down them but had to crawl on all fours. I took the long shaft with me and with all the strength I could muster tried to push her off from the bank. Nothing whatever happened; Susan came and helped, but it was no good. We next tried a trick which can be very useful, that is bringing the butty up between the motor and the bank and trying to push her off that way. In this case it did nothing.

Susan then decided, rightly as it turned out, that we were caught up on a rock; at the same moment it started to rain heavily. Arrayed in oilskins and sou'westers we went ashore again, this time with the shore plank and attempted to prise the motor off her eminence. At the end of some twenty minutes of this, when the only result was that we were both soaked and very bad-tempered, we gave it up and decided we must wait for help. It was not long before an empty pair came round the corner, but in spite of their willingness to help they said they hadn't got enough weight with their empty boats; we must wait for a loaded pair.

At the end of a further interval of rain and a feeling of deep incompetence, the welcome pop-popping was heard and round the bend came the cheerful faces of the three Beachy brothers. They roared with laughter when they saw our shameful motor but knew at once what was expected of them. They slowed down and as their butty came past, threw us a line. Quickly we made it fast to the motor fore-end, and George Beachy accelerated; the line took the strain, tightened, held and with a most terrifying splash the motor came off her rock and flopped into the water again.

We undid their line, thanked them warmly and collected our dejected selves. Wet and miserable we progressed to the top of Marsworth which we knew would now be well and truly against us; luck, however, decided to give us a break. The Beachy boys were well ahead, at the bottom by this time no doubt, and there was a pair coming out of the top lock to meet us.

Much restored to find fate on our side we went on happily enough to Nag's Head 3, half a dozen locks before Leighton Buzzard, where we tied up for a few minutes for our dinner and to get some dry clothes as it was still pouring with rain. Your socks and the bottoms of your trouser legs get horribly wet in spite of the enveloping oilskins and it is rather nice, too, to be able to dry your hands and face and neck, even if it is only for a minute or two.

At Leighton another excitement awaited us. This was the not

uncommon occurrence of getting the boat caught on the gate in the lock. It can be frightfully dangerous and may even result in the boat being sunk, but this can only happen if you are not paying the slightest attention to the lock emptying. We were not guilty of that and what did happen was not our fault. As the lock emptied the fore-end of the motor caught on one of the beams of the gate at the bottom end and was held up out of the water, with the result that the stern-end started to go under. Susan was up, drawing the paddles, and from the top it is very hard to see that the angle of the boats is not right.

It didn't dawn on me at first; then I suddenly realised that the bows were tilting up in front of me and, looking round, I saw that water was beginning to wash over the motor counter. There are no hatches on the motor and in one more minute the water would be in the cabin . . . when that happened, heaven help us. Every second the angle was getting worse as the water in the lock fell. Of course, all this went through my head like a flash of lightning; I screamed to Susan at the top of my lungs; with the noise of the rushing water she didn't hear me and I yelled again: "Let them down. . . . DROP them ! ! !"

As I have said, from the top of the lock it's nearly impossible to judge what is wrong and Susan appeared to think that I had gone mad because, to my despair, she went on drawing the paddles as if nothing was the matter. To argue with her at this moment meant sinking the boats, and I did the only thing there was to be done. I shinned up the lock-side, how I don't know, but I think I must have got up with my foot on the butty chimney; anyway I went up in one movement, faster than I've ever been before or since, and dashed to draw the top paddles and put some water back in the lock again. (This is the only crisis which justifies having paddles up at both ends at once.)

As it was nearly empty by that time there was a tremendous head above the lock and the pressure was terrific, but I tore across the gate and had the second paddle up before I dared to stop and look for any result. I did hear Susan calling out and asking me what on earth I was doing; for answer I pointed to the lock. We looked down and saw the motor gradually come up at the stern and then with a fearful wallow she came off the gate and floated even again. I dropped the top paddles and mopped my brow. We were saved again !

Several times that had happened to me but that was the

nastiest moment of them all and I did really think we were
for it.

That was a day of violent extremes. In the middle of all these
excitements came the pleasant thrill of collecting our things from
Frank's paint shop. My dipper was simply heavenly and I was
delighted with it; Susan did not like the tea-caddy she had
ordered and I promptly bought it from her so I now had three
pieces of boat painting in my cabin. The dipper went on a nail
on the cabin side of the back-end door, where it hung down
exhibiting on its under side the traditional castle, river and
mountains of the cut.   No one seems to know where or how
this legend or tradition arose, but it is there in some form or other
on practically every boat you see; sometimes on the panels of the
doors, sometimes on the under side of the table in the cabin
and very often on the side of the dipper; and it only varies
according to the style of the painter. In essentials it is always the
same; the castle very Eastern, almost Moorish in design, the
river bright blue and winding, and the mountains in the distance.

(In this connection it is interesting to note that on some old
engravings dated 1827 which I have in my possession there is no
sign of any of these pictures. There is an indication that the
boats were painted with diamonds and a certain amount of
ornamental scroll-work but of the castles and roses there is no
trace at all.)

I am so much of a Philistine that I can find nothing very
beautiful in this picture but I wanted to have an example of it,
so I had told Frank to put it on the bottom of my dipper where it
would only show when it was hung up. I am glad I had it now;
it hangs in my kitchen on the wall and makes a very pleasant
splash of colour against the cream distemper, quite apart from
the usefulness of the dipper as an accessory to home laundry.

One would think that we had had enough for that day but the
ever unexpected cut had another trap for us, into which we duly
fell. This took place almost as soon as we left Leighton lock, in
the treacherous Jackdaw pound. We went fast on to the mud
again and in a place where no one had ever been before; definitely
not our good day. We did everything we could to get off but it
seemed to be another case of waiting for a "snatch"; the butty
was on this time as well as the motor. Presently we heard the
sound of another engine coming along behind and with happy
smiles turned round to shout.

Susan has better eyesight than mine and to my dying day I shall not forget her face as she recognised the boats coming up.

"Oh, my stars !" she moaned, "it's the Beachy boys again !! !"

It was. They had emptied at the bottom of Mathers and so had got behind us once more. I think I had better draw a veil over our feelings as they pulled us off for the second time in one day; also over the moment when the motor came off and we started down the cut, only to discover that in the general excitement we had forgotten to hitch the butty on again and were rapidly drawing away from her where she lay, coyly nestling on the bank . . . we tied up at Finney, ruffled, tired and inadequate, a thoroughly-deserved feeling which having a new washing receptacle (that did not have to be shared with the potatoes) did little to mitigate. Definitely one of those nights when an unshared cabin is a necessity.

The next two days up to Hawkesbury were uneventful but for a howling wind, which with empty boats is really a cursed nuisance. They are so high out of the water that they get blown about all over the cut unless you can keep going at full speed; hanging about waiting for other boats to come out of locks is a misery and always ends in going on the mud; you are blown there and nothing you can do with a shaft will stop you.

We got to Hawkesbury and collected our orders on Friday but there was no chance of loading before Monday, so when we had moved round to the Newdigate arm we had nothing more to do for two days which was a very pleasant thought.

It was an opportunity for some shopping, which we did in Coventry which boasts, among other amenities, a most excellent book shop. Here I was lucky enough to pick up a copy of a wild flower book that I wanted badly and which was very hard to get at the time. Susan and I ate extensively while we had the chance and went to the pictures, as usual. Over the week-end we came across the second pair of Barlow boats to go on the Oxford, Margaret and her crew; they all came in and had coffee with us after supper on Sunday. By that time Susan had a friend staying with us on the boats, so we were a little congested, six of us in my cabin and all of us with plenty to say. The "Barlow girls" on the subject of Knapton locks gave me special delight !

Susan's friend stayed with us two nights and had the motor to herself, Susan coming in with me, which we thought would be better for her friend. She, poor thing, was longing to be gliding up and down the waterways of the Midlands but all we could offer her was the very disgusting little Newdigate arm in which we sat for two days. I think she enjoyed it though; it was all new and strange which hides a multitude of shortcomings, and on the first morning she gave us great delight by saying at breakfast how lovely it had been lying in bed listening to the fish popping in and out of the water by her head. Susan and I with commendable gravity agreed that it was indeed lovely, and allowed soulful expressions to creep on to our faces. We never disillusioned her; her "fish" were an outsize in rats, holding their nightly aquatic sports on the mud of the smelly bank opposite.

She was in on the loading which took place first thing on Monday; getting out of the arm was beastly as the wind was still very high and it is really better to have three people to get round the angle into the main cut, even when it is not windy; but we managed it in the end and even made the visitor steer the butty which she did with an expression of terror on her face, as if she expected it to blow up in her hands.

We went with her to Coventry and after we had seen her off, took ourselves to the Public Baths and there removed the coal dust from our grimy persons; we ended up with a large high tea in the town and got back cleansed and refreshed in time for an early bed.

One of the best things about a cabin to yourself, was being able to read in bed as long as you liked without feeling that perhaps the light was keeping your stable companion awake. I used to take full advantage of this and sometimes read for hours after I was in bed. It was the feeling that this time was my own that was so very pleasant, for by the time I became the *Dodona's* tenant I was hardened to the work and was nothing like so tired in the evenings. At the end of the day to lie in bed (which now seemed extremely comfortable) with my "Shepherd Boy" on the wall before me, the brasses shining and the stove irreproachably black, a great sheaf of scabious and purple loose-strife in the brass bowl at the end of my bed, a cigarette in my hand and three good pillows under my shoulders and the cabin lighted by the warm glow from the candle in the silver candle-stick on my little shelf; the cool night sky over me for ceiling, the water lapping round the side of the wall against which I lay, the only other sound the occasional hoot of an owl . . . what more could the heart of man, or woman, want?

Sometimes I read so late that I was hungry again before I went to sleep; I had only to sit up and stretch to the cupboard to provide myself with a large and sustaining piece of bread and treacle or a mug of cocoa. How many people can do *that* in their bedrooms ?

I see from my diary that we took six days to get from Hawkesbury to Slough where we were unloading. That does seem rather a long time but the only bad hold-up we had was half a day lost at Leighton while I indulged in a splitting head: most of the delay was due to our being two-handed. That means that if the locks are against you, you have got to stop the boats and tie them up before every single lock, get it ready, untie the boats again and take them in. Multiply this by a hundred and forty and it is easy to see where the time goes to.

We met Iris on the way down and were surprised to find that she had joined up with Kay (of the mutton chops) so it looked as though we should go on being two-handed for a bit. We also met Kit with three new trainees, but as they were coming out of the lock that we were about to go into, it was impossible to hold much conversation, especially as the trainees chose that moment to place both Kit's boats on the mud ! We went on our way (I was laughing I'm afraid), with the well-known sounds of: "Well now . . . IF you'd done as I said . . ." in our ears.

The only snag we encountered on the way down was getting our towing line very badly in the blades at Sweeps 2. This was our fault, of course, though the cause of it was not. A pair of boats coming up committed the really unforgivable cut crime, and drew off our lock from us. The lock was ready for us to go into and against the other pair coming towards us and, although they could very well see us coming, they deliberately shut our gates and emptied the lock for themselves. Besides being considered bad manners this is a horrible waste of water, which is why it is considered a very low form of behaviour. Each lock holds, as I've said 56,000 gallons of water; you do think twice before doubling the amount.

In this particular case we were on the higher level, which meant that the 56,000 gallons were being drawn away from under our boats, there being only a short distance behind us to the next lock. The result was that we sank lower and lower on to the mud, and in the general scene of hate and recrimination that followed, our towing line went in. I rejoice to say that so badly were we stuck in the mud and so completely across the cut, that we held up the offending boats so that they could not pass us without a lot of hard work on their part, pushing us out of the way. While this was going on we lost no opportunity of telling them at close range what we thought of them. When they had disappeared Susan put on a bathing dress and descended into the mud to try to grapple at arm's length with the knot of rope and propeller.

There was a timber yard at the other side of the cut and, being late in the evening, the sun was down behind it; this meant that very soon Susan was blue with cold and the rope as tightly caught as ever. It can be a very long and wearisome job getting it out and is better with three people and one of them a man, if possible. The best way to do it necessitates the brawniest going into the engine-room and constantly turning the engine over with the handle, to alter the position of the blades. As this is only effective if the engine is in gear and accordingly almost impossible to turn at all, it will be seen that women, however hearty, do not shine at this performance.

It was with great relief that we heard other boats coming up, relief that almost turned to hysteria when we recognised the Beachy boys! But this time it really was not our fault, or at least we could pretend it was not, and soon the angelic boys were spread all over our boats, doing incredibly muscular things with engine and rope. One of them lay flat on our counter hanging out over the water with his right arm up to the shoulder reaching for the trouble underneath, while his brother manhandled the engine inside. They were at it for a good hour with very little result, but they would not leave us till they had done some good, and eventually, after we had begged them repeatedly to go on and not waste any more time on us, a long length of towing line appeared and it was possible to start the engine again; we would be able to get out the rest afterwards.

When we tried to thank them once again for their kindness, all those boys did was to grin at us and say quietly: "You're welcome." That is what I call being a gentleman, even if you can't read or write.

Neither of us had ever been to Slough before and we were not very sure of the turning, which is below Cowley lock. The result was that when we arrived we overshot it and had a wretched time making up for the mistake and getting round the angle.

The arm we were entering is not very wide, and bang opposite some helpful soul had tethered three large barges which made our path narrower still. Every time we got into position, or thought we had, a pair of boats would come up or down and we had to get out of the way again to let them pass. As they were all deeply interested in our plight and all offered conflicting advice as they went by, life became rather complex. When we were finally left to ourselves we got on better !

The Slough arm is practically dead straight for an hour . . . about four miles. The only thing of interest that morning was the number of fishermen on the banks; it was Sunday and I counted three hundred and eleven of them before we tied up. It was a heavenly morning and we spent the whole hour steering from the cabin tops, which is quite possible when the cut is without bends. It is very restful to be able to perch up there and just keep the boat under control with one hand. We met no traffic, other than fishing lines which were all lifted as we went by, accompanied by thunderous glances from their owners. One man didn't bother; his line was sucked into our propeller at once and, of course, broke; in spite of his rage it was no one's fault but his own.

I spent the afternoon until tea-time perfecting my Turk's head technique; then we did the unsheeting and had tea with our labours over for the day.

The unloading arrangements here were most primitive. A sort of toy railway came on the gunwale bearing a truck on top, into which four men had to shovel the coal from the hold. When the truck was full it was whisked away and emptied on to a heap and then returned again. We gave the men draughts of tea at intervals; it was a very hot day and just watching them was filling our eyes and throats with coal dust, so it is surprising they could swallow at all. It was a poor show and a shocking waste of labour, in my opinion; this was deeply underlined when presently, to my amazement, I noticed that the evergrowing heap of coal on the shore was being *reloaded* by another man into a horse-drawn cart. Perhaps the firm in question had made valiant efforts to bring the machinery for unloading up to date and been prevented by war-time restrictions; I don't know, but it did seem absurd.

There were so many instances like this one, and we were constantly coming across them. I suppose we noticed them more by very virtue of the fact that we were doing hard and unaccustomed men's work because we had understood that the shortage of men was so acute; yet on every side you saw the men who were left (in reserved occupations all of them) wasting their time and labour from one cause or another. At times the doings of the stronger sex are a source of surprise and bewilderment to the weaker.

Susan and I ended that trip in a blaze of self-congratulation which was as edifying as it was novel. We had to go farther on to wind the boats after they had emptied us; when we got to the end of the arm we had only commonsense to tell us how to set about turning the boats in the narrow basin we found there. So brilliantly did we deal with the situation that our only regret was there was not a soul about to witness the perfection and polish of our technique, which was based on the telegraph pole at Long Ford.

We also managed the turn into the cut proper without a hitch; this, in spite of the presence of what appeared to be the entire local population, swimming, diving, canoeing and generally disporting themselves all round us; catching hold of the butty stern, trying to race the boats, diving under them and all manner of other horrors.

It is, actually, very nerve-racking all this; the small boys slip about in the water like eels and it's impossible to watch them all at once, yet if one of them did get too close to the motor there might have been a ghastly accident in a flash, for which we should have felt responsible.

Being somewhat used to dealing with the young, I knew that if the voice be authoritative enough it will be obeyed without the authority being questioned; I accordingly used to select the life and soul of the party (there always is one), and fixing him or her with a malignant eye issue my ORDERS in words of one syllable, giving short but pithy reasons for what I was saying. They no doubt thought me an utter spoilsport and a perfect brute; I was not concerned with finding my way to their hearts but only with preventing their small and naked bodies finding their way into our blades.

It was always like this at week-ends in the summer; if the weather was specially hot the late evenings would crowd up too. The worst of all was when some bright spirit had shut the top gates of a full lock and with some hefty companions was using the resulting "box" of water as a swimming-pool. This would always collect a big crowd to watch the fun; they made such a row that they did not hear the boats coming and we would get quite close before it dawned on anyone what was happening. They would all look up with great interest, diving off the gates and swimming to meet us with loud shouts of joy. But did they ever have the sense to open the gates for us? Never. You ploughed your way through a sea of flailing arms, bawling at them to keep clear and at the same time making frantic signals to those left on the gates to "OPEN THEM! . . . Yes that's right. . . . OPEN . . . WIDE OPEN . . . we want to come in . . . no, OPEN THE GATES . . . oh, God, are they all half-baked? We shall have to stop the boats and tie up."

Finally it would dawn, but not before we had completely slowed down, with all the resulting paraphernalia of the butty running up and having to be checked before she banged the gates. As the lock sides would be crowded with the eager throng the checking took on a nightmare quality, and as you ran you wondered how many legs would crack this time in the taughtening rope.

The next stage in the proceedings took place when the boats were safely in the lock and we were down at the far end drawing the paddles; this was the signal for a general move, *into* the boats themselves. In two seconds they would be swarming with large glistening naked bodies but here we knew where we stood, and they were promptly ordered off. " No unauthorised person is allowed on the boats, please."

The last scene is a comic one; it was the expression on the faces of the bathers when, and as, they realised that their swimming-pool was being drained away through the open sluices. Collecting our bits and pieces of line, picking up the towing rope and reinserting the tiller handle we would glide peacefully away, gentle smiles on our faces, leaving them pool-less . . . until another pair should come up and refill it for them.

Of course they didn't mean to be a curse; equally, of course, they were one . . . hundreds and hundreds of curses in fact. I often wondered idly what the reaction would be if I explained our sanitary arrangements to the bathers and the method of disposal? A case in which ignorance was very productive of bliss. . . .

Next day we had three days' leave meted out to us; as Susan

had not got anything particular to do I took her home with me, and we were nice and lazy all the time, when we weren't washing ourselves or our clothes or our hair. It was 19th June; I had plenty of time for another trip before the children's summer holidays began.

Chapter xiv—CURRENTS, CROWDS AND
SAFETY-PINS

Susan went back ahead of me; I arrived at the lay-by in a state of unutterable gloom; for the first time I did not want to go back. Without Susan's comforting presence my leave had been a depressing one and, filled with worries, I felt that I ought to be at home and not careering about over the Midlands.

There is a saying that theatre people use when they are not well and ought not to be playing: "Don't worry; I shall be all right when I've got my make-up on. Doctor Grease-paint will do the trick." It is quite true and it works every time.

I should like to coin a similar phrase for the cut, but I find it impossible to attribute to any one single thing the magic that at once started to exert itself over my drooping spirits, when I got back to my cabin. Perhaps, as with grease-paint, it is the old safe familiar *smell* that soothes the jangled nerves more than any form of reasoning can do. Whatever it is, I bless it and give thanks for it, it cured me of my doldrums; by the time we'd had our tea and were starting for Brentford, to load aluminium for a short load to "Maffas," I was ready for anything again.

We made a good start, coming out of the lay-by breasted-up and very neatly; then we found that we had all the locks ready for us, so our run down was quick and peaceful. We tied up at supper-time with four other pairs, three of whom were old friends. It was Saturday night; there would be no loading before Monday and even then we were the fifth on the list.

I tried to find some friends in London with whom I could play on Sunday, but everyone I knew was out of town; I was not surprised, it was very hot indeed. I was not sorry either; being forced to stay where I was, Susan and I explored Brentford and found it delightful. I suppose it is London and yet it has the strongest flavour of *village* in spite of being away from the country.

When I was on leave I had collected an old skirt to bring back with me; it was nothing to write home about but it was better than trousers; I do rather flinch at going to church in bell-bottoms, which I had had to do previously. Now, more suitably attired, Susan and I visited the parish church of St. Lawrence on Sunday evening.

The light that evening was perfectly heavenly. After church I sat on the top of my cabin and tried to sketch the basin where we lay. In front of me were the old red-brown tiled roofs of Brentford, and the spire of the church, just showing through the elm trees against the deep blue of the evening sky, in which the moon had already risen. Behind me the sky was brilliant with light from the setting sun, gilding the water and warming my back where I sat.

They loaded us after dinner next day, 42½ tons of aluminium, a very light load. There was the most awful plague of green-fly hovering round the boats; after tea and sheeting-up I decided to go "up to town" to see a friend and get out of it. Imagine my feelings when I arrived at Victoria and met another swarm of fly in St. George's Square! However I enjoyed my evening, so much so that I lost my last bus home and had to walk from Chiswick Park Underground to Brentford. In the middle of this trek I developed a nasty blister from a loose shoe lining; on the principle of "if thy eye offend thee !" I duly "plucked" off my shoe and then, finding myself very one-sided, I took the other off too and with complete comfort walked barefoot home through the summer night.

I recommend this form of walking to anyone who has never tried it. I admit I was lucky in my road which was a newly made, very smooth, town pavement and I carefully steered a wide detour round the doors of pubs in case of broken glass; but the difference in freshness at the end of my walk was astonishing. My feet felt brand new and delightfully cool and, surprisingly enough, were not very dirty when I got home and had a look at them.

I was starving . . . as usual . . . when I got in; the only food we could find between us was Susan's porridge for breakfast the next day, which she nobly offered to me. I ate it then and there and have seldom enjoyed porridge so much. It was midnight when I supped but it was also Midsummer Night. . . . I think that must have had something to do with it !

Next day was a muddled one. We were slow getting to the locks and then wasted a long time back at the lay-by, collecting a new towing-line and having the accelerator seen to. We had our dinner there, too, as we had to wait anyway; finally, we got off at 3.15 but for some reason we were both tired and we got no farther than the top of Denham Deep; the only lock on the cut which is too deep to allow one to jump down on to the cabin-top from its side.

It was while we were tying up at the top that the "Peaselum" family hove into sight and we had the touching reconciliation scene that I have already described. It is the most lovely tie up, the cut being very wide and thickly wooded. It seemed many miles from the roofs of Brentford and to heighten the contrast everything was fresh and sweet-smelling after the rain, which had just come down in a heavy shower.

On Wednesday we did a fourteen-hour day from Denham to Broadwater . . . thirty-four locks, fish and chips again at Sweeps and the snubber badly in the blades on the bends of Albert's 2. On balance a bad day, really.

The next day was one I like to look back on. It was a fine morning and much cooler after more rain. We got to Mathers at dinner-time but found "Brooky" tied up waiting to unload . . . the dockers were on holiday. Besides being an awfully nice man and a good friend to us Brooky is rather a marvel. He has only one arm, yet to see him get the paddles up and manage the ropes and tiller you get the impression that he has one more than most people instead of one less, so quick and neat is he.

Coming down Mathers I had collected the most glorious bunch of wild flowers for my brass bowl; muskmallow—which has enormous pale pink flowers—blue scabious, hedge wound-wort—like a red nettle only much more handsome—knapweed and water-mint; wild flowers every one of them but when I had arranged them carefully in my bowl I was staggered by the beauty of them. They would have stood comparison with the choicest garden flowers. Ever since then I have been an ardent champion of wild flowers as a floral decoration for the house. They don't all die in water by any means; some of the solider kinds, like the ones mentioned above, last very well indeed.

Susan is an ideal horticultural companion; we had the greatest fun with our twin flower books and a sort of friendly rivalry existed as to who could spot the most rare and unusual speci-mens. It was agony if you could see what you wanted growing on the bank but were unable to get the boats in close enough to pick it; it was, as a rule, only safe to try to get the butty in but we were very fair with one another and if I, from the motor, saw something I wanted to add to my collection and could

manage to make Susan understand which of the hundred varieties
of flower it was that I was after, then she would do her best to
bring the butty in after I had gone past, and pick it for me;
and of course I used to do the same for her. It requires a good
deal of co-operation, this kind of hunting, but my steering
improved enormously and I got quite brilliant at pulling the
butty right over as far as I dared and then hanging out by the
skin of my teeth to grab at the flower I wanted with the tips of
my fingers.

Coming down Marsworth I had been able to pick my bunch
while I was lock-wheeling and that had meant that I could choose
the best flowers and buds. They did look so lovely when they
were up in water.

After tea we both went into Tring and spent a wasteful hour
or so in the antique shop there. I got two horse brasses which
looked grand one each side of my "Shepherd Boy" when I got
home and hung them up. Susan and I had tea in the hotel and
picked up some very excellent ice-cream on the way home. We
also roasted a leg of mutton in the rather doubtful oven but, to
my surprise, it was a great success.

I had spent a frenzied time organising the visit of a cousin of
mine, who was in the Canadian army and there had been a good
deal of wiring to try to get her to meet us at some specific point
at the precise moment that her "seventy-two" started. I thought
I had arranged it rather well and set off after supper to meet her
off a bus at the top of Marsworth. Greatly to my surprise there
was no sign of her at all so, after meeting all the buses up to the
last possible, I returned home to await some news next day.

I went into Tring again first thing in the morning to buy some
miniature brass candlesticks about which I had not been able to
make up my mind the day before. These and some other purchases
caused such a drop in my financial level that I thought it prudent
to go to the local branch of my bank and recoup a bit—there was
no hope of any more cash till we got to Hawkesbury and that
would be three days at least; we were still loaded. All this took
so much time that I found they had started the motor when I
got back.

Just as they were finishing the butty I was called to the telephone in the office and there found Mr. Kempton on the end of
the line, in the Southall office, literally with me in one hand and
my missing cousin in the other. . . .

She had not had *any* of my numerous telegrams and, having some idea that she was supposed to be meeting me in Coventry, had gone there when she had not heard from me. Not finding me there she applied to the Coventry office, who in their turn rang through to Southall where the masterly organisation of Mr. Kempton at once came into play. He hoped we should be able to hear one another on the two lines but as this did not work he acted as interpreter between us and it was a simple matter to tell my cousin that we should be at Leighton by 8.30 that night and leave her to find us if she could.

As we had finished unloading we got away sooner than we thought and had time on the way to Leighton to ask for the keys of the tiny little church at Church lock and to look over it. Parts of it date from the tenth century and it holds about thirty people; it was well worth a visit and we were still ahead of time when we tied up at Leighton.

Zillah duly turned up, having perseveringly hitch-hiked from Coventry via Banbury and Buckingham. The cold roast mutton was excellent and we were conscious of having impressed our visitor with our "table." She shared my cabin of course, and Susan lent her something to sleep on: we turned in rather late with Zillah swearing she was comfortable, which I did not for a moment believe—you have to be very tired indeed to be comfortable your first night on the boats. . . .

Her reaction to the lock in the morning was very amusing; she looked as bewildered as we remembered feeling when we saw our first lock, but by the time we had done a dozen or so she was getting the hang of it and was really very helpful. Later in the day it came on to rain and we were glad to tie up at Gayton Arm End after a twelve-hour day.

I biked up to the hotel at Blisworth station and asked if we might have baths ? and then tore back and warned the others that I was about to step into mine, and would they hurry up and come along if they wanted one ? When we had all had baths the hotel provided us with a very good dinner and the day ended with a tremendous argument about the hour we should have to let go in the morning if we wanted to clear Hillmorton before they locked up at one o'clock. Susan and I worked it out that we should have to be off at five if we were going to make it; no one had an alarm so it was doubtful if we should ever wake up in time but we decided to have a crack at it.

What actually did wake me in the morning was the sound of
the engine being started up; I crawled out of bed and thrust a
dishevelled head out of the cabin. Susan had let go and was
popping triumphantly down the cut by herself without having
asked for any assistance. We were empty and there was practically
no steering needed on the butty so Zillah and I had breakfast and
got dressed leisurely. Time 5 a.m.

The time-table which I had so carefully worked out the night
before with the assistance of "The Book," went all haywire at the
bottom of Bugby; we arrived at 8 to find no less than *eight* pairs
waiting to go up and all being prevented by a pair of boats,
immovable in the very lock itself. In reply to our amazed inquiries
the pair in front said that there had been a wedding the night
before and the subsequent party had been of such magnitude
that the gentleman in the first pair had so far resisted all efforts
to waken him !

As the remaining eight pairs were all beers and, therefore,
unused to being kept hanging about while people slept off their
hang-overs, the efforts were soon successful and it was not long
before the unhappy reveller was routed out and sent panting up
the locks with all the beers in hot pursuit. We followed on
behind but Hillmorton was now hopeless.

While waiting to go up we were amused to see the "bridal
boat," as it were, tied discreetly at the cut side with no sight of
life coming from it. They had evidently decided to lie low till
the uproar outside had died down and thereby escape the inevitable chaffing their appearance would have caused.

Just behind them was the bride's old home; when boat people
get married it is as easy as that. The bride who was one of a
family of three sisters who worked with their mother, had left
one pair of boats on her wedding day and had returned to her
husband's pair at night—both pairs were tied up together and
would in all probability finish the trip one behind the other;
there was no question of a honeymoon and the work went on
with the minimum of fuss and delay.

Missing Hillmorton did not matter, as it turned out. When we
got to the top of Bugby and called for our letters at the toll office,
we were asked if we would like to go to Leicester for a change ?

It was a very rare trip and I was doubtful about it as we were
two-handed. We neither of us knew the way but Susan's enthusiasm was so great that she filled me, too, with the desire to see as

much of the canals as we could while we had the chance. So it was settled and instead of going straight on to Brum we turned right into new and unknown country.

We had a bit of a job getting round the turn; there was a bad wind blowing and the arm we were to go down was not very wide. However, with the three of us we managed at last and set off with great excitement. The cut was much narrower than we were accustomed to and very weedy; so weedy, in fact, that there appeared to be a narrow channel of clear water down the middle and the rest looked solid. It floated out of our way to a certain extent, but if we allowed the stern to get too near it we found we had picked up a mass of it on our blades and had a long job with a shaft, clearing it out before they would work properly.

Going into the blue like this made me wonder what on earth was going to happen to Zillah who was due back in camp in the south of England at midnight—how she was going to get there or where from I did not see at all. In an hour or so we came to the first set of locks, seven of them, all single and known as the Watford locks from the village nearby. We were still fairly well in civilisation and I knew Rugby could not be far away; in any case the main road ran close to the cut here so it did seem the obvious moment to cast off Zillah.

While we did the first lock she rapidly packed up her belongings and I walked with her to the road, where a useful number of lorries were dashing by—in uniform I knew she would be all right. She said she had thoroughly enjoyed herself and I don't doubt her: it was an original story to take back to Canada and we had enjoyed having her and her help.

What a very good thing that she left when she did! After Watford we entered into a twenty-mile pound without lock, house or road in the whole stretch. Unloaded as we were and able to travel comparatively fast, it took us six and a half hours to do that twenty miles, so overgrown and muddy was the cut.

The country was open and beautiful: wide, rolling Leicestershire fields and hills, with some large houses standing upon rising ground from time to time, but for the most part absolutely empty of human habitation. A notable exception was one of the most attractive houses I had ever seen, which we came upon suddenly as we rounded a bend. It was set back, perhaps only twenty-five yards from the water, with its garden sloping down to the towpath. The house itself was Queen Anne or early

Georgian—a perfect gem and quite unspoilt. In the flower-beds were masses of white tobacco plants whose scent drifted out to us as we went by. The house was soft orange coloured in the evening sun and had white roses climbing and tumbling over the lower half of it.

I turned and looked across the cut; the view must have been wonderful; nothing but the rolling Leicestershire scene as far as I could see, the little fields marked off with their hedges and low walls, here and there a road winding or a hill gently rising, a great clump of elms or a line of oaks marked clearly on the tapestry of the country. We both hoped that whoever owned the house appreciated it as we felt sure we would have done.

It was nearly nine o'clock before we got to Foxton where the next locks are, and we were very tired indeed after our early start. We tied up and called it a day, but before we went to bed had a nice depressing talk with a pair who were tied on the other side of the cut. They said it was "terrible farther on," and we plied them with anxious questions but all we could get out of them was that we might expect to have motor tyres wound round the blades every few yards, the engine choked with weed, a ghastly time going down the locks and, with much head shaking and indrawing of breath; " . . . they didn't ought to have sent you, women and two-handed and all." On this encouraging note we went to bed rather dreading what the morning would bring forth but still, on the whole, very glad we had come.

The Foxton locks once seen are never to be forgotten. There are ten of them, all single, and they fall down the side of the hill like a very steep back staircase. From a few yards behind the first one, all that can be seen is the sky with the balance beams of the lock standing out against it in silhouette; move a step or two forward and the wide Leicestershire plain unrolls itself at your feet. You feel like a small insect standing on the edge of the dining-room table, and long to take a big jump on to the flat carpet below you. (I was reminded of Tom in *The Water Babies* wanting to throw a stone down the chimney of the cottage in the valley below him.)

The single locks of Foxton are not quite the same as the other single ones we had met; they have side-ponds and are built in groups of "risers," that is to say that the bottom gate of one lock is also the top gate of the lock below, with no pound of level water intervening. There are one or two pounds, a couple of boat lengths long, on the way down the ten locks, to enable traffic to pass. If it were not for this, one lot of traffic would have to wait till the entire ten had been negotiated by a pair travelling in the opposite direction, a delay of nearly an hour.

Another thing that makes Foxton memorable is its lock-keeper. One-legged and one-eyed, he presided over our descent like a beneficent genius, talking all the time, teaching us without seeming to do so and nipping back and forth from lock to side-pond with astonishing agility. To see him prop his stick against the wooden upright while he wound the paddles up (and very stiff they are on Foxton) then hop down to the motor and issue instructions and encouragement before taking his one leg and his stick back again up the steep hill to watch over the butty's progress, was a remarkable sight as well as being an example of patience and the overcoming of physical disabilities, which was very sobering to watch. He is a big man and no longer young; the constant running backwards and forwards up and down the hill from lock to lock must be a great strain, but he was always cheerful and spurred us on with a positive spate of advice and help.

Feeling that we had left a real friend behind, we proceeded out at the bottom into the unknown wilds of Leicestershire, wondering what the day would bring forth to corroborate the awful forebodings of the previous night.

We need not have worried; in spite of what we had been told we got along perfectly all right without any hitch at all. By dinner-time we had another pair of G.U.s on our tail, two-handed like ourselves but, being boat people, considerably quicker than us. All the locks were against us and we met no traffic at all . . . Mrs. Lane was lock-wheeling for her pair and Jack was bringing both boats along by himself; it soon became clear that we should have to learn to do the same thing or else let them through.

We asked Mrs. Lane to show us and she explained how the butty was loosed off and the checking strap thrown to the lock-wheeler on the bank, as both boats came into the lock. The lock-wheeler helped with about half the lock and then tore on, on the bicycle, to prepare the next one. Soon we had mastered it and feeling very pleased with ourselves we steamed ahead in much better time, with no waiting for the lock to be got ready.

It was one of the hottest days of the year but we had no time to pause and contemplate it or even to feel sorry for ourselves at having to work so hard in such heat. Any spare moment was devoted to the much more important job of making tea, with which we kept Mrs. Lane—and ourselves—liberally supplied; in return for this first-aid she helped us with our lock if she came along before we had got away.

Our accelerator kept slipping all day long, which is simply fiendish; it nearly always chose to do it going round a bend, that needed both hands to negotiate anyhow. Somehow or other one hand had to be spared with which to fumble in the ticket-drawer for the screwdriver and then, without slowing down or losing direction, the wretched screw would be tightened—or inadvertently loosened, so that the engine died altogether. . . .

It was with relief that we came to the outskirts of Leicester and found that the last two locks had lock-keepers to ease our load. We tied up with the Lanes at 7.30; after a washing down of the cabin-tops and hatches I went to bed and had my supper there. We were still very glad we had come.

Next morning Susan went off to the office and returned with the news that we were to go up to Langley Mill, about nine miles north-east of Derby and midway between Belper and Nottingham. On the way we might have a chance of a load at Nottingham or Newark, which I was very keen on for personal reasons, but we should be told when we got to Trent lock and the parting of the ways. Also, we were to have a waterman to take us.

Much of the way would be along the river and the boats were always offered the services of a waterman if they wished for him. We most certainly did, having no desire to find ourselves grappling with tidal waters in our unwieldy narrow boats with their length ten times as great as their beam. He would not arrive till dinner-time so Susan and I set off to visit the town.

There are all sorts of things to be seen in Leicester; I regret to say that we merely concentrated on the best bookshop in the town, our rations and a jolly good dinner at a cabman's café. I found five new King Penguins that I had not got and several postcard size reproductions of some modern paintings that I liked very much and knew would look good on the cabin walls.

At 2.30 Joe Roberts arrived to take us to Langley Mill and off we went with him steering and us having a holiday, which we found restful but very strange. As soon as we got clear of the town, which is the same as any other town is beside the cut, very unpleasant, the scenery got lovely, open and countrified;

the Soare on which we were now travelling was very wide in parts. We were glad we had Joe with us and had not tried to tackle it ourselves. The swiftly flowing water was such a change from what we were used to that we looked at it with eyes of awe, and felt great respect for the way in which Joe was conducting us up the river.

He got us to Loughborough that night and then took a bus home, after promising to be with us by 9 next morning. I forget where he lived but I remember thinking that he must have rather a nice life combining, as he did, all the best things of water and land life. After supper I cleaned my bicycle from top to bottom and then biked into the town to have a look round and to post a letter. In the centre of things I ran into the Conservative candidate leaving his last meeting amidst much cheering, which was all I ever had to do with the General Election. (I only discovered too late that it was possible to vote by proxy, but had hoped that I would be near enough to rush home and vote when the day came. This ingenuous idea had been completely wrecked by coming up to Leicester and I finally spent polling day loading coal which worried me very much at the time. Later I discovered that my vote had been quite unnecessary to my candidate and I felt better.)

I tried to visit the church at Loughborough but found that it was locked—as usual. I do think this is such a pity, though I know the practice has become so widespread by reason of the many thefts from open churches. It is quite possible to get a key, I know, but when one is in a hurry this generally means that you cannot spare the time and do not go at all. I don't know how many times I have been prevented from visiting the churches up and down the Midlands, and in London, too, for this reason; we were always in a hurry. Besides, getting a key is such a performance when all one wants is to turn aside into the cool quietness of the church for a few moments, leaving the bustle and rush of work and business outside, while one sits still and collects one's thoughts. At least, that is what I like to do and I cannot believe that there are not hundreds of other people who feel as I do. I think that is what the Archbishop of Canterbury must have had in mind when he let us women off hats in church!

From my diary:

" 4th July:—Joe didn't turn up till 9.30 so we had a late morning in bed. More lovely country till after we had passed over the Trent and then it gets ugly. No orders at all for Nottingham so on to Langley Mill for coal. Found several other pairs above Trent lock and farther on the Jack Lanes still waiting to load their coal. Just above the lock several house-boats tied up in a colony, for all the world like a row of bungalows and, as a last insult to life on the water as it ought to be lived, all connected up to the mainland telephone ! After this, horrid little towns, all red brick and dark green iron bridges and railings. All the mud smells awful and at Stanton, where the ironworks are, the most dense green weed all over the cut which stuck to the boats and smothered everything it touched. Tied up at 6.30 and Joe helped us to re-do our cratch with very smart twirls and rosettes of cotton-line, before going off for the night. We are to get our-selves up to the loading place above the lock before he arrives tomorrow; this will save time as they are ready and waiting for us. Went and had a look at the town and wished we hadn't: no cigarettes anywhere but we found some very expensive chips, which were better than nothing, and I got a cobbler to mend the broken upper of my boots. In the same shop found a miner's belt for A, the man very kindly chopping a long length off the end and making some new holes so that it will fit his very small waist. Have sent it to him with the information that it is "a real miner's belt" and hope he will be suitably impressed. What impresses *me* is that in this very poor district it is possible to buy such a thing of real leather, soft and pliable, for the sum of 1s. 6d. while down in the gilded south I have never been asked less than 3s. 6d. for a rotten little piece of webbing with a cheap tin buckle, worth 6d. at the most and with a week of life in it."

[Adam is still, after two years, wearing his miner's belt.]

" *5th July:*—Up to the loading place which involved some com-plicated winding above the lock and then a procession backwards till we came under the chute. Not far, the winding was the difficulty, but we had plenty of time to work it out and a subsi-diary neck of water to help us. They loaded us very quickly with 46 tons of D.S. (hurray !) and by 10.30 we had sheeted up the butty and were off again with Joe in command. He turned up while we were sheeting the motor. We had a bad day and were thankful he was with us. The oil-feed snapped but, by the mercy of heaven, we had a spare which Joe put on. (This is one of the few repairs that we both know how to do—but no oppor-tunity to show off with Joe there to do it for us. . . .) We went on the mud several times and got stuck in locks, all of which

Joe dealt with, but the depths of misery were plumbed when a tree caught my chimney and sent it flying down the steps into the cabin, landing on the hob of the stove and cracking it in two. As Susan was steering at the time she has heroically offered me her hob in compensation but as a pair of boats we shall be maimed internally till we can replace it from the depot. Tied up at 6.30 at Trent lock where we found a lot of friends from the G.U. and had a nice gossip all round, ending up with pints at the very attractive pub which also produced sausage rolls and mince pies. How *do* they do it ?"

" *6th July:*—Joe turned up at 8.30. Uneventful day really, broken by various excursions on to the mud in spite of our very light load. I don't wonder the boat people hate coming up here; it wants dredging very badly indeed. Susan biked off to shop in Loughborough and picked us up as we came through. Unable to buy fresh milk (in plentiful supply) because we hadn't got our ration books. As nine times out of ten we are never asked for them when buying milk, we took a poor view of this but were forced to leave pints of lovely milk and return to our tinned variety. Reached Leicester again at 7.30 and said good-bye to Joe, who has done his job with us and will now wait till someone else wants a waterman."

" *7th July:*—Went to the office to draw our money, shopped, and finally let go at 10. Got stuck in the first lock of all which we knew was a brute and had carefully not breasted-up for this reason. No power on earth would get the boats in and while we wrestled the engine lost power and conked out altogether. Cycled back to the wharf to ask for help. Found a boater there who could be of no assistance as his missus had gone shopping and had left him in charge of the baby. Left a message with him to send help from the office as soon as anyone came back—they were all out—and cycled back to Susan whom I found holding the fort with rows of onlookers and children doing all they could to get on to the boats. As there was nothing but a magnetic eye and a barrack square voice to prevent them, she was having a busy time. Had sundry meals till the lock-keeper turned up— a priceless man—and finally fitter and office manager. Being Saturday afternoon we were lucky to have caught them both. The engine trouble was only one of the tappets that had got stuck but it took the fitter a little time to locate the trouble. He also redid the fender for us, which had once again developed its middle-aged sag. Finally cleared the lock at 3.45 picking up some home-grown lettuces from the next lock-keeper, and with no further troubles tied up at Blaby—where the ghastly pub is—at 7.30. Had a gorgeous fillet steak supper and a long chat with the people in the cottage beside the lock, who have promised to screech out of the window at four o'clock tomorrow morning in order that I may make a shot at going to early church at Kilby."

"*8th July:*—Called at 4 as arranged but my clock was slow and we didn't leave till 5.15 which made me miss church by about half an hour. Simply infuriating but it was the most heavenly morning and so early that it was cold and fresh and heavy with dew. More than a sprinkling of early fishermen which increased as the day went on and by afternoon we were tripping over bathers at every lock and feeling slightly hysterical. One fat, hairy body turned up about six locks running, having sped down the path on a bicycle ahead of the boats; we daren't catch one another's eye but worked like maniacs, clearing the other bathers off the locks and scooping them off the boats in between times. The day culminated in a Blackpool pier effect at the bottom of Foxton, where every type of thing that will float on water was doing so, in addition to many dozens of human bodies. Some of the canoes seemed to be made of paper, and all came far too close to the wash of the motor for my peace of mind. Was thankful to get round the corner to the foot of the locks but was totally unprepared for the sight which met our bulging eyes. The entire hillside was crowded with happy holiday-makers and their picnic baskets, reminding me of Hampstead Heath on a Bank Holiday. Even I was a little shaken by the sight of them and I daren't think what poor Susan was feeling. She *loathes* crowds of people. Mercifully George spotted us at once and came hopping down the hill to help; not a minute too soon, because the crowds, as one man, had risen up at the sound of our engine and were now thronging the lock-sides the whole way up. Working two boats up single locks requires a good deal of co-operation between the two steerers, but I found it extremely difficult to pick Susan out from the crowds, in spite of her red sail-cloth trousers and white sweater. Up we went, doing our parlour tricks before a fascinated audience which stood silently thronging the path beside us. Some faithful souls came from lock to lock with me and I made the utmost use of them, training them to open and shut the gates for me as I negotiated the rather complicated technique of single locking. They were very good by the time I'd finished with them! Tied at the top, very exhausted, at 9. Susan completely done in with her 'first-night' audience."

I have only made a passing comment in my diary on what proved to be one of the wildest things that ever happened to us. There is a tunnel between Leicester and Foxton called Saddington, truly a suitable name for us that day. As we were going through, with Susan on the motor, I suddenly heard the engine race like mad and after a tumultuous moment of crashing din, it stopped altogether. It did not take me many seconds to realise that the butty would shoot ahead, break her strap and pass the motor, and in the darkness of the tunnel I should lose Susan and be marooned on the butty and unable to help with whatever the crisis was. As I came up with her I threw a cotton-line round where I judged the stud on the motor stern must be, with such good aim that it promptly snapped: I was travelling too fast for it to hold me, and ought to have used something stronger but in the dark it was all I had time to find. Luckily I had another on the cabin-top and made another shot as I went past the fore-end of the motor. This one held; with great relief I was able to tie the two boats up together while I clambered back down the top-planks, armed with a torch to find out what was wrong.

Susan was in the engine-room inspecting the engine. We had no bulb in the socket in there so it was difficult to see more than two square inches of engine at once, but we soon came to the trouble. A split-pin had dropped out of the arm holding the rack-rod in position, so that the accelerator no longer controlled the speed of the engine: a tiny piece of steel no longer or thicker than a match was all we needed. We hadn't any spares and we were in the middle of a jet-black tunnel on the Leicester cut where traffic is very infrequent, and we could not move an inch without the engine. I wondered vaguely how long it took to starve to death and decided that, in any case, I didn't want to die that kind of death nor in this particular spot.

I forget who had the brilliant idea of using a safety-pin . . . it is quite clear that no one but a woman would have thought of it, though. With some difficulty Susan made her way back to her cabin and found the pin that she "thought she had somewhere": it fitted perfectly, and gingerly we started the engine up again. All appeared to be well: the pin held and it was again possible to control the engine. I returned along the top-planks to the butty

and Susan came up with the motor, we recoupled the boats in
a more normal position and proceeded on our way . . . two
boats, two women and forty-six tons of coal, all held together
with one safety-pin.   Surely a record?

We were very late letting go next day, being somewhat exhausted after the tunnel episode and the heat and the bathers and
then the Foxton fray to top it off.   We had the interminable
twenty-mile summit in front of us and knew we should take hours
to do it, so there was no vital need to be away quickly.   We
could go on till midnight if necessary.

Actually it took us about ten hours to do the twenty miles.
We left at 10 and tied up at 10 at night, nearly, but not quite, at
the end of it.   There was very little water and it was impossible to
hurry.   Mile after mile we crept along: I don't remember a day I
disliked as much as that one.   It was boiling hot and almost impossible to keep awake, standing at the tiller for hour after hour
without lock or mud or bad bend even, to vary the monotony.
(People of the "lovely, lazy life" school of thought, please take
note.)

We tied up at Husband's Bosworth, just before the tunnel,
and did some shopping in the village—to wake us up as much
as anything—and inspected the church, which was miraculously
open.   After we had eaten our dinner we slept for half an hour:
personally, I could not have gone on in the heat and boredom
without a sleep, if I had had the German army at my heels.

Considerably restored by our nap, in the most fairy-like
surroundings at the mouth of the Bosworth tunnel, we pushed on
again; on and on, apparently with no expectation of *ever* reaching
the locks at Watford.   There was a second tunnel we knew, but
even that seemed to have disappeared and I wondered wildly if
we could have taken a wrong turning, until reason told me that
there was not one to take.   In the late evening our pilgrimage was
enlivened by the presence on the towpath of a party of goats,
dozens of them all having a good tuck-in at the hedges.   One of
the ladies decided we were worth closer inspection and proceeded
to walk beside us for several miles.   Whenever I slowed down for
a bridge-hole she tried to climb on to the counter beside me, her
hairy face unfrightened and quite expressionless, except for a
faint glint of curiosity in her yellow eyes.   She wanted milking
badly, which was extremely tantalising; we had had no fresh
milk for a week and more. . . .

A little later we came up with a farmer's wife feeding a pet lamb through the bars of the farm gate with a bottle of milk and asked her if she had any milk to spare ? She sold me three quarts and a dozen eggs: in that heat it was not safe to try to keep milk for long so that the rest of my journey was made far pleasanter by frequent draughts of cold, creamy milk. Susan, I rejoice to say, doesn't much care for milk or eggs—it is not really surprising that I had put on two stone by the time I had finished with the cut.

By ten o'clock there was still no sign of any landmark and we felt we had just about "had it." In desperation we stuck crowbars into the towpath and tied-up under a bridge-hole, hoping that no one would want to come by in the night: if they did it would be just too bad. We were so tired that I don't think we even said good night to one another, but stumbled down into our cabins to the blessed sanctuary of bed, without a single word.

We were a little startled next morning to find that we had spent the night under bridge No. 13. . . .

Nothing happened after we got going, except that the fine weather turned to a downpour as we got out into the cut at Norton Junction again, after an interval of eight days; we had our dinner tied up in the rain at the top of Bugby. We got to Stoke Bruern that night and, in a misguided moment next morning, let two pairs down ahead of us which resulted in a bad road all day, every lock against us and just about double the work. In order to get a good road for Marsworth and all the locks on the southern side of the Tring summit we worked like the proverbial niggers all day long, in an effort to be first at the bottom of Marsworth, ready for the next day. We landed up at 10.45 p.m. to find ourselves behind the two pairs of Ovaltine boats which we had let through in the morning. Evidently we had been far quicker than we had thought but the sight of them was the end: we were too tired even to swear.

We woke to pandemonium in the morning. At least seven pairs of boats were all waiting to go up the locks: we looked at them with dislike and decided to let them all go. To hold your place in the middle of a stream like that demands more effort than we were capable of, at this stage of the trip and with no one to do our lock-wheeling for us. It turned out to be a wise move to let them get on: fortune favoured us and we spent the rest of the day meeting boats just when we most needed them, which was an enormous help all the way to the "Fishery."

Here fortune abruptly withdrew her support as we went into the full lock. I was on the motor and to my horrified consternation the engine started racing like mad—just as it had done in the tunnel—and at the same moment the gear stuck in reverse. Thank heaven it *was* reverse and not ahead, or nothing could have saved us from charging the bottom gates and going clean over the top. As it was we banged them fairly heartily, or rather the motor did. The butty was unaffected by this pile-up of disasters and Susan was able to jump off and check her as usual, while I raced round the gunwale to stop the engine.

On examination we found that the pin from the *other* end of the rack-rod had now fallen out but that our dear little safety-pin was still with us and doing its stuff! The obvious solution seemed to be to insert another safety-pin—indeed there was nothing else to be done—and when another pair of boats had done something to improve the gear position for us, we went on with our innards held together by two of these particularly feminine aids to canal boat-women.

Susan decided a little later that we really were being rather risky and after a long discussion with some other boats she told me that she had made up her mind to tie up above Nash's 2, which we did just before 7.

It was swelteringly hot again and maddening to have to sit about waiting for the fitter who could not, at the earliest, get to us before noon the next day. It wasn't a very thrilling tie up either; just before the lock with an unpleasing outlook on to the Nash paper mills in front and the Apsley paper mills behind. In the middle distance were row upon row of red brick bungalows, the sun beat down upon us and there was no shelter. Feeling very dispirited I went off for a walk to see what "the village" had to offer.

Only two things stick in my mind in connection with that walk. One is the beautiful old inn, several hundred years old, which a local inhabitant told me was shortly to be pulled down to make room for "a really up-to-date road-house" . . . and the other, the conversation I had with a gentleman who was clipping his hedge.

Susan and I had been vainly trying for some days to recall the name of the flower known to both of us by the name of "Red

Hot Poker." It did not in the least matter if we remembered or not; it was just one of those things that get on your mind and drive you nearly mad. We had no books to consult and every time we had been in, or near, shops we had forgotten all about it. Seeing the neat little villa gardens and the owner busy with his hedge trimming I thought here was a golden opportunity to set our minds at rest.

Accordingly I got into conversation with him and told him of our stupid dilemma, explaining the flower I meant and adding that he probably knew it, as I did, by the ordinary name of "Red Hot Poker." I suppose I was prepared for him not knowing the horticultural name but it certainly never occurred to me that he would not have any knowledge of the plant—yet such appeared to be the case. In vain did I describe it, its colour, height and shape; all I got was a mystified shaking of the head. Finally, by a brilliant stroke of fancy, he suggested: "Do you mean a *foxglove ?*" . . . I gave it up.

(Have I been peculiarly brought up in my part of the world? where the Kniphofia grows in profusion and without difficulty and is always called by the name I know ? Are there really none in Hertfordshire ? or are they as plentiful as they are here in Surrey but under a different name from ours ? I wish I knew.)

Dazed by this encounter, I made my way thirstily to the "Three Crowns," where I found some excellent cider and an evening's entertainment that kept me out till after ten o'clock, this being a lesson in nautical knots administered by an N.F.S. man and an ex-sailor, in which I took part with the greatest interest. The sailor and I became such friends that he ended up by lending me his *Manual of Seamanship Vol.* i and providing me with his name and address in case I should like to keep it for a bit.

No one came near us all the next day and by evening Susan and I were nearly at screaming point with absolutely nothing to do. This is the only occasion on which I have ever bathed in the cut—intentionally.

I was sitting on the hatches, I remember, kicking my heels and watching Susan do the same.

"I'm *so* bored," I said, "that for twopence I'd bathe in the cut . . . drains and all."

"Will you *really?*" inquired Susan, with an expression of throbbing interest. "You can have my bathing costume—if only you will."

This was a slight indication of the pass we had come to, that Susan should be able to regard as an entertainment *par excellence* the idea of me bathing! I took the small shaft and tried the cut all round the boats; it was gravel everywhere so far as I could make out—if it had been mud I don't think I *could* have gone in, even to entertain Susan.

It was cool in the water and lovely to be totally immersed, so long as I kept my mind off what it was that was immersing me. I swam across to the other side of the cut and then back again and in the middle put my foot down to see how the bottom was just there. I could stand quite easily with my head out of the water; from one side to the other I walked and nowhere was the water any deeper. I know I measure 5 ft. 6 in.—allowing eight inches from my chin to the top of my head, that means the cut was under five feet in depth. I began to see why we so often got stuck on the bottom.

I quite enjoyed that bathe in spite of my imagination and the variety of cans that I encountered with my toes; at any rate I was cooler than before and felt freshened up. After I had had a jolly good hot wash from head to foot, shampooed my hair and found some clean clothes to put on, I went back to the pub and, over reinforcements of cider, poured our woes into the sympathetic ears of His Majesty's Navy.

My new friend told me he worked for Ovaltine's, about a mile down the road. Of course we knew the factory well from always going past it; its boats were the smartest and best painted and most well-cared for on the cut and were a joy to behold. Why didn't we, said my sailor, ring Ovaltine's or go round in the morning and see if they couldn't provide us with our missing bit?

I was much taken with this suggestion and in the morning, as no one had put in an appearance from the depot, Susan phoned, and I biked down to the works where they received me with the greatest kindness and offered to do anything they could. By great good luck they had one of our brand of heavy-oil engines in the shop—they had just bought it from the G.U.—so it was easy for me to point out exactly which bits had dropped off ours. In about ten minutes they had made me the exact length and thickness of steel rod that we needed and had provided me with a handful of split-pins to replace our safety-pins, and I was on my way back to the boats.

The piece fitted perfectly; we started up the engine and were away as fast as we could go.

It was appallingly hot and thundery, there were bathers every-where and all the locks were against us; by the time we got to Rickmansworth we felt we'd had more than enough; it was nearly 7 o'clock and we had done fourteen locks and were only five hours away from the Bridge. Tomorrow would be Sunday, so we had all day to do the five hours in, and could go down late Sunday night or early on Monday to our destination which was the Celotex factory at Alperton, an hour and three-quarters from the Bridge. We tied up and tried to do some shopping but found we were too late for anything but bread and some fish and chips.

This was the night of the phenomenal thunderstorm—though we did not know that yet. We went for a walk in the town to try to get some air but there was not a breath of it anywhere. The sky was copper-coloured and a thick blanket of mist was lying over the fields at the edge of the water; everything was very still and waiting—even the cows hardly moved, where they stood legless in the smoky white grass.

The storm broke at ten o'clock; by that time we were both in our own cabins and to hold any communication with one another was quite hopeless. The rain was lashing down, plastering the boats and the water all round us and producing unexpected streams and drips inside my butty. I arranged cake tins and bowls all over the floor at strategic points and covered myself in a ground sheet. Even with the light on I could see the ceaseless lightning, flashing over every part of the sky at once.

Very soon I started to get thoroughly scared. I don't in the least mind thunder or lightning as a rule—in fact I rather like it and look forward to the wet, cool smell that follows it, but now I was none too sure how safe we were. We were lying in water, in boats of iron and wood, conditions, it seemed to me, that are eminently desired by the heart of electricity. I should very much have liked to go and consult Susan, but to put my nose outside the door would be to get drenched to the skin at once—it was wet enough *inside*—so I had to nurse my groundless fears in private. It was far too hot to sleep but I put the light out and lay watching the pattern of the flashes on the ceiling, till I dozed off into a rather uneasy sleep. The noise inside the cabin had to be heard to be believed; what with the thunder in the sky and the rain clattering on the roof and sides of the small cabin, and pinging into all my bowls and tins, I felt as though I were out in the middle of the storm. It was suffocatingly hot because I had to have everything shut up in order to try to keep dry.

I woke several times in the night but the stormy weather seemed to be continuing without any signs of abatement; also the drip receptacles required emptying again and again and I began to wonder what I should do when my bucket was full? The last time I woke it was five o'clock and still the storm was carrying on with undiminished vigour, but by then I was too tired and sleepy to care what happened, and had got used to the orchestration of sounds.

When we poked our heads out in the morning the freshness of the earth and grass and trees was a reward for the terrors of the night. I could have worked for twenty hours that day if I had had to, but it was Sunday and for once we were in a position to lay off a little as befitted the Sabbath.

I went off to church; it was a heavenly day and the church quite close. My breakfast, eaten out of doors in the hatches with the wet earth smell all round, was like a meal for the gods. Later, yet another of Susan's sisters turned up—she has got dozens— and came with us for the rest of the day. We collected our mail at the Bridge on our way through and, as there was no one specially interesting in the lay-by, we went on down to Alperton and tied up—very *cold* by this time—at 9.35.

We were up at the unloading place in good time next morning —at eight o'clock—but by the time the men had had their cups of tea, without which it is apparently impossible for them to get going, it was ten o'clock before they touched us. (Never let me hear again that constant cups of tea are a womanly failing. . . .) We went off to buy rations and left the men to get on with it, having our dinner in the works canteen before we tidied the boats up again.

I knew that with all the setbacks and the abnormal length of this trip I should not have time for another before the holidays began. It was 16th July—I couldn't hope for a short trip even, before I would have to be home for the children's return; besides, I was tired after this long two-handed trip and was looking forward to a rest. In any event, I did not think two months was too long to be off the cut, with the war with Japan still being waged with all our force, and felt confident that the job and the boats would be waiting for me when September came.

Kit came in to see us when we got back to the lay-by and then went home for the night. I borrowed her Bradshaw of the cut before she went, and worked out what Susan and I had done on the way to Leicester and back; it was an impressive total. Three hundred and forty miles, three hundred and thirty-eight locks, eighty-eight tons of cargo and twenty-two working days. We certainly had got about and seen life.

Susan went home next day and I spent it packing and tidying up my things. Kit and I had dinner in the canteen and I talked to several of the other women who were all in the throes of going and packing. *Still* I did not realise. . . .

It was very quiet when everyone else had gone; the cabin looked strange with all my bits and pieces taken down and packed away in the store against my return in the autumn. I kept out my diary, but everything else was packed up in my two kit-bags. I didn't know who would have my butty when I had gone but I left her swept and garnished for whoever it was, and cleared the larder so effectively that I was reduced to bread and marge and sugar for my supper.

Next day I took my bedding-roll up to the store, arranged for my bicycle to be sent home by rail and locked the *Dodona* for the last time. It was only two months but you never know—it did not bear thinking about, and I walked quickly away from the cut; as quickly as my luggage would allow, hating its cumbrous awkwardness every bit as much as I had on my arrival ten months before.

Chapter xv—HOW IT ALL ENDED

FOR some time after VJ day I went on thinking that I should be able to go back; I thought it would be several months before the men could be got back again from the forces and the switch-over to peace-time accomplished. But by the end of the summer holidays I knew it was a vain hope. On every side I had news of the women packing up and going home—when I heard that even Kit had chucked it I knew my number was up too.

There was nothing left but to go and collect my stuff from the store, which I did; an ultra-depressing business, with no one in the lay-by that I knew well, piles of dusty possessions belonging to my fellow-workers, waiting like mine to be collected—the only bright spot was the warmth of the welcome I got from the women in the canteen. They laughed when I said I was "a lady of leisure again"—as I meant them to do—but I felt more like crying.

It did seem quite impossible to believe that it was all over; that the boats had no more use for me and that I was merely getting in the way by being there at all. Everything *seemed* the same—I kept catching myself expecting to see Kit come tearing round the corner on "Otto Blink," or running into Susan trying to get a new towing-rope out of Frank in the oil store—there were ghosts everywhere.

We often used to say that we would be bound to get together, when it was all over, at least once a year, for the pleasure of indulging in a good boat gossip. This has actually happened now and I hope it will become an annual event—the very nature of the work was such that we can only relive it to the full in one another's company—and with considerably less risk of boring the rest of our friends!

And, looking back, it is so well worth reliving—this extra-ordinary slice of existence into which we were all pitchforked.

For so many millions of people all over the world the war brought horror, torture and loss, that it seems almost wrong to have found anything good in what it brought to me; but it would be less than honest not to admit that it *did* bring me good. So there is an immeasurable amount of enjoyment that I can look back upon, knowing that I have paid the score on the debit side too.

All these things I have enjoyed and loved: the work of the boats, the pleasure of slowly learning to manage them, the shape and the colour and the noise of them; the homeliness of the cabins and the friendship of my fellow-workers; enormous appetites and the hundred per cent feeling of physical fitness, the tiredness and the heavenly rest at the end of the day; the colour of the cut through the seasons, the never-ending anticipation of what lay "just round the corner," the open fields and the wooded cuttings between high banks, the cottages, houses, factories, wharves and docks, amongst all of which my days were lived so fully. The pubs and the people in them, the butchers, bakers and all the other shopkeepers who were good to us and became forever part of the pattern; the early mornings and the late evenings and the quiet black nights; the noise of the lock gates banging shut, the feel of the sun soaking into me as I lay full stretch on the balance beam, listening to the water boiling and racing below me; even the wetness of the rain on my face and the scrunch of the snow under my boots; the complete stillness that suddenly fell when the panting engine was stopped at the end of the day.

But very much more than all these things I am grateful for the chance to have known the people of the cut, for the way they accepted us into their way of life and for the help they were so ready to extend to us. Indeed, I am grateful to all the people who might so easily have sneered at "the lady bargees playing at boats," but instead met us on an equal footing, with a "Watcha, mate" and an offer of help. If there is any way—and I think there may be—in which I can help them, I shall do what I can with a very genuine feeling of "You're welcome."

Of the other side, of the things I hated there seem to be very few in retrospect. The permanent dirt for one, the agony of chapped hands; carrying the filled-up water cans which, even to the bitter end, pulled my arms out of their sockets; breasting-up; hanging about doing nothing and waiting for other people— all very small things and of importance to no one but myself.

But of the things that do matter, and matter very much to other people—to the boat people:—the living conditions, small children doing heavy work, pregnant women bow-hauling, the illiteracy of the vast majority, the sight of the men, women and children of the cut steering the boats through sheets of rain with no waterproofs to protect them, broken boots and ragged coats, the necessity to go on working without a let-up to keep the family fed, the shortage of food and not even the same extras that are given to the agricultural labourer, the bewilderment in the face of illness, the hopelessness of not knowing how to deal with it. . . .

There was a lot of talk before the war about the scandal of our slums. I never heard anyone mention the slums on the water—the bright paint of the boats and the golden summer fields through which they glide is so idyllic a picture with which to lull the conscience—picturesque is the word, or gipsy-like.

The boat people may be picturesque and gipsy-like—(they are both, only I don't advise you to go telling them so—and I for one hope with all my heart that they will remain so)—but don't you think they would much rather be clean and well fed and properly clothed and able to read and write as well? The two things are not incompatible if they are gone about with tact and understanding. The canal companies cannot do it all without help, and I am, therefore, glad to note that since I started to write this book a society has been formed to look into, and try to improve, the conditions on the canals. It is called the Inland Waterways Association, Sir Alan Herbert is its President, and its address is 11, Gower Street, W.1. It would be good if all the people who have felt an interest in the canals—and to judge by the interest that has been expressed to me alone, there must be very many—would write to the Secretary, for particulars of how they could help in a practical way.

Well—that seems to be the end of the trip, good roads and bad roads and all. My sudden impulse turned out a hundred times better than I had any right to hope. I found so much to make me happy in my job—health, contentment and satisfaction—so much for which I am so deeply thankful that I know I have neither the words nor the skill to express it. If what I have written gives only a small idea of the variety and interest of my year on the cut, of the fascination the life held for me, of the kindness and humanity of the simple people amongst whom I worked and of the good comradeship of the other "Idle Women," I shall be well repaid. And far more than that, perhaps I shall be able to feel that I have repaid some of the debt I owe to my fellow-workers, a debt which I am so fortunate to have incurred—may their road be ever as good a one as they made mine.

People still ask me: "Don't you miss the boat life?" Well—what do *you* think?
November, 1946.

APPENDIX

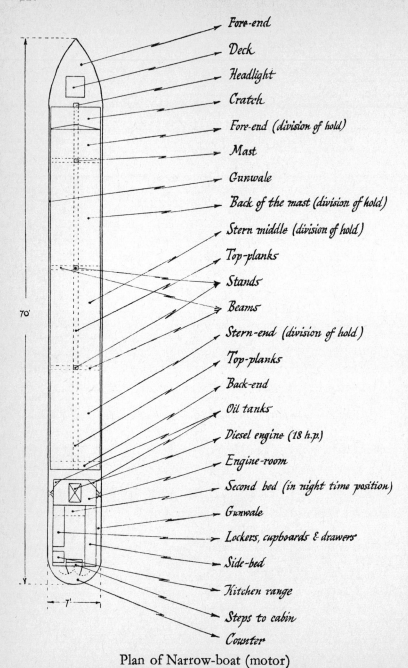

Fore-end

Deck

Headlight

Cratch

Fore-end (division of hold)

Mast

Gunwale

Back of the mast (division of hold)

Stern middle (division of hold)

Top-planks

Stands

Beams

Stern-end (division of hold)

Top-planks

Back-end

Oil tanks

Diesel engine (18 h.p.)

Engine-room

Second bed (in night time position)

Gunwale

Lockers, cupboards & drawers

Side-bed

Kitchen range

Steps to cabin

Counter

70'

7'

Plan of Narrow-boat (motor)

BAD ROAD.—Usually meaning that all the locks are against you; a trip beset with difficulties.

BARGE.—To be a barge a boat must have a beam of at least 14 ft.; on the Grand Union Canal the barges are always either horse-drawn or without any supplementary method of propulsion.

BOAT.—Long-boat, Narrow-boat or Monkey-boat; the names are synonymous for a seventy-foot boat with a beam of seven feet.

BOTTOM ROAD.—The route to the North East of Birmingham by which the boats travel to Coventry for loading coal. The locks are all single.

BOW-HAULING.—Pulling a boat—usually the butty—into a lock by hand.

BREAST-UP.—To tie the boats abreast; used at night for tying up or, in some cases, when going into locks empty.

BRIDGE-HOLE.—The arch under any of the innumerable canal bridges.

"BUGBY."—Long Buckby; the seven locks there.

BUTTY.—The boat on tow.

CRATCH.—The semi-permanent, tent-shaped structure at the fore-end of butty and motor-boat.

CUT.—Any canal.

DIPPER.—Metal utensil with a handle, with which every boat is provided by the Company and which is used for washing, cooking and laundry.

DRAW.—To draw the paddles up when filling or emptying a lock.

FLY-BOAT.—Slang name for the boats which do the London to Birmingham trip non-stop, in something under sixty hours.

GAUGING.—The process which is gone through at intermediate points in the journey of a loaded boat to ascertain that the weight of the cargo is the same as that which was originally loaded.

GOOD ROAD.—Usually meaning that the locks are, or will be, ready for you; a good trip in general.

"ELUM."—Boater language for the rudder or helm.

"FINNEY."—Fenny Stratford.

HOLD IN, HOLD OUT.—Steer nearer to the towpath side of the cut; steer farther away from the towpath side.

HORSE BOAT.—A boat or pair of boats drawn by one or more horses. These are rare now but there are some to be seen still, usually plying between places which are situated close together.

"JOSHER, JOSSER."—Slang name for boats belonging to the firm of Fellows, Morton and Clayton, Ltd., in friendly memory of the late Mr. Joshua Fellows.

LAY-BY.—The strip of canal at Bull's Bridge where the boats lie while awaiting orders.

LET GO.—Cast-off.

LOCK, TO.—To work through locks.

LOCK-WHEEL.—To go ahead on foot or bicycle to prepare the lock for one's own pair of boats.

LOCKED-UP.—To be unable to go up or down the locks on account of a padlock placed on top and bottom gates. Some locks are locked up every night at a specified hour; in a drought any lock may be so put out of action at the discretion of the lock-keeper, at any hour of the day, so as to conserve water.

"MAFFAS, MATHERS."—Marsworth or the Marsworth locks.

MUD BOX.—Filter to keep mud and other solids from entering the water-cooling system.

NARROW-BOAT.—See "Boat."

NUMBER ONES.—The name given to the boaters who own their boats, in contrast to those who work under contract to the various Companies.

PADDLE—The sluice in the bottom of a lock gate by means of which the lock is filled or emptied.

POUND.—The stretch of water in between locks.

RAM'S HEAD.—In the butty, the post at the top of the rudder, usually highly decorated with Turk's heads and/or horse-hair; in the motor, the steering column.

SHAFT, TO.—To manipulate the position of the boat by means of the shaft (boat-hook).

SILL.—The stone or concrete slap against which the lock gates rest when closed.

SNUBBER.—Towing-rope made of coconut fibre and used between fore-end of butty and stern of motor; as distinct from the overhead towing-rope.

STANDS.—The upright planks which are slotted into the hold at intervals and support the top-planks when the boats are loaded.

STEMMED-UP.—On the mud, in a general muddle or getting

the motor into such a position in the lock that it is impossible to bring the butty in alongside.

STRAPS.—The ropes used for tying-up, checking or short-length towing.

STUD.—The T-shaped iron cleet on the fore-ends of both boats and on the butty stern used for towing and tying-up. The stern of the motor carries an iron hook and small bollard, known as the "dolly," to which the towing-rope is attached.

TIPCATS.—The sausage shaped fenders at the stern of the motor.

WIND.—To rhyme with "pinned." To turn the boats round.

WINDLASS.—L-shaped crank handle used for winding up the lock paddles.